LITERARY BIOETHICS

CRIP: NEW DIRECTIONS IN DISABILITY STUDIES

General Editors: Michael Bérubé, Robert McRuer, and Ellen Samuels

Committed to generating new paradigms and attending to innovative interdisciplinary shifts, the Crip: New Directions in Disability Studies series focuses on cutting-edge developments in the field, with interest in exploratory analyses of disability and globalization, ecotheory, new materialisms, affect theory, performance studies, postcolonial studies, and trans theory.

Crip Times: Disability, Globalization, and Resistance
Robert McRuer

Accessible America: A History of Disability and Design
Bess Williamson

Literary Bioethics: Animality, Disability, and the Human
Maren Tova Linett

Literary Bioethics

Animality, Disability, and the Human

Maren Tova Linett

NEW YORK UNIVERSITY PRESS
New York

NEW YORK UNIVERSITY PRESS
New York
www.nyupress.org

© 2020 by New York University
All rights reserved

Library of Congress Cataloging-in-Publication Data
Names: Linett, Maren Tova, author.
Title: Literary bioethics : animality, disability, and the human / Maren Tova Linett.
Description: New York : New York University Press, [2020] | Series: Crip: new directions in disability studies | Includes bibliographical references and index.
Identifiers: LCCN 2019039472 | ISBN 9781479801268 (cloth) | ISBN 9781479801251 (paperback) | ISBN 9781479801299 (ebook) | ISBN 9781479801336 (ebook)
Subjects: LCSH: English fiction—20th century—History and criticism. | Bioethics in literature. | People with disabilities in literature. | Human body and technology in literature. | American fiction—20th century—History and criticism.
Classification: LCC PR888.B53 L56 2020 | DDC 820.9/362—dc23
LC record available at https://lccn.loc.gov/2019039472

New York University Press books are printed on acid-free paper, and their binding materials are chosen for strength and durability. We strive to use environmentally responsible suppliers and materials to the greatest extent possible in publishing our books.

Manufactured in the United States of America

10 9 8 7 6 5 4 3 2 1

Also available as an ebook

For Dominic, Ruth, and Lev
And for my mother, Deena Linett

CONTENTS

Introduction

Reading Fiction, Valuing Different Kinds of Lives

In a 2005 *New York Times Magazine* article about human-animal amalgamations, Jamie Shreeve discusses possible hybrids, remarking that "strictly from a biomedical perspective, a human-ape chimera could be the ultimate research model for human biology and disease—one that is completely human in everything but its humanity" (n.p.). With this paradoxical statement, Shreeve signals the instability of the category of the human and hints at the myriad ways scientists, bioethicists, and the general public conceive of and patrol its borders. The article directly addresses the slippery boundaries of humanness, asking, for example, whether there is "a clear biological distinction between us and the rest of creation, one that should never be confounded by the scuffling of strange new feet in laboratory basements?" But it nevertheless relies on such a distinction, as if the lineaments of humanness were unproblematic, in that it fails to raise ethical questions about animal experimentation.[1] Such equivocations about the category of the human and its ethical implications are common not only in contemporary biomedicine, bioethics, and news coverage of biomedical techniques, but also in literature, and these equivocations are both fascinating and illuminating when we come to consider the bioethical questions that are of pressing importance in contemporary life.

Bioethical questions come to the fore as scientific and technological advances make it possible to inject human brain cells into non-human animals, genetically edit embryos, offer genetic testing and selective abortions for a growing number of genetic anomalies, gain deeper insight into animal consciousness, and create meat in laboratories. Furthermore, social developments such as the aging of the human population, varying accommodations for physically and intellectually disabled people, and intensive animal agriculture are sparking heated bioethical debate in the public and academic spheres.

Literature has a key role to play in such debates. Imaginative writers have long been considering bioethical and biopolitical questions—think of Frankenstein refusing to create a mate for the Creature lest (among other worries) they breed more of their kind: a eugenic decision, *avant la lettre*, that certain kinds of beings must not reproduce. Exploring literary treatments of bioethical questions can supplement conversations within bioethics proper, helping to reveal our existing assumptions and clear the way for more considered views. Bioethics has its own "habitus," Pierre Bourdieu's term for the habits, skills, and assumptions that govern an area of knowledge, or what Jackie Leach Scully describes as "pretheoretical, prereflexive knowledge" ("Moral Bodies," 34). "The habitus of professional bioethicists serves to naturalize their imported moral, epistemological, and other assumptions, so that they fade from sight as needing justification: they *just are so*" (Scully, "Moral Bodies," 39). While I am certainly not arguing that exploring bioethical problems through literary analysis is superior to exploring them through philosophical argument, doing so does catapult us outside this habitus (and into the habitus of one or another form of literary criticism), making possible alternative perspectives.

Literary texts can serve as thought experiments that help us envision the ramifications of given values. Peter Swirski has argued that this capacity to generate thought experiments is one of literature's strengths. Not all literature works this way, in Swirski's account, but fiction can sometimes create "an intellectual and emotional laboratory" that "contains the narrative and cognitive machinery for examining issues that challenged thinkers of yesterday, and will continue to challenge thinkers of tomorrow" (11). In this study I read four novels as though they are such laboratories: literary-philosophical spaces in which simmer experiments with bioethical questions.

To do so is not to forego attention to the particularity, or what Derek Attridge calls the "singularity," of literature. My goal is not simply to use a literary text to provide an answer to a bioethical question raised within it. I remain cognizant of "what we lose when we ask reading and criticism to pursue clearly defined, public ethical ends" (Altieri 34). Novels are not philosophical arguments, after all, but complex representations of characters and their worlds, rendered through the instability of language. The chapters therefore attend to the nuances of the texts under discussion—to allow for which, I focus on a single novel per chapter—while exploring how they represent the stakes of bioethical views. The result is a tapestry in which strands of literary analysis interweave with strands of bioethical investigation.

Tony Hope writes that ethical inquiry requires "not only intellectual rigour but also imagination. Ethics uses many tools of reasoning, but it is not just a question of learning how to use the tools: there is always the possibility of a leap of the imagination—of a different perspective or an interesting comparison that . . . takes our thinking forward" (59). My contention throughout this study is that literary treatments of bioethical questions encourage such imaginative leaps. Novels have the virtue of presenting vividly imagined worlds in which certain values hold sway, casting new light onto those values; and the more plausible and well-rendered we find these imagined worlds, the more thoroughly we can evaluate the justice of those values.

Literary Bioethics draws from literary and cultural theory, disability studies, age studies, animal studies, and bioethics to consider the value of different kinds of lives as presented in fiction. That is, I am using "bioethics" broadly; rather than treating practical issues of medical ethics, I take "bioethical questions" to mean (1) questions about the value and conditions for flourishing of different kinds of human and nonhuman lives, and (2) questions about what those in power ought to be permitted to do with those lives as we gain unprecedented levels of technological prowess. As Rita Charon writes in a note about the origins of "bioethics," the term as used by Van Rensselaer Potter includes "a recognition that the biological life interacts with the moral life" (217). In understanding bioethics in these terms, my approach has been guided by Cary Wolfe, who suggests that we ought to reclaim the "bio" of bioethics, taking account of what Derrida calls "the living in general" and moving past the entrenched valorization of the human (*Posthumanism*, 49). My work is also shaped by Melinda Hall's assertion that because many bioethical questions center on "what makes life worth living and who should live," disability is "a major fulcrum for bioethics" (ix). Such commitments keep this study within the borders of humanistic rather than medical fields.

Literary Bioethics raises questions of value about nonhuman animals, old human beings, intellectually disabled human beings, and cloned human beings. It begins at the turn of the twentieth century, as H. G.

Wells asks us to think through the morality of animal experimentation in *The Island of Doctor Moreau* (1896). Next it considers the absence of old people in Aldous Huxley's *Brave New World* (1932) and the contested value of intellectually disabled people in Flannery O'Connor's *The Violent Bear It Away* (1960). It ends at the turn of the twenty-first century, with Nobel Prize winner Kazuo Ishiguro's 2005 novel, *Never Let Me Go*, where cloned human beings are used by the government as organ donors. By analyzing novels published at widely spaced intervals over the span of a century, this study offers snapshots of grapplings with questions of value.

Attridge claims provocatively that "the impulses and acts that shape our lives as ethical beings—impulses and acts of respect, of love, of trust, of generosity—cannot be adequately represented in the discourses of philosophy, politics, or theology, but are in their natural element in literature" (*Coetzee*, xi). Even if Attridge overstates the incapacity of philosophy, politics, and theology to represent ethical impulses, literature certainly depicts human action and motivation with great perspicacity. Such a capacity for insight into human experience makes literary texts well suited to serve as material for ethical inquiry. In this study, without leveling the ambiguities of fiction, I lead readers through the textual laboratories, seeking fresh ways to think about questions of value.

Reading Ethically

As Thomas Murray notes, "Most people, most of the time, learn most of what they know about morality from narratives of one kind or another" (6). As a result, "much, if not all, moral discourse, including moral theory, is embedded within, conditioned by, and conducted in narratives" (10). This does not mean that reading literature is always ethically productive; but it does mean that fiction has a role to play in our moral reasoning and our refinement of moral ideas. Becoming immersed in a literary treatment of a situation, feeling that characters are so real to us that we begin, as Virginia Woolf puts it, to see "all sorts of things through [their] eyes" ("Mr. Bennett," 200), helps us to move past instrumental views that can stymie ethical treatment of others.

Resistance to viewing people (or animals) instrumentally can happen even when the text or its author accedes to instrumental views of nonnormative characters. Experiments by Daniel Batson have shown that "the key variable distinguishing those in whom a story of woe elicits compassion from those in whom it does not is the experience of vivid imagining" (Nussbaum, *Political Emotions*, 146).[2] For this reason, fiction's power to depict even devalued characters in their full particularity can lead to readers caring about them and resisting their devaluation. The author's vivid representation of a nonnormative character may work on readers such that we value him or her more than the author seems to have intended.

This is the case, as I show in chapter 3, with O'Connor's character Bishop Rayber, an intellectually disabled boy who comes to imaginative life, who garners (many) readers' sympathies in spite of O'Connor's ultimate indifference to his value. And it is the case in another way in William Faulkner's *The Sound and the Fury* (1929). In Faulkner's appendix (written in 1945), he dismisses the value of Benjamin Compson's emotions by claiming that they do not quite exist *as* emotions. Faulkner claims that his character lost nothing in losing his sister, in being castrated, and in being committed to the state asylum because he did not remember the things he loved (and therefore, by implication, his love was not to be taken seriously). Faulkner writes, "Gelded 1913. Committed to the State Asylum, Jackson 1933. Lost nothing then either because, as with his sister, he remembered not the pasture but only its loss, and firelight was still the same bright shape of sleep" (213). But Faulkner's artistic talent in representing those losses contradicts his statements in the later appendix. He represents the awful events *and* Benjy's responses to them in a way that renders them heartbreaking to many readers. As Michael Bérubé notes, "There are good reasons, both theoretical and practical, to resist Faulkner's characterization [in the appendix] of the character he created" (*Secret Life of Stories*, 77).

Often, novels' commitment to their characters means that they solicit readers' sympathy for them—for all of them. In a series of articles and books, Martha Nussbaum has explored the ability of literature to work against viewing human beings purely instrumentally or in abstract terms. It is not simply that reading literature increases our empathy for others with whom we can imaginatively engage, though that frequently does happen. It is more that literature's particularity and imaginativeness work against viewing people as abstract entities. Zeroing in on the capacity for "fancy," Nussbaum lauds its "ability to endow a perceived form with rich and complex significance; its preference for wonder over pat solutions; its playful and surprising movements, delightful for their own sake; its tenderness, its eroticism, its awe before the fact of human mortality" (*Poetic Justice*, 43). And fancy, for Nussbaum, is another way to describe "the metaphorical imagination," or the imagination that is active when we read literature (*Poetic Justice*, 36).

In "The Literary Imagination in Public Life" Nussbaum sets literature, especially the Victorian realist novel, against a mindset, often active in policy decisions, that "attends only to an abstract and highly general version of the human being"; literature, on the other hand, confronts readers with "a diverse concreteness" (883).[3] In philosophical thought experiments, characters, if so they can be called, are often defined by single attributes, such as disability. This abstraction is necessary to thought experiments but can act to prevent readers from envisioning specific people, temping us to think about them instrumentally. Literature, however, as Susan Squier writes, "is able to hold open a zone of exploration that other mediations (political, social, scientific, and economic) foreclose" (22).

Moreover, as Nussbaum argues in "Equity and Mercy," another aspect of reading fiction affects our ethical thinking: narrative itself teaches us to view human actors as beings who have developed out of certain conditions and "whose errors emerge from a complex narrative history" (104). Engaging with a story about how a person came to be the person he or she is, even if he or she has committed evil deeds, humanizes him or her, and this leads to an attitude of mercy.[4] We see this merciful attitude in O'Connor's novel *The Violent Bear It Away*, where the narrative portrait of young Tarwater makes us understand, though not excuse, his murder of his young cousin.[5] Nussbaum attributes this attitude, again, to the particularity or specificity of literature: her inquiry "construes the participatory emotion of the literary imagination as emotion that will frequently lead to mercy, even where a judgment of culpability has been made. And this merciful attitude derives directly . . . from the literary mind's keen interest in all the particulars" (110).

Even when novels or short stories do not solicit our sympathy for certain characters—for example, when one character's identity is stigmatized—fiction's layered and dialogic (to use Bakhtin's term) quality makes space for readers to view those characters slantwise, to value them in ways beyond what the text, or its implied author, seems to expect.[6] My argument for reading literature bioethically, then, does not depend on literature's arguably inherent ability to promote ethical relations to others.[7] It depends instead on the ability of literary analysis to extract ethical meaning from the complexity and "diverse concreteness" of imaginative texts. One example requires a short detour through another of Nussbaum's claims.

In *Political Emotions* Nussbaum discusses the mechanisms of compassion in democratic societies. She observes that although we usually have compassion for the suffering of people who are already important to our lives and projects, we are also regularly capable of viewing people as important *because* they are suffering. Nussbaum writes, "The thought of importance need not always antecede the compassionate response; the vivid presentation of another person's plight may jump-start it, moving that person, temporarily, into the center of the things that matter" (145). This capacity to feel compassion simply because someone is suffering may explain Suzanne Keen's observation that "*empathy for fictional characters may require only minimal elements of identity, situation, and feeling, not necessarily complex or realistic characterization*" (69).

In literature, the plight of a character such as Bishop Rayber or Benjy Compson may similarly jump-start our compassion in spite of the fact that in important ways the texts seem to dismiss their importance. This readerly response brings us into conflict with the texts themselves. While each text seems to want to lead readers to accept, for example, that there is "no great loss" involved in the murder of Bishop or the castration and institutionalization of Benjy, readers are free to—and are indeed invited to by textuality itself—respond differently. We may read the text against its grain, foregrounding the suffering of characters we are expected to sideline. Resistant reading practices long employed in feminist studies help open up ethical meaning even in texts not particularly committed to a given arena of social justice. Deconstruction has shown us the ability of texts to work against themselves, and resistant readings illuminate those nodes of contradiction.

The power of literature for ethical analysis stems in large part from this complexity that makes space for difference. As Nussbaum puts it, literature "contains within itself an antidote" to its own efforts to "inhibit imaginative access to the stigmatized position" (*Not for Profit*, 109). Whereas a philosophical thought experiment offers a flattened narrative designed to lead the reader to a particular conclusion, literature's open-endedness makes possible various ethical responses, including those that conflict with the author's stated views or the general import of the text.[8] This is why instead of cursorily referencing the plots of the novels I discuss as if those plots in themselves offer definitive answers to bioethical questions,[9] in the chapters that follow I take the time to "sit with" each of the texts, considering their complex meanings and implications in depth. This approach helps to "reposition fiction and literature as contributors to social knowledge" (Squier, 23).

This is not to say that reading novels carefully and caring about characters necessarily alters our behavior, although it sometimes does. Keen has questioned the assumption that caring about characters will translate into caring about others in the real world. She even wonders "whether the expenditure of shared feeling on fictional characters might not waste what little attention we have for others on nonexistent entities" (xxv). Arguing against claims by Nussbaum, Steven Pinker, and Lynn Hunt, Keen "questions the contemporary truism that novel reading cultivates empathy that produces good citizens for the world" (xv). Keen gives pertinent examples of readers being invited to laugh at stigmatized characters in eighteenth-century novels: "Anyone who has read a fair number of eighteenth-century novels will be able to think of examples of stigmatized characters who are held up for ridicule and humiliation, to the delight of protagonists and implied readers alike. The elderly, the fat, and the gout-ridden all seem to be fair game" (xix). It is true that implied readers are invited to laugh at stigmatized characters, and it is true that many do. But my claims here diverge from both of Keen's points.

First, arguing that vivid stories make possible wider identification does not imply that such identification will necessarily change readers' behavior in the real world. But neither does reading a convincing (bio)ethical argument—one whose claims one assents to as one reads—necessarily change one's behavior. The students in my most recent class in literature and bioethics, for example, read articles about animal rights and the horrors of factory farming, and though they raised a few objections, nearly all of them assented to the claim that factory farming, as David DeGrazia puts it, causes "massive unnecessary harm" (74) to sentient creatures. But when I asked them if they planned to change their behavior because of their agreement with DeGrazia's claims, many of them admitted that it would probably be too much trouble to change their eating habits. Ethical or bioethical inquiry may not lead (or may not lead immediately) to practical outcomes, whether that inquiry is the result of philosophical argument or literary analysis. And yet both of these routes toward exploring and committing to ethical views are essential for democratic debate about values.

Keen's second point about the "elderly, the fat, and the gout-ridden" being fair game for humiliation in eighteenth-century novels resonates with my analyses in the chapters that follow. While some texts revalue nonnormative human characters, asking readers to see past the stigma that would have hidden the fullness of their humanity, other texts indeed build their plots and/or humor around the humiliation or dismissal of nonnormative characters. But as I have been arguing, the very presence of these characters in novels in which we are immersed leaves room for alternative responses.[10] It is readers' job—with help from the text itself, from the contradictions, instabilities, and layers that make up narrative—to analyze and resist the norms that govern such texts; and doing so can often be more instructive about ethical or bioethical issues than analyzing texts that do not require resistance for ethical reading.

So I am not claiming that literature is in itself necessarily ethical; clearly literature can rely on and reinforce discriminatory norms. But I am suggesting that literary richness makes possible multiple readings, readings that, for example, respond with compassion to the humiliation of characters at whom we are invited to laugh. Flannery O'Connor's story "Good Country People" is a good example. In that story a man steals the wooden leg of a woman who disdained him and yet planned to seduce him. Instead of a sexual consummation, the story presents comeuppance for a highly educated, arrogant, atheistic woman who finds in this moment that she "ain't so smart" (*Habit*, 170). O'Connor claimed that "the average reader is pleased to observe anybody's wooden leg being stolen" (*Mystery*, 98). But she acknowledged that the story has multiple layers, that it "does manage to operate at another level of experience" (*Mystery*, 99), and that other readers as a consequence might respond quite differently to the theft of the leg. In the chapters that follow I explore responses actively invited by the texts as well as some of those made possible by the complexity of narrative, seeking more fully to understand questions of value raised by each of the novels.

Conceiving the Human

Definitions of the human are changing in postmodernity; but they were not stable in the modernist period either. As Julie Livingston and Jasbir Puar write in the introduction to *Interspecies*, their special issue of *Social Text*, "What counts as 'human' is always under contestation" (6). An article on the website of *Discover Magazine* points out that the only stable definition of the human being has been the Western theological one: the idea that human beings and no other living beings are made in God's image and given immortal souls. This definition privileges "the naked ape over all other creatures" without ambivalence (Fuller). Other discourses and definitions of humanness have been less stable. Even before Darwin, for example, human beings had been pushed off their pinnacle in some scientific circles. In 1735, Carl Linnaeus published the first edition of *Systema Naturae*, in which he placed human beings within the category Anthropomorpha, along with the other apes (Edwards, 39). He explained this decision in a letter, saying that he could find no "generic difference between man and simian which is in accord with the principles of Natural History" and that perhaps he ought to have called "man a simian or vice versa," even though that would have brought "all the theologians against [him]" (Edwards, 40). In later editions of *Systema Naturae* Linnaeus gave in to pressure and moved humans into our own subcategory of primates, where we remain in contemporary taxonomies. The key tenet of the Western religious view of the human being, then, that we are fundamentally separate from the other animals, is reinforced in evolutionary schemas.

This self-understanding, of course, cannot exist without understandings of what it means to be not-human, to be animal. In *The Open*, Giorgio Agamben writes, "It is as if determining the border between human and animal were not just one question among many discussed by philosophers and theologians, scientists and politicians, but rather a fundamental meta-physico-political operation in which alone something like 'man' can be decided upon and produced" (21). The boundaries and terms of this question change over time as certain characteristics come to the fore. For example, Agamben notes that "up until the eighteenth century, language—which would become man's identifying characteristic par excellence—jumps across orders and classes, for it is suspected that even birds can talk" (*Open*, 24).[11]

Since the Enlightenment, in addition to language, the identifying characteristics of the human have been rationality and control of our environment. Myra Seaman summarizes the "subject of traditional liberal humanism":

> The human long presumed by traditional Enlightenment and post-Enlightenment humanism is a subject (generally assumed male) who is at the center of his world (that is, the world); is defined by his supreme, utterly rational intelligence; does not depend (unlike his predecessor) upon a divine authority to make his way through the world but instead manipulates it in accord with his own wishes; and is a historically independent agent whose thought and action produce history. (246)

This supposedly autonomous and world-making subject is not only male, of course, but also white/European.[12] Neither disability nor race was ever far from sight for nineteenth- and twentieth-century scientists who contributed to definitions of the human (claims by Darwin and his protégé T. H. Huxley about "primitive races" are quoted in chapter 1). Nor were disability and race entirely separable. Ellen Samuels establishes that "the discourses of racial identification institutionalized by physical anthropologists developed in intimate connection with nineteenth-century efforts to measure and classify forms of physical and mental difference we would now understand through the rubric of disability" (178).

Nineteenth-century American geologist J. P. Lesley, for example, articulated his society's belief in the equivalence of animals, disabled people, and members of nonwhite races. In his view, as Sunaura Taylor describes it, "human evolution was demonstrated not only by the discovery of so-called primitive or apelike populations (in other words, non-Europeans) but by examining the 'idiots' and 'cretins' of all societies." Taylor further notes that the dehumanization of nonwhite populations relied on "classifications that were inextricably entangled with definitions of inferiority, savagery, sexuality, dependency, ability/disability, physical and mental difference, and so forth" (*Beasts*, 18).[13] The very concept of the *primitive* links nonwhite and nonhuman beings by associating both with that which "we" have transcended through evolution.[14]

Posthumanism questions this exclusive and exceptionalist account of humanness, pointing out first that the label "human" was "granted by and to those with the material and cultural luxury to bestow upon themselves the faculties of 'reason,' autonomous agency, and the privileges of 'being human'" (Seaman, 247). Seaman describes various forms of posthumanism that aim to counter the arrogance and narrowness of humanism. My understanding of posthumanism accords with that of Wolfe, who argues that posthumanism is not the celebration of what we might call "the posthuman," the transcendence of embodiment and materiality (implanting our minds in computers, for example) that is more often known as transhumanism and that extends rather than diverges from humanism. Instead, posthumanism is post-human*ism*, not posthuman; that is, it seeks to move past the ideology of humanism that elevates the human animal over all others and that, through its insistence on the value of certain typically human capacities (primarily reason), also elevates human beings who possess them over those who do not. For Wolfe, the human being is, moreover, "fundamentally a prosthetic creature that has coevolved with various forms of technicity and materiality, forms that are radically 'not-human' and yet have nevertheless made the human what it is" (*Posthumanism*, xxv). Posthumanism, then, adapts to what Freud called the Darwinian "outrage upon [humanity's] naïve self love" (246). It accepts a more humble understanding of the human as one among other animals and as one life form among an enormous variety of living and nonliving entities on the earth.[15] It further accepts an understanding of the category of the human as itself in flux, as biotechnological advances continue to put pressure on the boundaries of humanness. In her consideration of liminal beings such as embryonic stem cells or animals grown with human organs for xenotransplantation, for example, Squier calls for an acknowledgment of "the shifting, interconnected, and emergent quality of human life" (6).

I have chosen the novels considered here in part because each suggests a reconceptualization of human being. In Wells's *Island of Doctor Moreau*, the Beast People are constructed, through multiple surgeries, out of nonhuman animals. Although their resemblance to human beings is imperfect, they pass for human, and the narrative raises multiple benchmarks of humanness that they meet when Prendick exclaims, for example, "These things—these animals *talk!*" (125), and "I never before saw an animal trying to think" (122). The novel thereby sharply questions what we think we know about humanness, which is, first of all, that we are *not* animals. It counters the conception of the human that Wolfe describes as an anthropological dogma: "that 'the human' is achieved by escaping or repressing . . . its animal origins in nature, the biological, and the evolutionary" (*Posthumanism*, vx).[16] In *Moreau*, the human is revealed as a category with arbitrary demarcations, even though, as I show in chapter 1, the text does not abandon hope for a transcendence of embodiment, a hope that lies at the core of humanism.

Huxley's *Brave New World* reimagines humanness in ways that are well known: people are engineered (bred in bottles) and multiple (genetically identical Bokanovsky groups) instead of the unique results of the genetic lottery that we know ourselves to be. But it also reimagines humanness in ways that are not as obvious. The Controller explains that the people's characters, bodies, and tastes do not change from young adulthood to the end of life: they never ail, and they never age. Their lives, as I discuss in chapter 2, have duration, but no shape.[17] This makes the people in the Brave New World unlike any human beings who have ever existed. If, as Gilbert Meilaender puts it, "living things retain their individual existence over time only by *not* remaining what they are" (*Neither Beast*, 10), then this scenario changes what it means not only to be human, but to be alive. By gesturing toward transhumanism within its dystopia, the novel critiques the tenet of humanism that views human beings as essentially minds tethered to unimportant bodies.[18] That is, like *Moreau*, *Brave New World* exposes the desire of humanism to transcend embodiment; and like *Moreau*, it is ambivalent about that desire.

In O'Connor's *The Violent Bear It Away*, the definition of human beings is debated among characters on opposite ends of a spectrum of theological commitment. While one character believes that humanness is defined by being made in God's image and having therefore an immortal soul (an a priori transcendent value), another rejects that definition and replaces it with one of usefulness that underlies many of our own society's values: one is human if one can be productive and useful to one's community. In the latter view, one is human because of certain abilities or capacities. These have been the dominant ways of understanding human-ness and its value: either we are human because we are created in God's image, or we are human because we can use tools, or walk upright, or reason, or speak, or conceive of ourselves through time, etc. (the capaci-ties change depending on the argument). What my analysis shows is that in *The Violent Bear It Away*, even the first definition of humanness, which seems to be neutral with regard to capacities, turns out to depend on a ca-pacity after all. For O'Connor, the capacity to struggle with religious faith makes one "more completely in God's image" than one would be without that capacity (*Habit*, 104). In this view, intellectually disabled people are less completely in God's image than those who have the mental capacity to doubt and to struggle with theology and belief. In this particular the two opposing definitions of humanness, the religious and the secular, collapse into each other, both devaluing and to varying extents dehuman-izing intellectually disabled human beings.

In Ishiguro's *Never Let Me Go*, by contrast, having capacities does not suffice to make one human; one must have been begotten, not made, as the Nicene creed puts it. The cloned human beings in the dystopian sce-nario are genetically identical to human beings, and they feel and think and create just as we do. Indeed, they are what Rosemarie Garland-Thomson calls "severely able-bodied" ("Eugenic World Building," 135). But they do not count as human beings in their society. This exclusion counters definitions of humanness that rely on capacity. While God is not used in the text as an explanation for the clones' devalued status, the frequent use of the word "God" in casual conversation (e.g., "God knows what she meant" [108]) suggests that perhaps a religious understanding of the human soul as implanted in embryos during "natural" conception might motivate the society's understanding of the clones as nonhuman. Created by human beings and not by God, the clones cannot, in this view, themselves be human beings. Whether or not this idea helps the imaginary society justify its abuse of the cloned people, the text's refusal of capacities as touchstones of humanness is instructive: it demonstrates that it is not only capacity-based understandings of humanness that can exclude and devalue some human beings. Even metaphysical under-standings of humanness have the potential to leave some people out, and thus rob them of the value and rights the category is supposed to confer.

In the textual analyses that follow this introduction, the category of the human remains indeterminate; the novels make visible the ways the category is constructed and adjusted to include and exclude, to empower and disempower. Recognition of full humanity has been withheld from women and from racial, ethnic, religious, and sexual minorities as well as disabled people, not merely on interpersonal but on systematic and governmental levels through slavery, forced sterilization, mass murder / "ethnic cleansing," and other forms of eugenics. Livingston and Puar label as "biopolitical anthropomorphism" the "biopolitical processes that bring about the centrality of the human and of certain humans" (8).[19] While I dissent from many of Leon Kass's bioethical positions, he is right to point out that "our successful battles against slavery, sweatshops, and segregation . . . were at bottom campaigns for human dignity—for treating human beings as they deserve to be treated, *solely because of their humanity*" (298). Academic work allied with social justice movements aims to foster the recognition of all human beings' humanity.

But at the same time that we must ensure that the category of the human includes all of us, we must interrogate the category itself and come to recognize the ways it excludes nonhuman animals from moral consideration. Eva Kittay argues that "the objection to [the] human's special place should be lodged at the claim of superiority and its concomitant right to dominate those lower on the scale, not at moral parity [among human beings]" ("Moral Significance," 31).[20] That is, although some philosophers have set up what seems to be a zero-sum game, we need not discredit the idea of equal inherent dignity for all human beings in order to condemn attitudes and actions of human dominance over and exploitation of nonhuman animals. Agamben writes poetically at the end of *The Open*:

> To render inoperative the machine that governs our conception of man will therefore mean no longer to seek new—more effective or more authentic—articulations, but rather to show the central emptiness, the hiatus that—within man—separates man and animal, and to risk ourselves in this emptiness; the suspension of the suspension, Shabbat of both animal and man. (92)

Allying Animal Studies to Disability Studies

Animal studies and disability studies have a simple common tenet, one they share with other social justice-oriented fields of study: difference does not justify exploitation. Together the fields rethink, as Wolfe puts it, "questions of subjectivity, bodily experience, mental life, intersubjectivity, and the ethical" (*Posthumanism*, xxix). But for the most part, animal rights work has been devastatingly unconcerned with disability justice—indeed, it has contributed a great deal to the devaluation of disabled human beings—and disability rights activists have been wary, for obvious reasons, of making common cause with animals.

Peter Singer, the author of *Animal Liberation* and the most famous animal rights pioneer, regularly relies on comparisons between animals and disabled human beings to make his case that animals deserve equal consideration of their interests in cases where they and we have similar interests (the interest in avoiding pain is the most salient example).[21] Writing on his own in *Practical Ethics* and elsewhere and with Helga Kuhse in *Should the Baby Live?*, he has argued that people should be legally allowed to kill "severely disabled" infants at birth. He consistently argues that people with disabilities are "worse off" than others and that their lives are therefore of less value than other lives ("Shopping," 35). He makes these arguments both separately from his animal liberation arguments and within them. Indeed, his arguments for equal consideration of animals' interests *depend* on his contrasting disabled people with animals. Because Singer is attacking the view that human beings automatically deserve consideration merely because they are human beings—a position he labels "speciesism"—he seeks to show that some human beings are less deserving of consideration than some animals.

To do this he relies on the belief that certain capacities are what grant human beings more value than most animals: capacities such as rationality, self-consciousness, and self-awareness through time. This leads him to devalue people with intellectual disabilities even though, as Kittay has shown, he has little knowledge about such people and shows little interest in learning about them ("Personal," 402–403). For example, in *Animal Liberation* he explains speciesism:

The only position that is irredeemably speciesist is the one that tries to make the boundary of the right to life run exactly parallel to the boundary of our own species. Those who hold the sanctity of life view do this, because while distinguishing sharply between human beings and other animals they allow no distinctions to be made within our own species, objecting to the killing of the severely retarded and the hopelessly senile as strongly as they object to the killing of normal adults. (19)

Here Singer moves beyond his initial claim that the right to life ought not to be based on species alone and suggests that one is a speciesist if one believes that killing someone with a severe cognitive disability is just as bad as killing a neurotypical person.

In spite of Singer's reliance on Jeremy Bentham's famous question "Can they suffer?" as the most important question to ask in granting moral consideration, he grounds his views not on this passive capacity to suffer but on active capacities that he insists confer value and create "persons" out of most adult human beings and many nonhuman animals. As Sunaura Taylor writes,

If Singer had left his argument in its simpler form, with the principle of equal consideration based on sentience, *Animal Liberation* would have been a remarkably anti-ableist book. But . . . in the end he rethrones rationality as the arbiter of personhood by arguing that the life of a full person is more valuable—because of the interests and desires that would be frustrated were it to end—than the life of a nonperson, who couldn't have desires and interests that would be frustrated. (*Beasts*, 128)

This sense of a sliding scale of value for human beings within Singer's and other animal ethics scholars' work makes clear why animal rights and disability rights have not yet been able to join forces.[22]

Taylor has provided a trenchant critique of Singer's views. In a chapter of *Beasts of Burden* entitled "All Animals Are Equal (But Some Are More Equal Than Others)," Taylor adopts George Orwell's maxim from *Animal Farm* to respond to Singer's chapter "All Animals Are Equal." She points out that Singer relies exclusively on the medical model of disability as a biological problem within the person, ignoring the powerful role social attitudes and barriers to access create in constructing disability (129). She argues convincingly against Singer's focus on particular future-oriented desires, saying that it is "presumptuous to assume that certain concepts of the future and death are the only capacities that can allow individuals to value their lives" (131). And most forcefully, Taylor claims that Singer himself is being speciesist in valuing the capacities he does. She writes:

> Perhaps the most striking proof of the linked nature of disability and animal oppression is that the things in Singer's argument[] that make it ableist also make it speciesist. By holding up particular capabilities related to rationality as the registrar of personhood (and of the protection from being killed that personhood offers), Singer's arguments reinforce not only a hierarchy of ability but also a hierarchy of species. Within this framework, species whose capabilities resemble (neurotypical) human capabilities are granted more protections. Those whose capacities we don't understand, or whose qualities are debatable, are then at risk of continued exploitation, ownership, and death. (146)

This critique correlates with the notion within animal studies that we ought not to value animals only to the degree that they are like us; instead, we ought to value their difference.

When we focus only on the ways animals are similar to us, we may reify their position of inferiority to human beings: their communication strategies are almost as complex as ours, their tool use almost as varied, and so on (Weil, 4–7). If, however, we allow animals' alterity and approach them with compassion, we can work against speciesism without simultaneously excluding some human beings from equal consideration. Richard Sorabji remarks that Plato made "the important point that we may treasure others because they belong with us or are akin (*oikeioi*) and that this is different from treasuring them because they are like us. The value may lie in the unlikeness" (131–132). Kelly Oliver makes a related claim when she asks, "Why must animals be either things or persons? Is there no way to extend our moral community without making animals persons? In other words, can they enter the moral community as animals?" ("Service Dogs," 248).

The sense that only humans can be persons, discussed further in chapter 1, forms the core of the humanism that underlies even many animal rights philosophies. As Wolfe writes in the introduction to *Zoontologies*, "One of the central ironies of animal rights philosophy . . . is that its philosophical frame remains an essentially humanist one . . . , thus effacing the very difference of the animal other that animal rights sought to respect in the first place" (xii). Or as the fictional Elizabeth Costello says in J. M. Coetzee's *The Lives of Animals*, "Reason is neither the being of the universe nor the being of God. On the contrary, reason looks to me suspiciously like the being of human thought; worse than that, like the being of one tendency in human thought" (23). As Costello suggests, many philosophers, including philosophers of animal rights, overvalue a particular kind of thinking in a sort of self-congratulatory and self-enclosed valorization of "one tendency of human thought."

On the other side of the story, disability rights activists shrink from associating their struggle with that for animal rights. In an article on the website of the organization Not Dead Yet, Stephen Drake exemplifies this wariness: "When disabled people are equated with animals, it never works out well for us." In her article "Unspeakable Conversations," Harriet McBryde Johnson details a visit to Princeton at the invitation of Singer, whose ideas about disability she loathes. Upon her admission that she eats meat, one of Singer's students asks her how she can have so much respect for human life, but so little for animal life. In her closing meditations on the visit, Johnson writes, "Because I am still seeking acceptance of my humanity, Singer's call to get past species seems a luxury way beyond my reach" (519). This position is understandable, but it too readily accepts humanness as the sole source of rights and consideration. Philosopher Cora Diamond stresses that we do not need to "get beyond humanity" or "see this from the point of view of the universe" in order to perceive the injustice in the way we treat animals (142).

Indeed, it is important not to treat disability rights and animal rights as opposed to each other. As historian Douglas Baynton has shown, in the late nineteenth and early twentieth centuries, groups such as women, African Americans, and immigrants sought to distance themselves from disability in order to claim their rights, thereby leaving unchallenged the assumption that if they *were* disabled, it would be acceptable to deny their rights ("Disability," 17–18, 30).[23] There is a similar conundrum facing disabled people now: if, when we are animalized, we seek to distance ourselves from other animals in order to claim just treatment, we leave unchallenged the assumption that it is acceptable to exploit nonhuman animals. As Taylor writes, "It is important to ask how we can reconcile the brutal reality of human animalization with the concurrent need to challenge the devaluing of animals and even acknowledge our own animality" (*Beasts*, 20).

In recent years scholars have begun to argue persuasively that disability liberation and animal liberation are linked. Work by scholars such as Daniel Salomon, Oliver, Wolfe, and (in the most sustained discussion) Taylor has sought to make clear that Singer notwithstanding, disability and animal oppressions result from similar mindsets. Taylor writes: "All animals . . . are devalued and abused for many of the same basic reasons disabled people are. They are understood as incapable, as lacking in the various abilities and capacities that have long been held to make human lives uniquely valuable and meaningful. They are, in other words, oppressed by ableism" (*Beasts*, 43). Kari Weil similarly points out that norms of humanness that depend on "thought, reason, agency" have not only justified unethical behavior toward nonhuman animals but also defined "the human in ways that exclude some humans" (21). Both speciesism and ableism fault beings for not adhering to cultural norms that solidified and intensified, as Lennard Davis has shown, with the rise of industrialization (23–49).

Moreover, Oliver argues, the interdependence highlighted and valorized in disability studies extends to nonhuman animals. We are "indirectly and directly as dependent upon animals as we are on other human beings" ("Service Dogs," 249). And so disability studies is a promising locus for an ethics of interdependence that can cross the species barrier. "If, as Kittay argues, our dependence on other humans for our very being obligates us to them, then it also follows that our dependence on nonhuman animals morally obligates us to them" (Oliver, "Service Dogs," 249). Kittay's and Oliver's emphasis on interdependence steers the discussion away from capacities and toward what we owe to our fellow creatures.

From another angle, Wolfe too moves the discussion away from capacities by critiquing specific arguments for the superior rationality of human beings. In his discussion of Jacques Lacan's and Daniel Dennett's views of animals, he assesses arguments that, having granted certain forms of complex reasoning to animals, begin moving the goalposts farther afield. He points out the oddness of making subjectivity depend, for example, on an ability to employ a "meta-meta-communicative frame" or to "pretend to pretend" (*Posthumanism*, 37, 39). His point that this is "question-begging in the extreme" resembles a point Michael Bérubé makes when he debates Singer about the capacities of people with Down syndrome:

> I note that in the 1920s we were told that people with Down syndrome were incapable of learning to speak; in the 1970s, we were told that people with Down syndrome were incapable of learning how to read. OK, so now the rationale for seeing these people as somewhat less than human is their likely comprehension of Woody Allen films. Twenty years from now we'll be hearing "sure, they get Woody Allen, but only his early comedies—they completely fail to appreciate the breakthrough of *Interiors*." Surely you understand my sense that the goalposts are being moved around here in a rather arbitrary fashion. ("Equality, Freedom," 106–107)

The injustice of this kind of strategy is important to identify because these arbitrarily moved goalposts work to remove certain kinds of sentient beings from the sphere of moral consideration.

Animal studies and disability studies, then, both reject the idea that beings need to have certain valued abilities in order to have rights; but Diamond goes further to reject the concept of rights as the basis for justice. Presenting a reading of Simone Weil's discussion of rights and justice, Diamond argues that rights are not necessarily coextensive with justice. Rights were originally meant to protect property, and they can still have the effect of protecting interests while maintaining "a moral noncommitment to the good" (128). Justice, on the other hand, in Diamond's reading of Weil, comes from a sense in all of us that expects the good, that aligns with the good, and that is brought up short when we observe someone harmed or when we ourselves are about to harm someone. Whether one has rights may depend on capacities, Diamond concedes, but whether one deserves justice is quite another question. She concludes that "tying justice and injustice closely to rights encourages misunderstandings of the complex relation between justice and compassion, and between acting unjustly and being pitiless" (123).

Diamond proposes, therefore, that we respond to the exploitation of animals in the language of justice, not of rights. She writes, "I spend as much time as I do on Weil because I think that what underlies the animal rights movement is a responsiveness to the vulnerability of animals in the face of the relentless exercise of human power, and that the articulating of that responsiveness calls for a grammar akin to the grammar of justice as Weil describes it" (120). If we accept this argument, then those capacities that may justify rights become irrelevant to questions of how we must treat other beings. Wolfe agrees with Diamond on this point, arguing that animal studies and disability studies come together to "pose fundamental challenges . . . to a model of subjectivity and experience drawn from the liberal justice tradition and its central concept of rights, in which ethical standing and civic inclusion are predicated on rationality, autonomy, and agency" (*Posthumanism*, 127).

I am not sure we should cede the entire concept of rights to beings who are believed to have "rationality, autonomy, and agency," or that we must abandon the liberal justice tradition to arrive at just treatment for animals (and I'm quite sure we do not need to abandon it to arrive at just treatment for disabled human beings). Tom Regan and Martha Nussbaum, among others, propose ways to include animals in the circle of rights-bearing beings to whom we have obligations. As Nussbaum writes, "There seems to be no good reason why existing mechanisms of basic justice, entitlement, and law cannot be extended across the species barrier" (*Frontiers*, 326). Regan's account of animal rights rests on the fact that animals, like human beings, are conscious, experiencing beings who are "subjects-of-a-life" (*Case for Animal Rights*, 243 and passim); they experience a sense of their own welfare. Their lives matter to them and therefore they must not be treated as mere tools. Regan argues convincingly that "the animal rights movement is a part of, not antagonistic to, the human rights movement. The theory that rationally grounds the rights of animals also grounds the rights of humans" ("Case for Animal Rights," 24). Though Regan does not mention disability rights in this passage, the subject-of-a-life view would apply to any conscious human being, no matter how severely disabled.[24]

Nussbaum, for her part, advocates the capabilities approach as a framework flexible enough to understand and seek to protect various sorts of dignity and flourishing (*Frontiers*, 327). Her claims about why we should move beyond social contract theory to account for our duties to animals demonstrate both types of arguments about animals: that they share qualities of intelligence with us (that they are like us) and therefore should be understood to have rights, *and* that beings do not have to be able to "join a contract as rough equals [to be] primary, nonderivative subjects of a theory of justice" (*Frontiers*, 327) (that they deserve justice even though or even when they are not like us).

Wolfe counters that we should not just add animals and disabled human beings into the category of rights-holders, but should rethink ethics completely. Like Weil and Diamond, Wolfe suggests that if we leave the liberal justice tradition behind and base compassion on the fact of the passivity of suffering, on the fact that others are our fellow creatures, then "new lines of empathy, affinity, and respect between different forms of life, both human and nonhuman, may be realized in ways not accountable . . . by the basic coordinates of liberal humanism" (*Posthumanism*, 127–128). In this he is influenced by Derrida's conception, based on his engagement with Bentham, of the shared finitude of all living beings. I agree that our shared finitude matters morally and should help delineate our behavior. But Wolfe's suggestion that Nussbaum's capabilities approach dehumanizes disabled people—a suggestion he makes by quoting Geoffrey Harpham (*Posthumanism*, 68)—misunderstands her list of the central human capabilities (whatever its other merits or insufficiencies).

Wolfe (following Harpham) claims that in Nussbaum's account, if someone inherently lacks any of the capabilities, that person is rendered less than fully human. But Nussbaum's list is not about what someone is able to do physically or mentally, but about what someone is able to do *politically*—that is, what one's government makes it possible or impossible for one to do. Nussbaum writes that she has used the capabilities approach in philosophy (while Amartya Sen has used it differently in economics) to "provide the philosophical underpinning for an account of core human entitlements that should be respected and implemented by the governments of all nations, as a bare minimum of what respect for human dignity requires" (*Frontiers*, 70). So it is not the case, as Harpham says, that Nussbaum's theory inadvertently dehumanizes someone like the late Stephen Hawking. Instead, the capabilities approach entails that Hawking would be dehumanized by his government if that government, for example, locked him away so that nondisabled people would not have to confront their own fears of disability.

The capabilities approach may at first *seem* to suggest that someone who cannot, for example, "move freely from place to place" (Nussbaum, *Frontiers*, 70) cannot attain to human flourishing and is therefore dehumanized; but it actually focuses on what can be done *to* people (and animals). As long as one is not prevented by powerful forces in one's sociopolitical world from exercising one's central capabilities, one is not being dehumanized or prevented from flourishing. After all, consider someone who is physically capable of moving from place to place but who does not desire to leave her own neighborhood; she is not dehumanized by her decision not to take advantage of the capability to move freely from place to place. It follows that someone who is physically or mentally unable to perform any of the activities listed by Nussbaum is not dehumanized by not performing them.

In the section of *Frontiers of Justice* where she applies the capabilities approach to animals, Nussbaum focuses similarly on what forces enable or inhibit animal flourishing. She points out that human compassion is not enough to ensure animal flourishing. We have compassion for someone who is suffering, even if that individual's suffering is not anyone's fault (for example if someone is suffering from disease). But we ought not merely to have compassion for animals, but also to be aware that their suffering is our fault and to acknowledge that animals are *entitled* not to suffer. "Where that suffering is caused by a wrongful act, a duty of compassion would involve acknowledgement of that wrongfulness. That is, a duty of compassion would not be just a duty to have compassion, but a duty . . . to refrain from, inhibit, and punish acts of the sort that cause the suffering occasioning the compassion" (336). This brings us back to a conception of rights and duties: the liberal justice tradition. "When I say that the mistreatment of animals is unjust, I mean to say not only that it is wrong *of us* to treat them in that way, but also that they have a right, a moral entitlement, not to be treated in that way" (337).

In combination, animal studies and disability studies ask us to rethink what grounds rights and, more generally, what grants beings moral value. They ask us to stop short before we dismiss a living being, human or nonhuman, from the sphere of moral consideration and question the basis for such a dismissal. In this way, the two fields work in tandem to acknowledge and respect the subjectivity of living beings whose subjectivity has long been denied. They come together, I hope productively, in three of the chapters that follow. In chapter 1, we find that Wells's disability rhetoric, in its linkage to ideologies of cure, works in tension with the text's attack on human exceptionalism. In chapter 3, we see the ways animality is used to assist in the dehumanization of O'Connor's mentally disabled character Bishop. And in chapter 4, we see Ishiguro's clones disabled by the fictional society and treated as though they are free-range animals, ready to sacrifice themselves for normate human beings. While chapter 2 focuses more squarely on aging and disability among human beings, it briefly shows the ways animality works as that which humanity in the Brave New World must transcend.

Analyzing Literary Thought Experiments

The topic of each chapter that follows can be described both in terms of a thought experiment that explores a particular view and in terms of literary analysis that brings out the singularity (to rely again on Attridge's term) of each text. The first chapter, "Beast Lives," combines animal studies and disability studies approaches to explore the ways *The Island of Doctor Moreau* grapples with human exceptionalism, an ideology still prevalent in bioethics and Western culture generally. Human exceptionalism, as should be clear from the foregoing, holds that human beings are so different from other animals as to be existentially unique, that we are the only beings who deserve to be understood as "persons," with the rights that personhood confers. This ideology is called into question by Wells's "Beast People," beings who are on a continuum between "beast" and "man." By depicting people who turn out to have been crafted—via multiple intensive surgeries without anesthesia—from nonhuman animals, *Moreau* offers a thought experiment that invites readers to revisit our assumptions about our unique value and inviolability.

While the novel seriously questions human exceptionalism, the dynamics of its exciting plot nevertheless depend on readers accepting that nonhuman animals but not human beings can be experimented upon and that animals but not human beings are (to use Donna Haraway's term) "killable" creatures. The Beast People resemble deformed and disabled people, and I use the novel's disability rhetoric to identify a belief in a "curative imaginary" (Kafer, 27) that, in spite of the novel's purported acceptance of human animality, seeks to transcend both animality and disability. What we learn from exploring this issue in *Moreau* is not simply that human exceptionalism is a self-serving aspect of humanism, but that this ideology underlies many types of assertion about the animality of human beings. That is, even a view that accepts that humans are animals can give rise to a desire to transcend such animality. And this desire for transcendence of human animality is akin to the insistence on cure that sees disabled human beings as objects to be fixed. As Eli Clare writes in his exploration of the ideology of cure, cure only sometimes saves lives: "Cure [also] manipulates lives; cure prioritizes some lives over others; cure makes profits; cure justifies violence" (xvi). In Wells's novel, both animality and disability are cast as inaccuracies that must, with great violence, be corrected. Such adherence to cure reveals a lingering belief in at least the possibility of transcendent value for human beings.

Chapter 2, "Old Lives," turns to the question of the value of old age and old human beings. Influential physician and bioethicist Ezekiel Emanuel has proposed that it would be a good thing for everyone to die at around age seventy-five, when it is no longer likely that they will contribute anything substantial to society, and before they become ill or disabled. In Aldous Huxley's 1932 *Brave New World*, people die at around age sixty, never becoming elderly, frail, ill, or disabled. Such a literary thought experiment allows us to tease out the implications of Emanuel's view, a view that, through the search for "compressed morbidity," has come to dominate age studies and the "healthy aging" movement. I explore the ways *Brave New World* implicitly critiques the compulsory youthfulness (to use a term coined by Hailee Gibbons) of the society it depicts.

By reading *Brave New World* in conversation with ideas about aging and the life span presented by Emanuel, Gilbert Meilaender, and Alasdair MacIntyre, I show that the fictional society has made it impossible for its citizens to have or create life narratives, which are a significant part of how we make meaning of our lives. The novel demonstrates two main reasons why this sacrifice of life narratives is not worthwhile. First, people who know they will never experience frailty or decline are less likely to have compassion for those who do. By showing the society's mistreatment of the only character who does experience aging, Linda, the novel suggests a moral cost to the unvarying health and able-bodiedness of the Brave New World's citizens. Second, the novel exposes how the society's control of embodiment trivializes bodily experience and divorces people's bodies from their emotions. The excision of old age, then, though overlooked by critics as a target of Huxley's critique, forms part of the novel's dystopia. Realizing this may prompt us to cast a more critical eye on our own society's pursuit of able-bodiedness and youthfulness throughout the life span.

Chapter 3, "Disabled Lives," inserts Flannery O'Connor's representation of the murder of an intellectually disabled boy, Bishop, into a debate in contemporary bioethics about the value of disabled lives. Philosophers Peter Singer and Jeff McMahan have each argued that to kill an intellectually disabled person would not be as bad as killing "one of us." That is to say, they hold that intellectually disabled lives are not worth as much as nondisabled lives. In *The Violent Bear It Away*, Bishop's value is a matter of debate among three characters: a self-styled prophet, who believes that Bishop's soul is as valuable to God as any other; the boy's hyperrationalist father, Rayber, who believes that if Bishop were to die it would be "no great loss"; and the murderer, young Tarwater, a fourteen-year-old boy who is resisting a calling to be a prophet himself and whose murder of Bishop is the desperate culmination of that resistance. By dramatizing this debate, O'Connor's novel asks readers to confront the import of claims such as Singer's and McMahan's.

As a devout Catholic, O'Connor finds views such as Singer's, McMahan's, and her character Rayber's repugnant. She would agree with her prophet character who asserts, though with telling condescension, "Precious in the sight of the Lord even an idiot!" But as I demonstrate, her novel colludes with the eugenic rationalizations she aims to critique. Her narrative—and not just Rayber and Tarwater—devalues and dehumanizes Bishop, making his life seem expendable. Many critics unthinkingly accede to this devaluation. And yet in a paradox key to literature's suitability for bioethical investigation, O'Connor's artistry enables readers to grasp the ways in which the narrative has performed this devaluation. Bishop's mere existence in a well-rendered fictional world allows readers to read the novel against its grain, to feel the pain of Bishop's loss even as his father waits in vain for pain to come. The novel's richness, as opposed to the purposeful flatness of a philosophical thought experiment, makes possible resistant readings that understand Bishop's worth as part of a diverse and inclusive world.

In chapter 4, "Cloned Lives," I turn to the question of what duties human beings have to those in their power—cloned human beings in the fictional world of Ishiguro's *Never Let Me Go* and farm animals in our own world. Michael Pollan, author of the *New York Times* bestseller *The Omnivore's Dilemma* and other widely read books that critique factory farming, advocates eating humanely raised meat and returning to a more natural diet. He argues that as long as an animal has had a good life and a respectful death, it is ethical to kill him or her, even at a fraction of his or her natural life span. In *Never Let Me Go* cloned human beings are raised in a progressive school, Hailsham, enjoying idyllic childhoods before donating their vital organs as young adults. They have what Pollan favors for animals: good lives and respectful deaths. This parallel between Pollan's ideal situation for animals and the situation of Ishiguro's fictional clones makes for a textual laboratory in which to consider the humane meat movement's aims and assumptions more carefully.

Readers' reaction to the fictional social system is generally one of horror. But are we certain that what is horrifying if it happens to genetic human beings is ethical when it happens to nonhuman animals? In this chapter I show how the novel illuminates the complex ways societies handle or suppress the knowledge of the suffering they inflict and more broadly, how they make certain beings "killable." Multiple critics have applied Agamben's distinction in *Homo Sacer* (for which he draws on Hannah Arendt's discussion of the Greek terms for what we simply call "life") between *zoë* or "bare life" and *bios*, or socially meaningful life, to the clones in this novel. They suggest that because they are killed with impunity, the clones exemplify *zoë*. I argue, on the contrary, that the Hailsham clones actually have *bios*. This makes it all the more surprising that they are viewed as killable by their society. It is because of this paradox that the novel sheds light on our relationship to humanely raised animals. *Never Let Me Go* highlights the cognitive dissonance inherent in treating beings well while valuing them solely instrumentally and preparing to kill them; it thereby provides an instructive thought experiment about the humane meat movement.

In a brief epilogue I analyze some of the ways the ideologies considered here play out in contemporary, real-world devaluation and exploitation of certain kinds of beings. Animals are exploited more relentlessly as we develop "better" industrial methods for processing them. Older people, whose numbers are growing, are routinely abused and neglected. Disabled people continue to be incarcerated (now mostly in jails) and sterilized, even if no longer in the context of a national eugenics program. I then compare some of the logic shared between the old eugenics and the new "liberal eugenics" advocated by many contemporary philosophers.

By inviting readers into vivid fictional worlds, these novels establish literary-ethical laboratories where we can examine human exceptionalism, ideologies of cure, compressed morbidity, the devaluation of disabled people, and humane farming. As Terry Eagleton has argued, literature has "the most intimate relations to questions of social power" (20). In each chapter, accordingly, I bring imaginative writers into bioethical conversations, allowing their voices to mingle with those of contemporary philosophers and bioethicists as we debate the relative value of different kinds of lives and consider what those in positions of power may do with and to those lives.

1

Beast Lives

Wells's *The Island of Doctor Moreau*

In "Eating One's Friends: Fiction as Argument in Bioethics," Tod Chambers describes two ways fiction can work bioethically on its readers. Fiction presents "an argument for a particular perspective on the world" either by setting up the story so as to value one perspective or by defamiliarizing the issues, allowing "the reader to re-see the world" (81).[1] Chambers writes that "through defamiliarization and other techniques, art seeks to make us aware of that which has become invisible, prompting a reckoning with the way things are and helping imagine the way things could be" (81). Focusing on speculative fictions that involve one species eating another, he argues that fiction can alter readers' perspectives by confronting speciesism (90). While H. G. Wells's 1896 speculative novel *The Island of Doctor Moreau* does not focus on the issue of *eating* other species, it certainly uses defamiliarization techniques to reshape readers' views of the human/animal divide.[2]

The assumption that human beings are absolutely separate from other animals is the basis of humanism. Human exceptionalism reaches toward its apotheosis in "transhumanism," an effort to "transcend the bonds of materiality and embodiment" (Wolfe, *Posthumanism*, xv) through science and technology. In Wells's time, the standard Western view of the human as the unique pinnacle of creation was beginning to shift as Darwin's work encouraged people to understand themselves as more closely related to other animals.

H. G. Wells was an admiring student of Thomas Henry Huxley, the scientist known as "Darwin's bulldog" for his passionate support for and explication of Darwin's theories (and the grandfather of Aldous Huxley). T. H. Huxley is mentioned in the novel as the protagonist's former tutor. One of Wells's biographers writes that "Huxley's teaching gripped and held his imagination" (Brome, 35).[3] Having been trained in Darwin's theories and having studied zoology at the Normal School of Science and the University of London, Wells had no doubt that humans had evolved from an ape-like ancestor. But further questions were still up for debate: to what degree and for what reasons are human beings superior to other animals? Should we be classified in a category by ourselves, or are we simply a type of ape? As Richard Costa notes, "The newly posited entanglement of species in the destinies of one another reopened the question of man's relation to the entire universe," a question central to Wells's early work (11).[4]

In his 1863 lecture "Evidence as to Man's Place in Nature," Huxley asks, "Is Man so different from any of these Apes that he must form an order by himself? Or does he differ less from them than they differ from one another, and hence must take his place in the same order with them?" He concludes that "the lower Apes and the Gorilla would differ more than the Gorilla and the Man" (Harris, 203). Ronald Edwards notes that this lecture "was the first really public, evidence-based demonstration that human beings were properly considered a type of animal—specifically, an ape" (22). While placing human beings in the same category as the apes, Huxley does not, as is clear from this passage, abandon ideas of "higher" and "lower" animals; this rhetoric implies that "man," though in the same order as the apes, is nevertheless "higher" than they—that human beings are, as Wells puts it in "Human Evolution: An Artificial Process," the "culminating ape" (Philmus, 193).[5]

Of course, the hierarchies laden within the category of "man" also included intrahuman hierarchies. Although Huxley's claim that human beings had a single origin was influential, he and his colleagues in the natural sciences (including Darwin) nevertheless held that "some races . . . occupied the very lowest rungs of the evolutionary ladder" (Brantlinger, 164). Indeed, as Patrick Brantlinger notes, Darwin's assertion about what he saw as the "almost certain" extinction of "savage races" was bound up with his assertion about the concomitant extinction of the "anthropomorphous apes" (167). Darwin wrote in *Descent of Man* that once these extinctions have come to pass, there will be a greater gulf between "man in a more civilized state, as we may hope, even than the Caucasian, and some ape as low as a baboon, instead of as now between the negro or Australian and the gorilla" (160). Conceptions of species in the nineteenth century and most of the twentieth often also invoked conceptions of race, with both categories inflecting definitions of humanness even as those definitions were in flux.

The view that human beings are the culmination of creation or evolution continues to underlie arguments about human rights and dignity not just in popular culture but in bioethics. It is used, indeed, to *ground* human rights by allegedly explaining and justifying human dignity. In *Human Dignity and Bioethics: Essays Commissioned by the President's Council on Bioethics*, for example, we find regular assertions of human exceptionalism, assumptions that we are unique not just as a species with particular features, but unique in a way "that merits special comment and consequences: 'uniquely unique'" (Edwards, 7). In essays written from both religious and materialist standpoints, our difference from animals is used to explain why human beings (but no other animals) should be granted moral personhood. Writing from a Christian perspective, for example, Robert Kraynack claims that the references in the Hebrew Bible to the *imago dei* "show that God created the natural world as a hierarchy with the human species at the top, possessing a special right of dominion over the lower species" (75). He grounds human dignity in this hierarchy and argues that such dignity "confers special worth to human life and procreation, although the lifeblood and procreation of other animals also receive certain blessings" (76).

Writing from within a secular philosophic tradition that valorizes human rationality, Holmes Rolston also finds the basis for human dignity in our difference from other animals, in "what is distinctively human" (129). He suggests that "we can make some progress toward recognizing distinctive human worth by articulating the ways in which humans differ from nonhuman animals. . . . Awareness of the gulf separating humans from all other species can sensitize us to our potential for dignity" (130). Elaborating throughout his essay on capacities that humans have but nonhuman animals allegedly lack, he argues that these capacities give human beings moral worth. He writes: "Only humans are 'persons,' enjoying 'existential uniqueness.' 'Human being' is perhaps a biological term, but 'person' refers to the further existential dignity associated with an experiencing subjectivity with personal identity, a phenomenological 'I' conserved with ongoing agency and responsibility" (143).[6] The regular reliance on human exceptionalism in this collection bolsters Wolfe's claim that within mainstream bioethics the notion of the human is still not only "uninterrogated but indeed retrenched" (*Posthumanism*, 49).

Both the existence of a gulf separating human beings from other animals and the moral consequences of the alleged gulf are questioned in Wells's early novel. In *The Island of Doctor Moreau*, Wells leads us to consider the ontological and moral status of human beings by depicting vivisection experiments that make human beings out of animals. Our protagonist, Edward Prendick, is saved after a shipwreck by men engaged in the unusual task of bringing a puma to a remote island. Once on the island, Prendick hears the puma screaming for so long and with such agony that "it was as if all the pain in the world had found a voice" (97).[7] As he later learns, Dr. Moreau has been experimenting on animals—performing multiple surgeries without anesthesia on members of various species—in an effort to create rational human beings. Although his creatures do pass as human beings, Moreau is never satisfied with them. Readers soon realize that he is seeking a perfection not available in any actual human beings, much less in his vivisected creations.

The intent to "improve" other beings serves as a focal point for readings of the novel in terms of race and imperialism. As Cyndy Hendershot points out, the Beast People function as "natives" who are "coded with racial theories which view the non-European as an intermediary between animal and human" (6). Moreau's effort to remake "native" beings in his own image is a clear analogue to imperialism, and the fact that he imports most of the animals on whom he experiments adds the suggestion of slavery. As is clear from the work of influential scientists such as Darwin and Huxley, "categories of animality are not innocent of race" (Chen, 104). Neither are such categories innocent of disability. Moreau is captivated by the glimmer of improvability, what Alison Kafer calls a "curative imaginary"—"an understanding of disability [or in Moreau's case, animality] that not only *expects* and *assumes* intervention but also cannot comprehend anything other than intervention" (27). Such an imaginary is further evoked by the novel's repeated references to disability and deformity to describe the Beast People Moreau has created.

The Island of Doctor Moreau raises important questions about animal experimentation, about what exactly makes Moreau's project wrong. It also raises broader questions about our status as human beings. It therefore serves as a literary thought experiment, enabling us to consider what characterizes us as human beings, what rights we have over other animals, and what, if anything, makes human beings unique. The novel certainly questions human exceptionalism. But it retains a sense of the superior value of human beings. Further, its questioning of human exceptionalism does not break down the human/animal binary so much as challenge "the idea that there is anything beyond animality" (Gross and Vallely, 3). The novel suggests that Moreau's project is doomed to fail not because it goes against nature to blend species and create chimeras or because it is sacrilegious to create human beings, but because human beings are not ever the perfectly rational creatures Moreau imagines. We are part beast—beastliness is humanity.[8] However, in the novel's use of disability rhetoric to indicate the liminal status of the Beast People, we see that Wells cannot completely abandon hope in Moreau's curative imaginary.

Animal Experimentation and the "Advancement of Science"

The puma's constant cries "at last altogether upset [Prendick's] balance" (97). Finally he heads outside until he is out of earshot of the puma's screams. But instead of condemning whatever it is Moreau is doing to cause such agony, he muses on his physiological response to others' pain: "Yet had I known such pain was in the next room, and had it been dumb, I believe—I have thought since—I could have stood it well enough. It is when suffering finds a voice and sets our nerves quivering that this pity comes troubling us" (97).[9] Prendick casts his pity as weakness, a function of nerves that respond unwilled to vocally expressed pain.[10] His simultaneous sympathy for and evasion of the suffering of Moreau's subjects encapsulates the novel's own equivocation between a condemnation of a project that inflicts intense pain on nonhuman animals and an acceptance of animal experimentation as a means of advancing human knowledge.

Wells was an avowed supporter of animal experimentation, what was then called "vivisection." But the novel demonstrates a sharp discomfort with pain being inflicted on animals, to the extent that some contemporaneous reviewers saw the novel as an antivivisectionist parable.[11] Indeed, Wells's later writing on vivisection displayed his contradictory views about how much animals can be said to suffer and what might make their suffering worthwhile.

In "Popular Feeling and the Advancement of Science: Anti-Vivisection" (1928), Wells responds to an influential antivivisectionist movement that "touched enough of the public to ensure passage of the Cruelty to Animals Act in 1876, which protected research animals in particular" (DeGrazia, 103). In the essay, Wells spends much of his time pointing out the hypocrisy of antivivisectionists who restrict their objections to animal research but continue to support the meat industries. He astutely suggests that such antivivisectionists are not really against inflicting pain on animals, but "against the thrusting of a scientific probe into mysteries and hidden things" (Harris, 268). But while the article's most powerful aim is to critique the antivivisectionists, it does also set forth an argument in favor of vivisection. Wells claims that many experiments do not hurt at all, and many that would cause pain are "nearly always performed under anesthesia" (Harris, 266). He admits that some experiments are painful, however: "There is no denial on the part of the scientific experimentalist that a certain number of experiments are painful and have to be painful, and that they . . . have to be performed upon animals *of an order of intelligence that leaves one in no doubt of the reality of the suffering inflicted.* . . . It is an amount of suffering infinitesimal in comparison with the gross aggregate of pain inflicted day by day upon sentient creatures by mankind, but it occurs" (Harris, 267, emphasis added). With the mention of the "gross aggregate of pain," he returns to his accusation of hypocrisy on the part of the antivivisectionist movement. But here Wells clearly acknowledges the reality of animal suffering.

And yet at the end of the essay, Wells reverses himself, calling such an acknowledgment of animal intelligence and suffering a "mythology." The antivivisectionists, he asserts, want to protect a "delightful and elaborated mythology in which these poor limited creatures are humanized and have thrust upon them responses, loyalties, and sympathetic understandings of which they are, in reality, *scarcely more capable than plants*" (Harris, 268, emphasis added). One of Wells's tactics here (with words such as "delightful" and "poor limited creatures," and the suggestion of sympathies "thrust upon" animals) is familiar to our period as well: accuse those who care about animal suffering of sentimentality.

Josephine Donovan demonstrates an "inherent bias . . . toward ratio-nalism" running through contemporary discourses opposed to animal rights and, in response, through much rights-based animal liberation theory (59). This rationalism is in reaction to a more emotionally cen-tered rhetoric espoused by nineteenth-century "women activists in the antivivisection movement, such as Frances Power Cobbe, [who] viewed as their enemy the 'coldly rational materialism' of science" (59). Cobbe is just the sort of person whose hypocrisy in eating meat while campaign-ing against vivisection Wells targets in this essay. Donovan notes that women "became the primary activists and energizers of the nineteenth-century antivivisection movement" (70); it is clear that Wells's disdain for what he saw as feminine squeamishness motivates some of the dis-missive rhetoric he employs in "Popular Feeling." For example, he says that the idea of vivisection is "naturally repulsive to gentle and kindly spirits" (Harris, 277) and that the "idea of living substance cut while it quivers and feels is too powerful for [the anti-vivisectionist]" (Harris, 267).[12] The prevailing emphasis on rationality can be seen in the novel in the way Moreau dismisses Prendick's visceral distress at the vivisected puma: "At least spare me those youthful horrors" (122). And Prendick's belief, articulated later in the story, that he could have overcome his "squeamish" reactions to the animals' cries had there been a valid pur-pose to them (145) demonstrates Wells's belief in the priority of rational-ity over emotion.

But Wells's equivocation about whether animals can suffer suggests a suppressed discomfort with animal suffering. In an earlier essay entitled "The Province of Pain," he had affirmed that "the higher animals, like man, look before they act; with the distinction of approaching man in being less automatic and more intelligent, it seems credible that they also approach him in feeling pain" (Harris, 273). As Patrick Parrinder points out, Wells's ambivalence about animal experimentation can be seen in his *Text-Book of Biology* (1893), which "is virtually a dissection manual" but in one copy of which Wells drew a sketch of a rabbit dissecting a man (*Shadows*, 50). Indeed, using vivisection to "generate Gothic hor-ror endows [*Moreau*] with a deep ambivalence towards science" (Harris, "Vivisection," 99). One might speculate that Wells did care deeply about the suffering of sentient creatures—in *Experiment in Autobiography* he mentions the butcher's yard next door to his childhood home, where animals "were harboured violently, and protested plaintively through the night before they were slaughtered" (22)—but such feeling was in conflict with his view of himself as a man and a scientist.

Wells is similarly contradictory about the reasons why he believes causing animal suffering is permissible. In one instance he takes a utilitarian view, writing that "the medical profession is massively in support of vivisection, and its testimony is that knowledge derived from vivisection has made possible the successful treatment of many cases of human suffering. So far as we can measure one pain against another, or the pain of this creature against the pain of that, vivisection has diminished the pain of the world very considerably" (Harris, 268). This view has similarities with and differences from the views of the influential utilitarian philosopher Peter Singer, author of *Animal Liberation*. Both Wells and Singer believe that inflicting suffering on animals *can* be justified if it works to prevent a sufficient amount of additional suffering (Singer, *Animal*, 85). On this count Singer and Wells differ from animal rights scholars Tom Regan and Mark Bernstein, who take more definitive stands against inflicting pain on animals for the purposes of experimentation. Regan writes that the "rights view . . . is opposed to human utilization of nonhuman animals in principle and seeks to end it in practice. . . . Because those nonhuman animals who exist as ends in themselves are never to be treated merely as means, it is wrong to experiment on them in the name of advancing the wellbeing of others" (*Defending Animal Rights*, 24).[13] For Wells and Singer, on the contrary, advancing the wellbeing of others can be sufficient grounds for inflicting suffering under certain conditions, conditions that are far more stringent for Singer than for Wells.

Wells differs from Singer first on the matter of whether humanity has genuinely benefited to any great extent from animal experimentation. Whereas Wells thinks "vivisection has diminished the pain of the world very considerably," Singer believes that we have not benefited to anywhere near the degree we would need to in order to justify inflicting the suffering we do (*Animal*, 41, 52, 91–92). Second, he differs from Singer on how much consideration to give animal suffering. To Wells, it seems, human suffering matters more than animal suffering. Because he does not attempt to claim that fewer animals than human beings suffer in the grand scheme of medical research and disease, he implies that human suffering deserves greater consideration. To Singer, on the other hand, equal degrees of suffering of all sentient creatures have equal moral weight, and so the like interests of all sentient creatures must be given equal consideration (*Animal*, 8, passim). For Singer, then, causing suffering by experimenting on thousands of sentient creatures even in order to save hundreds of human beings the same amount of suffering would be unethical. Wells, for his part, remains vague about what sorts of suffering of what sorts of beings deserve what degrees of consideration.

But again, toward the end of "Popular Feeling and the Advancement of Science," Wells takes a different tack, declining to take animal suffering into consideration at all and instead laying out the views of a "supporter of vivisection" in approving terms:

> He regards the whole animal creation as existing not merely for its present sensations, but as a contributing part of a continuing and developing reality which increases in knowledge and power. His disposition is to see things plainly and to accept the subservience of beast to man in man's increasing effort to understand and control. He regards animals as limited and simplified cognates of our own infinitely more complex and important beings, illuminating inferiors, and he can conceive no better and more profitable use for their lives than to serve the ends of mental growth. Otherwise, what are their lives? A play of desires and fears, that ends in being devoured by other creatures great and small. (Harris, 269)

Reducing animal consciousness to "present sensations" and "a play of desires and fears" and romanticizing an almost personified "developing reality," Wells here idealistically enters into the mindset of a vivisector who proclaims an across-the-board "subservience of beast to man" in man's efforts to "understand and control." Since human beings are "infinitely more complex and important," the utilitarian argument that measures suffering against suffering does not even have to be adduced. Here, instead, the highest purpose of animal lives is to serve *our* "mental growth."

Wells goes so far in this section of "Popular Feeling" as to declare practical applications irrelevant to the vivisector's pursuit of knowledge: "I doubt if his work is largely determined by practical ends, or whether it would have much value if he undertook it directly for the sake of curing disease, benefitting humanity or anything of that sort. Sentimental aims mean loose, sentimental, ineffective work. He wants knowledge because he wants knowledge; it is his characteristic good. Practical applications follow unsought" (Harris, 269). Here, instead of providing the rationale for inflicting suffering, the pursuit of benefit is cast as a drawback that could lead to sloppy work. This description of the vivisector corresponds to Moreau's character. Indeed, in one of Prendick's most impassioned moments of thinking about Moreau's project, this is the very problem for him—that there are no practical ends to Moreau's work. He laments that the Beast People's "mock-human existence, begun in an agony, was one long internal struggle, one long dread of Moreau—and for what? It was the wantonness of it that stirred me" (145).[14] Considering the end of "Popular Feeling," one might think Wells would be entirely on Moreau's side against Prendick's accusation of wantonness: it is not just for practical applications but for the pursuit of knowledge that animal suffering can be justified. But the contradictions in Wells's essays are echoed in the novel, leaving far more ambivalence than the essay's ending would suggest. The novel asks readers to be outraged by Moreau's torture of the animals but at the same time to accept vivisection as something non-criminal and even useful—to maintain the view of animals as beings on whom with impunity we can inflict great suffering.

One of the textual dynamics that works against readers' sympathy for nonhuman animals is the suspense Wells added to the first half of the novel in the final draft. In the early draft, Prendick knows that the beings Moreau is experimenting on are not human and never fears for his own safety (Philmus, xx). When he catches sight of the puma after she has been partially transformed, he doubts whether it is an animal he sees, but Moreau immediately explains (Philmus, 128–129). For the revised version, however, Wells added an element of fear and suspense: Prendick is afraid that Moreau is experimenting on human beings, animalizing them through vivisection, and that Moreau might start experimenting on him next. "Could it be possible, I thought, that such a thing as the vivisection of men was carried on here? The question shot like lightning across a tumultuous sky; and suddenly the clouded horror of my mind condensed into a vivid realization of my own danger" (107).[15]

In an intense chapter entitled "The Hunting of the Man," Prendick runs away from Moreau's assistant, Montgomery, hides, and seriously considers drowning himself rather than submit to the torture he is sure is waiting for him. He is convinced that the creatures he has seen were "victims of some hideous experiment" and that the "sickening scoundrels," Moreau and Montgomery, must intend to "fall upon [him] with a fate more horrible than death—with torture" (108). In the next chapter, he joins some Beast People for a time, but Moreau shows up and orders them to capture Prendick. A violent struggle follows, adding to readers' sense that Prendick is in great danger. And so when Prendick and readers finally discover in the following chapter that he is not in danger, that Moreau is experimenting exclusively on nonhuman animals, we can hardly help but join Prendick in his relief. This relief draws us away from our concern that Moreau is causing excruciating pain ("a fate more horrible than death") to sentient beings and solidifies the human-centered values of the novel.

Other revisions Wells made detract from what could have been the novel's antivivisectionist message: in the first version, Prendick tells Moreau that "the bare thought of vivisection turns me sick" (Philmus, 104). Such a bald statement by our protagonist would be likely to encourage readers' agreement, but Wells cut it for the final version. Moreover, in the first version Moreau's wife is on the island with him. As she and Prendick try to chat over the puma's screams, Mrs. Moreau, in spite of long acclimation, begins to "shiver and [grow] paler as the discord of pain crept into the growing outcry." As they talk about books, "the sense of the helpless animal & its slow hopeless agony got at last unendurable." And Prendick senses that Mrs. Moreau is "fearful that I might remark upon this cruelty" (Philmus, 115). With the removal of the character of Mrs. Moreau, the sense of shared but not-to-be-spoken horror is excised from the text.

Also in the early draft, Prendick catches sight of Moreau in his lab with his hands and arms covered with blood, his face springing into "an expression of diabolical rage" (Philmus, 128). In this version Montgomery tells Prendick, "I hate this Moreau. I fear him. He has no humanity. He's simply the Devil. Mark my words, Prendick, Moreau's the Devil!" (Philmus, 137). This portrayal of Moreau as monstrous places readers on the side of the horrified Prendick and the fearful and disgusted Montgomery. But the final version of Moreau is calmer, making a virtue of being disinterested; and Montgomery does not criticize Moreau to Prendick in any such terms. In the later version of the scene where Prendick walks into the lab, Moreau's face is still "white and terrible," but the terribleness is mitigated by the explanation that he is worried Prendick will "ruin the work of a lifetime" (107). The published version of Moreau explicitly distances him from those who act from greed or self-interest. He tells Prendick that previous "study of the plasticity of living forms" was done "by tyrants, by criminals . . . by all kinds of untrained clumsy-handed men working for their own immediate ends. I was the first man to take up this question armed with antiseptic surgery, and with a really scientific knowledge of the laws of growth" (124). Like the disinterested vivisector of the end of Wells's essay, this Moreau obsessively pursues knowledge as an end in itself.

In his revisions, then, Wells clearly tempered the negative portrayal of vivisection. But in spite of his avowed support for animal experimentation, the novel on balance represents Moreau's work negatively. For example, even though Montgomery has been witnessing Moreau's experiments for years, he still winces and sits "in a state of ill-concealed irritation" as he hears the cries of the puma (96). Moreau himself refers to his laboratory as "a kind of Blue-Beard's chamber" even as he says it's "nothing very dreadful, really, to a sane man" (92). Prendick describes the enclosure where Moreau lives and works as a "pain-haunted refuge" from the wildness of the forest.

One important incident that adds weight to the antivivisectionist side of the novel's ethics is the mercy killing. Late in the novel, when Prendick comes face to face with the Leopard Man, who is about to be captured and returned to the laboratory for further torture, he shoots him between the eyes. Moreau is dismayed, and Prendick lies to avoid his anger, saying that it was an "impulse of the moment" (144). I discuss this killing further below. Because Wells represents Prendick's compassion for the Leopard Man in that moment, the immediate impact of the mercy killing is to underscore the horror of Moreau's laboratory—dubbed "the House of Pain" by his creatures. This scene recalls the antivivisectionist pamphlet that Prendick saw in London, entitled "Moreau's Horrors." And finally, the fact that the puma whose screams so disturb Prendick eventually breaks loose and kills Moreau (147, 151) lends the plot a sense of poetic justice, confirming many readers' sense that the novel ultimately condemns Moreau and his project.

Another major element of the novel's antivivisectionist bent is the fact that Moreau uses no anesthesia for his experiments, although anesthesia was available by the mid-nineteenth century and Wells cites its use as a defense of vivisection. As a contemporaneous critic wrote, "Mr. Wells must know that the delicate, prolonged operations of modern surgery became possible only after the introduction of anaesthetics" (Harris, 186). The screams of the puma dominate the first third of the novel, changing in chapter 10, as she is transformed, into the screams of "a human being in torment" (107). If Wells had had Moreau procure anesthesia on his trips off the island, the ethics of Moreau's project might seem much more debatable.

But Moreau is not interested in anesthesia because he does not care that the animals are experiencing pain. In his explanation of his work to Prendick, he tells him that pain does not matter, that it is the "mark of the beast," and will be transcended through evolution. He exalts his intellectual pursuits, telling Prendick, "You cannot imagine . . . what an intellectual passion grows upon [an investigator]! You cannot imagine the strange, colourless delight of these intellectual desires! The thing before you is no longer an animal, a fellow-creature, but a problem!" (127). Dismissing pain as inconsequential, Moreau sidesteps the questions Wells raises in his essay about what makes inflicting pain justifiable. When Prendick objects that the "thing is an abomination" (and it is not clear whether he is referring to the project as a whole or the puma herself), Moreau replies, "To this day I have never troubled about the ethics of the matter" (128). Dismissing ethics as irrelevant to the pursuit of knowledge, Moreau relegates the beings on whom he experiments to the status of inanimate matter. This sort of separation has deadly consequences. As Kari Weil claims, "The ultimate violence may result from the kind of thinking that concludes that there are beings against whom it is impossible to commit a crime" (Weil, xviii).

Wells's avowed support for vivisection, then, as can be seen from the essay's and the novel's vacillations about the ethical status of animals, is not as thoroughgoing as he represents it. Instead he has created in *Moreau* a dialogic representation of the ethics of animal experimentation. Sarah Cole argues that although Wells portrays himself as a polemicist on many issues, his works regularly incorporate opposing viewpoints, creating a dialectical vision that invites readers to consider multiple aspects of ethical and political issues (10). Further, she notes that "Wells's dialectical thinking is never greater than when science is the topic" (256). In this case Wells seems to feel both that animal suffering is justified if it arises in the pursuit of knowledge and simultaneously that it is intolerable—a set of emotions replicated by Prendick when he refrains from intervening to try to stop the puma's suffering, but runs from the sound of her screams.

"Hi Non Sunt Homines": Defining the Human

One of many reasons the question of animal suffering is left ambiguous is that the novel seriously questions the status of human beings. Along with the biologists of his day, Wells was asking—in his scientific and philosophical essays and in his fiction—what sorts of beings we are, and whether we are unique, classifiable as separate from all other primates. As I mention above, Thomas Henry Huxley argued that human beings should be placed in an order with other great apes, rather than in a category of our own. *Moreau* too works to dismantle the stark separation between human beings and other animals. As Robert Philmus points out, the story of the wreck that opens the novel, in which Prendick's companions were preparing to eat one another, "illustrates the feral instincts which privation can elicit in human beings" (xxvii) and thus initiates the novel's blurring between humans and animals. Such moments of blurring pepper the text, as when a hammock deposits Prendick on all fours, when he feels an animal comfort in eating (106), and when he says that even after he has returned to England, his "eyes have a strange brightness, a swift alertness of movement" (168).[16]

The novel suggests several characterizations of human beings based on capacities we often ascribe to ourselves alone, but which can be found in the Beast People. In the chapter entitled "The Thing in the Forest," Prendick finally gets a look at the creature who has been shadowing him and thinks, "It was no animal, for it stood erect" (103). Erect posture has long been seen as that which—as Chris Danta describes it while noting its masculinist associations—makes humans the "lords of all they survey because they stand erect with their faces toward heaven" (*Animal Fables*, 5).

As Prendick watches the Beast People, trying to figure out how to classify them, he offers a handful of other actions as definitive of human beings. When he is first caught by Moreau and learns that the Beast People are really animals, Prendick thinks that Moreau's work has been surprisingly successful: "They may once have been animals; but I never before saw an animal trying to think" (122). When he is listening to Moreau's subsequent explanation, he objects: "'But,' said I, 'these things—these animals *talk*!'" (125). When Prendick tells the Beast People that the murdered Moreau is watching from on high and will return with his House of Pain, he differentiates himself from them in explaining their credulity: "They were staggered by my assurance. An animal may be ferocious and cunning enough, but it takes a real man to tell a lie" (164). And Montgomery joins the game of defining humanness when he tells the Beast People to join him in a drink after Moreau has died: "'Drink!' cried Montgomery, 'drink, you brutes! Drink and be men!'" (155).[17]

Some of these capacities, such as speech and self-consciousness (if we might so characterize *trying* to think), have been taken seriously by philosophers defining humanness—or personhood, the status that for many philosophers affords one the right not to be tortured or killed, for example.[18] Others, such as drinking alcohol, are more humorous. The variety of suggestions indicates that Wells is playing with the tendency of philosophers to define humanness against animality; the text is concerned not so much with the specific capabilities being adduced, but with the assumption that there are capabilities that demonstrate humanness. As Eva Kittay writes, "much of philosophy depends on being able to make . . . claims about distinctive human capacities" ("The Personal," 393). But given that the Beast People have capacities that are usually reserved for human beings, ought we to conclude that Wells is debunking the uniqueness of human beings or that Moreau has successfully created human beings—or both?

Following Huxley and Darwin, Wells clearly believed that the superiority of human beings over other animals was exaggerated. He did not believe, for example, that humans are superior to other animals morally (a common form of human exceptionalism [Edwards, 8]). Darwin had noted in *The Descent of Man* (1871) that "besides love and sympathy, animals exhibit other qualities connected with the social instincts, which in us would be called moral; . . . dogs possess something very like a conscience. . . . Dogs possess some power of self-command, and this does not appear to be wholly the result of fear" (Harris, 208). In *Moreau,*

Wells's satire of religious morality is clear in the Law that the Beast People recite and follow, and in "Human Evolution: An Artificial Process," he glosses this aspect of the novel: "What we call Morality becomes the padding of suggested emotional habits necessary to keep the round Paleolithic savage in the square hole of the civilized state. And Sin is the conflict of the two factors—as I have tried to convey in my *Island of Dr. Moreau*" (Philmus, 193). More generally, Wells suggests in *Text-Book of Biology* that human beings and other animals are more alike than we seem—that studying biology demonstrates "the wonderful unity in life" and the "uniform and active causes beneath an apparent diversity" (Harris, 211). We are, that is, animated by the same biological and social forces that animate other animals. Wells asserts that "zoology is, indeed, a philosophy and a literature to those who can read its symbols" (Harris, 211).

If human beings are not different from other animals in ways that matter ethically, then the question of our right to inflict suffering on other animals (at least "higher" animals such as gorillas) should be identical to the question of our right to inflict suffering on other human beings. In *Moreau*, however, the identity of these two questions is never suggested. When Prendick is fleeing in fear from Moreau, Moreau is at pains to point out—in "schoolboy Latin" so as not to undermine his teachings that the surrounding Beast People are "men"—that his creatures are *not* men, but animals: "*Hi non sunt homines; sunt animalia qui nos habemus*—vivisected" (120). As much as the novel seeks to undermine this distinction philosophically, its plot—including our initial fear for Prendick and then our assurance that he is not in danger—depends on the distinction between animals, on whom one may experiment, and human beings, on whom one may not. As Derrida points out, the very term "the animal" violently confines "within the strict enclosure of this definite article . . . *all the living things* that man does not recognize as his fellows, his neighbors, or his brothers" (*Animal*, 34). This is particularly true of Moreau's reassurance to Prendick that the creatures are "*animalia*" (120), which suggests that their status as animals removes the taint of criminality or danger from his work. The degree to which *Moreau* debunks human exceptionalism, then, remains unstable.

Although Moreau creates beings who pass for human even at close contact, he is dissatisfied with the results. As Edwards points out, this is because Moreau has an idealized view of what a human being is, a view that Wells is critiquing. Moreau is not really trying to create human beings as they exist in the world, but to "make a rational creature of [his] own" (130).[19] The conviction that humans are driven by reason while animals are driven by instinct is one of the hallmarks of human exceptionalism. Prendick displays his belief in this distinction when he returns to civilization at the end of the novel and tries to convince himself that the people he sees are "emancipated from instinct" (173). In his discussion of Moreau's science, Edwards demonstrates that Moreau "cherry-picks the concept of humans as animals for purposes of comparisons and proxy research while ignoring its other implications about humans" (97).[20] That is, Moreau's exceptionalist view of human beings is at odds with his understanding that it is the very animality of human beings that makes his research possible.

Moreau explains his goal to Prendick: "Each time I dip a living creature into the bath of burning pain, I say: this time I will burn out all the animal, this time I will make a rational creature of my own" (130). Edwards sharply demonstrates Moreau's incoherence on this point, addressing the character directly: "What's this about getting rid of animality to result in a new creature that we know is in fact an animal? . . . We're already a species of animal, which is why your re-shaping works. This has nothing to do with 'burning out' anything. Your whole goal is a mystical phantasm" (99). Moreau is trying to have it both ways: humans are animals, so we can be concocted out of other animals; but we are rational creatures—with rationality implicitly defined as the opposite of animal instinct—and so the animality must be burnt out of us before we can be truly human.

Such incoherence about the animality of "man" has a distinguished lineage. For example, in describing Thomas Aquinas's claims about what aspects of humanity will be resurrected, Agamben writes, "The resurrection, he teaches, is directed not to the perfection of man's natural life, but only to that final perfection which is contemplative life" (*Open*, 19). Like Moreau's futuristic vision, Aquinas's vision separates perfected humanness from the "perfection of nature" (qtd. in Agamben, *Open*, 19). I agree with Edwards, then, when he argues that in *Moreau*, Wells challenges "the dichotomy of Man and Beast"; but in my view, the novel itself nevertheless clings to the same mystical phantasm. It clings to it in the text's separation of humanness from nature; it clings to it in the sense of relief readers experience when we discover that Moreau only operates on beings who begin as animals; and it clings to it, as I describe in what follows, by casting disability as chimera while sustaining a curative imaginary.

Disability as Chimera

Instead of creating rational creatures of his own, Moreau ends up creating chimeras, boundary-crossing beings that hover in the confused space between human and nonhuman beings.[21] A sense of the Freudian uncanny surrounds the Beast People: Prendick sees them as both strange and familiar, mysterious not in their parts, but in their totality. When he first has a chance to look at Montgomery's servant M'Ling on the ship after his recovery, for example, Prendick is "astonished beyond measure at the grotesque ugliness of this black-faced creature. I had never beheld such a repulsive and extraordinary face before, and yet—if the contradiction is credible—I experienced at the same time an odd feeling that in some way I *had* already encountered exactly the features and gestures that now amazed me" (79).[22] Even after he has become used to the Beast People, his sense of them is prone to alter suddenly. One moment he accepts them as fellow human beings, not that different from "some really human yokel trudging home from his mechanical labours" or from a woman he had "met . . . before in some city byway." But the next moment "the beast would flash out upon me beyond doubt or denial" as he catches sight of "scissor-edged incisors and sabre-like canines," "slit-like pupils," or a "curving nail" (136). As can be seen in the linkage between the animal and the woman in the "city byway," "species difference itself is fraught with anxieties about race and reproduction" (Chen, 148).

The chimera quality of the Beast Folk—their unprecedented combinations of features—is the source of their disturbing effect.[23] Such a disturbance may stem in part from fears of miscegenation; and it is definitely underwritten by a cultural fascination with transspecies being. In a discussion of government reports on the ethics of interspecies projects, Susan Squier proposes the existence of "xenogenetic desire—a covert but incessant obsession with transgressive, interspecies sex, hybridity, and interspecies reproduction" (95).[24] *Moreau* raises the question whether such boundary crossing is ethically acceptable or whether it threatens a mystical uniqueness about human beings—a uniqueness interrogated but not completely discarded by the novel. Indeed, the very strangeness of the hybrid creatures stems from the novel's lingering humanism—the species-typical human being remains the touchstone or standard from which the Beast People deviate.[25]

One contemporaneous critic objected to Moreau's "foul ambition to remake God's creatures by confusing and transfusing and remoulding human and animal organs so as to extinguish so far as possible the chasm which divides man from brute" (Harris, 189). Another wrote that "it is an offense against humanity to represent the result of the intermingling of man and beast" (Harris, 194). When Moreau explains his project to Prendick, Prendick asks why he has taken the human form as his goal, noting that "there seemed to me then, and there still seems to me now, a strange wickedness in that choice" (126). Prendick's response to Montgomery's assistant M'Ling is based in a related discomfort: "'He's unnatural,' I said. 'There's something about him—don't think me fanciful, but it gives me a nasty little sensation, a tightening of my muscles, when he comes near me. It's a touch—of the diabolical, in fact'" (96). The words "unnatural" and "diabolical," when we recall M'Ling's "black face" and "black coarse hair," suggest a racist taxonomy as well as indicate that like the reviewer, Prendick believes in a right and proper separation between human beings and animals, to bridge which is to go against Nature or God.

M'Ling's unnaturalness stems from his chimerical biology and his human appearance. As Prendick later relates, M'Ling is "the most human-looking of all the Beast Folk" and yet he calls him "it" in describing his origins: "It was a complex trophy of Moreau's horrible skill—a bear, tainted with dog and ox, and one of the most elaborately made of all his creatures. It treated Montgomery with a strange tenderness and devotion" (135). With the word "tainted" Prendick evokes the "nasty little sensation" he experiences in M'Ling's presence and suggests too a homophobic response to M'Ling's unusual devotion to Montgomery. By emphasizing M'Ling's devotion even when Montgomery kicks or ill-treats "it," however, he also stresses the dog-aspect of M'Ling's origins, which helps locate and stabilize M'Ling as a domestic animal-cum-servant, even though he is composed mainly from a bear.

Questions about the status and appropriateness of chimeras are aris-ing now as genetic engineering advances and scientists are able to insert human DNA into the cells of other species in embryo.[26] In explaining people's worries about hybrid embryos, bioethicist Insoo Hyun told NPR host Ray Suarez, "There's . . . great concern about the level of human-animal mixing that might result in animals that are not 100-percent animal and not 100-percent human. We may be flirting with an area of human dignity that we just do not want to cross, even if the scien-tific value of the work may be quite high" ("Chimera Quandary").[27] A similar concern is raised in another NPR story about chimeric embryos: "'One of the concerns that a lot of people have is that there's something sacrosanct about what it means to be human expressed in our DNA,' says Jason Robert, a bioethicist at Arizona State University. 'And that by inserting that into other animals and giving those other animals poten-tially some of the capacities of humans that this could be a kind of vio-lation—a kind of, maybe, even a playing God'" ("In Search for Cures"). As these descriptions make clear, human beings are still defending our status as separate from other animals, not just in the same sense that chimpanzees are separate from bonobos, but in the sense of being, as Edwards puts it, "uniquely unique."

Our investment in this status is similarly seen in defensive responses to Peter Singer's work on animals.[28] Singer quotes a German sponsor-ing organization that, in preparation for his visit, passed a motion that reads "The uniqueness of human life forbids any comparison—or more specifically, equation—of human existence with other living beings, with their forms of life or interests" (*Practical Ethics*, ix). Wells, like T. H. Huxley, questioned the need to ground human dignity on such unique-ness. Prendick eventually becomes accustomed to the Beast Folk, and what "seemed unnatural and repulsive speedily became natural and or-dinary" to him (135). Showing Prendick adapting to what had seemed unnatural and diabolical, Wells suggests that perhaps our sense of the naturalness of the man-brute divide is itself not natural, but socially con-structed, serving to buttress humans' sense of self-worth.

And yet Moreau's project, as we have seen, depends on the idea that human beings are or could be cut off from the rest of the animal king-dom, and that to create them he must purge his creatures' animality. His vision aims for a kind of perfection that excludes actual living beings.

Moreau is what we might now call a transhumanist, rejecting humanness as he has created it *and* as it is, seeking something superior.[29] It requires only a slight adaptation of Kafer's "curative imaginary" to see Moreau's "grandiose humanizing project" (Rohman, *Stalking*, 68) in its light: he sees living beings as projects to be perfected. The danger in such a curative imaginary lies in its link to eradication, as Eli Clare elaborates in *Brilliant Imperfection*. Discussing three permutations of eradication—of body-mind difference itself, of future people who have such differences, and of living people who do not conform to expectations of normalcy—Clare concludes that "as a widespread ideology centered on eradication, cure always operates in relationship to violence" (28).[30]

Moreau's goal is a future of enhanced humanity; and as Kafer explains, ideologies of futurity tend to enlist images of disabled people: "Futurity has often been framed in curative terms, a time frame that casts disabled people (as) out of time, or as obstacles to the arc of progress. In our disabled state, we are not part of the dominant narratives of progress, but once rehabilitated, normalized, and hopefully cured, we play a starring role: the sign of progress, the proof of development, the triumph over the mind or body" (28). We will see this exclusion of disabled people from the usual senses of temporality again in chapter 3, where I explore how O'Connor's intellectually disabled character is relegated to a mythical past—described, for example, as "grown backwards to the lowest form of innocence" (*Violent*, 111). Demonstrating the perception of disability as an obstacle to futurity, Moreau's desire for a perfectible future results in prevalent disability descriptors in the text. After all, as Michael Davidson confirms, "the biopolitical imperative to improve and create a better future was underwritten by fears of an ill, 'feeble-minded,' or deformed body" (*Invalid*, 11).

Prendick continually compares Moreau's imperfect creatures to deformed and disabled human beings. His narrative exemplifies Sunaura Taylor's assertion than "ableism is intimately entangled with speciesism" (*Beasts*, 57). Disability stands in for all that is "wrong" with Moreau's creations, all that Moreau believes and the text suggests ought to be fixed. When Prendick is still uncertain what Moreau has been doing, he wonders about the Beast People: "What were they all? Imagine yourself surrounded by all the most horrible cripples and maniacs it is possible to conceive, and you may understand a little of my feelings with these grotesque caricatures of humanity about me" (115).[31] Similarly he later asks readers to "Imagine the scene if you can! We three blue-clad men . . . surrounded by this circle of crouching and gesticulating monstrosities—some almost human save in their subtle expression and gestures, some like cripples, some so strangely distorted as to resemble nothing but the denizens of our wildest dreams" (140–141). In both of these passages Prendick is at a loss to make readers understand his horror; he draws on language of disability as a way to gesture toward the boundary-crossing, semihuman status of the creatures.

Prendick uses disability language throughout in his descriptions of and references to the Beast People. They are described multiple times as "deformed," "malformed," "queer," "strange," "distorted," "monstrous," "lunatic," "maniac," "dwarfed," and "crippled" (and in the early draft, also "hunchback"). The label "queer" alongside the more obvious terms of disability bolsters Jasbir Puar's claim, following Robert McRuer, that "historical entanglements . . . have produced disabled bodies as already queer (both in their bodily debilities and capacities but also in their sexual practices regardless of sexual object choice)" ("Prognosis Time," 165). The wide-ranging disability imagery serves to indicate the Beast People's liminal status between human and animal, or as Michael Parrish Lee puts it, "the ambiguity and slippage that precludes a clear distinction between 'human' and 'animal' categories in the first place" (261). In her study of unsightly beggar ordinances, or "ugly laws," Susan Schweik discusses the connections between the desire evident in the late nineteenth and early twentieth centuries to keep visibly disabled people out of sight, Jim Crow laws, which similarly regulated what kinds of bodies could be in what kinds of spaces (184), and even the desire to keep the streets clear of dogs (97). In the city ordinances as in freak shows, the line between disabled human being and animal was often blurred; "unsightly beggars" were both "punished for animality and punished by relegation to animality" (Schweik, 100).

Both within and outside of the text of *Moreau*, disability is represented as the condition *par excellence* that needs fixing.[32] One major source of this mindset was that disability was seen as evolutionarily backward, closer to animality, something that would eventually be overcome by nature or by eugenics. Darwin compared animals to "idiots" in explaining the status of disability as atavism. He asserts in *The Expression of Emotions in Man and Animals* (1872) that the "insane and idiotic" pull back their jaws when angry, much as do animals. Darwin quotes psychiatrist Henry Maudsley who explains this as "the reappearance of primitive instincts," more obvious in intellectually disabled people because "the brain of an idiot is in arrested condition" (244).[33]

The idea that disability was a signal of evolutionary backwardness was widespread by the late nineteenth century. Douglas Baynton explains that at this time, "both nonwhite 'lower' races and defective individuals were similarly described as evolutionary laggards or throwbacks" (*Defectives*, 67). Citing the work of sociologist James T. Trent, he notes that "Defective individuals and defective races were both ranked on the basis of how 'improvable' they were . . . and both were explained in terms of atavism or lack of evolutionary development" (*Defectives*, 67). Rohman contextualizes this idea further when she explains that in the late nineteenth and early twentieth centuries "our shared heritage with other animals resulted in anxieties about regression and atavistic 'leftovers' in the human person" (*Stalking*, 68). Insofar as Moreau aims "to improve on evolution" (Sherborne, 112), then, he is working to eradicate the conjunction of animality and disability.

This was the aim of national eugenics programs as well, as scientists, doctors, and policy makers sought to advance humankind away from its animal past and disabled present more quickly than by leaving such progress to nature.[34] Wells's views about eugenics were complicated: he did not approve of "positive" eugenics because he believed there were many different worthy types of people (Harris, 236, 237); he also thought Francis Galton overrated direct inheritance (Partington, 55). But he did agree that the modern world would need to somehow consign disability to the past. His early views about how this could be brought about were quite harsh. In *Anticipations* (1901), Wells recommended violent means of excising the unfit. He called poor and "undesirable" people the "people of the abyss" and described them as "breeding undesirable and too often fearfully miserable children." The parents of such children he described as "a mean-spirited, under-sized, diseased little man, quite incapable of earning a decent living for himself, married to some under-fed, ignorant, ill-shaped, plain, and diseased little woman" (331). He claimed that "the nation that most resolutely picks over, educates, sterilizes, exports, or poisons its people of the abyss" will have success—as though all of those options would be equally acceptable (230).

After critiques of *Anticipations* called it inhumane, Wells modified his views (Partington, 51–61). In *A Modern Utopia* (1905), his narrator maintains that a utopia must find a way to relegate its "congenital invalids, its idiots and madmen, its drunkards and men of vicious mind [to] the descendent phase[;] the species must be engaged in eliminating them: there is no escape from that" (136). After all, he says, "these people spoil the world for others. They may become parents, and with most of them there is manifestly nothing to be done but to seclude them from the great body of the population. You must resort to a kind of social surgery" (142). He assures readers that "there would be no killing, no lethal chambers" (143) but rather exile to islands where they will have as much freedom as the main society can give them without endangering itself (144–145). But even as Wells's narrator claims there would be no killing in his Utopia, he concedes that "no doubt Utopia will kill all deformed and monstrous and evilly diseased births" (143). In the words of O'Connor's character Rayber, Wells's narrator thinks that an advanced society will "have learned enough to put [disabled babies] to sleep when they're born" (*Violent*, 169).

As Wells's passage makes clear, it is not only the mentally "defective" who would be eliminated from a Wellsian utopia, but the physically "deformed" as well. In the novel where he predicted the atomic bomb, *The World Set Free* (1914), Wells depicts a "congenital cripple," a brilliant Russian named Karenin, who voluntarily undergoes an operation that he knows is likely to kill him (and the narrator tells us in advance that it does).[35] Karenin tells a friend not to assume that his brilliance was enriched by his disabled body: "There is no peculiar virtue in defect. I have always chafed against—all this. If I could have moved more freely and lived a larger life in health, I could have done more. But someday perhaps you will be able to put a body that is wrong altogether right again. . . . But meanwhile a few more of us must die in patience" (270). Karenin believes that "it will be good when you have nobody alive whose body cannot live the wholesome everyday life, whose spirit cannot come up into these high places as it wills." He is reassured by his friend: "'We shall manage that soon,' said Fowler" (273).

The most striking and relevant line about disability in *The World Set Free* comes when Karenin predicts that "the time is not far off when such bodies as mine will no longer be born into the world." This is because, he asserts, "deformity is uncertainty—inaccuracy" (270). Disability in Wells's speculative work represents the imperfection of nature writ large. It is this very imperfection, this inaccuracy, that Moreau is trying to eradicate. Under the guise of curing animals of their animality, Moreau is really trying to cure human beings of their imperfection—their disability, their humanity.[36] But Moreau's species mixing leads only to more of the undesirable condition of inaccuracy/disability/deformity. The Beast People's inaccuracy, the uncanny mixtures of their features, their chimera quality—all are focused by the language of disability and deformity scattered throughout the text. And this casting of disability as chimerical demonstrates that although the text actively questions human exceptionalism, it is nevertheless invested in Moreau's curative project.

Man-Beast

This is not so much a contradiction (though Wells contains multitudes) as a matter of what the text is suggesting about human status. Certainly it rejects the idea that human beings have immortal souls or are otherwise sanctioned by God in ways that make us absolutely distinct from nonhuman animals. This rejection is especially powerful in the moment when Prendick sees the Leopard Man crouching in his animal fear and realizes "the fact of his humanity." In this scene Moreau, Montgomery, Prendick, and several Beast People are pursuing the Leopard Man to bring him back to the "House of Pain" for further work/torture, because he has killed and eaten some rabbits, and eating flesh is against the Law for the Beast People.[37] Prendick is the one who catches sight of him: "It may seem a strange contradiction in me—I cannot explain the fact—but now, seeing the creature there in a perfectly animal attitude, with the light gleaming in its eyes and its imperfectly human face distorted with terror, I realised again the fact of its humanity" (144). It is at this moment, seeing the Leopard Man's humanity and his animality all at once (he calls him "it" and describes his gleaming eyes and "perfectly animal attitude"), that Prendick commits the mercy killing.

"In another moment, others of its pursuers would see it, and it would be overpowered and captured, to experience once more the horrible tortures of the enclosure. Abruptly I whipped out my revolver, aimed between its terror-struck eyes, and fired" (144). Without changing the pronoun he uses to refer to the Leopard Man, Prendick extends human sympathy to his fellow imperfect human, killing him precisely because he sees the animal fear in the human being, or the human being in the animal fear.[38] With the word "abruptly," Wells signals an emotional impulse that is far more moral than Moreau's disinterested science.[39] He has read the Leopard Man's situation as, in Martha Nussbaum's terms, an emotionally engaged reader of a narrative: with "attentiveness to particularity and . . . capacity for sympathetic understanding" ("Equity and Mercy," 105). Prendick has beheld the Leopard Man at that moment, seen the grammatically telling "fact of its humanity," and acted to save him from further torture—torture that, when he believed it would happen to him, he judged worse than death.

It is important to notice that Prendick does not even consider killing Moreau to protect the Leopard Man. As much as he sympathizes with the Leopard Man, his allegiance is with the human beings in that he does not see human beings as killable creatures. As Donna Haraway points out, "Every living being except Man can be killed but not murdered. To make Man merely killable is the height of moral outrage; indeed, it is the definition of genocide" (78).[40] The maintenance of this distinction between the killable and the not-killable is a key way in which the novel stops short of truly breaking down the distinction between human beings and other animals. But Prendick's mercy killing does nevertheless emerge from a moment of what Michael Sandel and Rosemarie Garland-Thomson have both called "beholding."

Garland-Thomson describes beholding as "holding the being of another particular individual in the eye of the beholder. . . . The work of a beholding encounter would be to create a sense of beholdenness, of human obligation" (*Staring*, 194). At this moment Prendick feels himself beholden to the Leopard Man in a way that Moreau could never recognize, and in a way that takes priority over his obligation to advance the interests of his fellow *Homo sapiens*, Moreau (though without changing his view of Moreau as unkillable). Moreau's interest in the Leopard Man is solely in remaking him. Sandel labels such a stance "molding": to mold, he says, is to seek mastery and domination, whereas to behold is to remain, in William F. May's phrase, "open to the unbidden" (Sandel, 45–46). Prendick's mercy killing, arising from a moment of sympathetic beholding, works as a counterpoint to Moreau's curative imaginary.

In the chaos that follows the killing, Prendick steps away from the others and muses on everything happening on the island. In this most contemplative passage in the novel, Wells has Prendick equate the Beast People with human beings: "A strange persuasion came upon me, that, save for the grossness of the line, the grotesqueness of the forms, I had here before me the whole balance of human life in miniature, the whole interplay of instinct, reason, and fate in its simplest form" (145). The Beast People are us; they are "wretched [because] the old animal hate moved them to trouble one another; the Law held them back from a brief hot struggle and a decisive end to their natural animosities" (145).[41] Much as Wells argues in "Human Evolution: An Artificial Process" that we are the same as our Paleolithic ancestors evolutionarily, only differing through the artificial cultures we have created, here we are asked to think of ourselves as animals who are trying futilely to transcend our animality through our legal and moral systems.

In a later preface, Wells further explained this aspect of the novel: "There was a scandalous trial [Wilde's] about that time, the graceless and pitiful downfall of a man of genius, and [*The Island of Doctor Moreau*] was the response of an imaginative mind to the reminder that humanity is but animal rough-hewn to a reasonable shape and in perpetual internal conflict between instinct and injunction" (Harris, 180). The novel is in this sense an allegory about the force of nature, "a vast pitiless Mechanism" acting to "cut and shape the fabric of existence" in ways that, as T. H. Huxley argued, do not make for greater happiness, but for greater misery.[42]

But this equation between us and the Beast People does not exactly break down the animal/human or beastliness/transcendence oppositions; instead it denies "that there is anything beyond animality" (Gross and Vallely, 3). R. D. Haynes notes that not only do "the 'human' beasts revert to their previous bestial state" but that the actual human beings revert as well, so that beastliness wins out in the text ("Unholy," 16; *H. G. Wells*, 24). And in his analysis of the novel's use of spaces demarcated initially as human and nonhuman, John Huntington shows that the human spaces all dissolve or otherwise fail, confirming that there is nothing other or more than animality.[43] Wells's own description of the novel as "written just to give the utmost possible vividness to that conception of men as hewn and confused and tormented beasts" (Harris, 180) makes this point explicit.

When Prendick returns to human civilization at the end of the novel, he "cannot persuade [himself] that the men and women [he] met were not also another Beast People, animals half wrought into the outward image of human souls" (172). He sees no people who "have the calm authority of a reasonable soul" (173). Gross and Vallely explain that such an attitude does not reject

> the division of the world into "the animal"—that is, the material world as known by science—and "the human"—that is, the material world imbued with something *more*: with soul as opposed to soulless beasts, with reason as opposed to irrational brutes, or with language and culture as opposed to animals that merely communicate and are driven by instinct. Often, to assert that "humans are animals" is precisely to accept the division of the world the human/animal binary implies. What is rejected instead is the reality of what religious practitioners call soul or the contention that *Homo sapiens* actually behave as rational subjects that freely create their own cultures. In many cases, to assert that "humans are animals" is to reinforce the dominant way of conceiving the category human and the category animal. (2–3)

Wells suggests that human beings are beasts with culture superadded, that we are driven by instinct.[44] This is his motivation for blurring species boundaries through Moreau's Beast People. But he is unable to embrace the full implications of our beastliness, instead retaining an investment in human exceptionalism.

Further, Wells retains a belief in a future transcendence of the beastliness that makes us human. As Karenin says in *The World Set Free*, "Every man is something of a cripple and something of a beast"; we see this belief also in *The Time Machine* (1895) where these aspects of human beings can be seen in the Eloi (like "cripples" in their fragility) and the Morlocks (like "beasts" in their brutality). But Wells, like Karenin, sees this condition as temporary. As Philmus and Hughes note in their edition of Wells's early science writings, "While rejecting 'each and every transcendentalism' actually offered him, Wells nevertheless admits the lure of the concept of some mystical, all-encompassing synthesis" (Wells, *Early Writings*, 18). In "Morals and Civilization" (1897), Wells opposes the "man beast" to the "inherent possibilities of the man" (Harris, 233). By viewing human beings as sites of potential, he holds onto a humanism (or transhumanism) that understands "man beast" as something that will someday surpass its own beastliness.[45]

With his utopian leanings, Wells surely agrees with Karenin when he says, "It's only now, when he has fully learnt the truth of that, that he can take hold of himself to be neither beast nor cripple. Now that he overcomes his servitude to his body, he can for the first time think of living the full life of his body" (273). Karenin makes explicit here the link between beastliness and disability that permeates *Moreau*. His faith that "man" can overcome his identity as "beast" and "cripple" echoes Moreau's obsession with perfecting his "rational creature" and Wells's own implicit endorsement of the curative imaginary that seeks to fix human inaccuracy and disability.

Much as scientists such as Darwin and Huxley believed in "the inevitability of ['primitive' races] vanishing" (Brantlinger, 190), and indeed participating in the same ideal of evolutionary progress, Wells marked out disability for extinction. He was unable to simply *behold* the chimera quality of human beings, our inaccuracy, our imperfection. He knew that evolution does not actually work to perfect the species of *Homo sapiens*—he rejected "the placid assumption of the time that Evolution was a pro-human force making things better and better for mankind" (Harris, 182–183)—and he knew that human beings are very little different from the great apes. But like Karenin he believed that we ourselves could perfect humankind through negative eugenics and rational, beneficent rule as he describes in *A Modern Utopia*. And like Moreau, he entertained the idea that evolution would at least rid us of pain, making life better for mankind: "the province of pain is after all a limited and transitory one; a phase through which life must pass on its evolution from the automatic to the spiritual" (Harris, 273–274).[46] In "Human Evolution" Wells ends by seeing in education the possibility for a salvation described in biblical terms: "in Education lies the possible salvation of mankind from misery & sin. We may hope to come out of the valley of death before the City Beautiful is attained" (Philmus, 194). Philmus describes the novel's ending, where Prendick finds solace in looking to the stars, as hopeful that "we as a species may yet become something other than the clothed and gabbling but mentally intractable ape that *Moreau* discovers us still to be" (xxxii).[47]

As Sarah Cole points out, "Wells toggles between seeing evolution as a world system with its own logic and unstoppable directionality, and his many schemes to plan and imagine our way into a harmonious future that has little in common with evolution's demands" (246). Much as his scientific training led him to endorse vivisection even while emotionally he clearly recoiled, so too did his abiding interest in utopia, in moving humankind forward, conflict with his certainty that human beings are animals, leading to an uneasy but persistent affirmation of the curative imaginary, and more generally of humanism, in *The Island of Doctor Moreau.*

2

Old Lives

Huxley's *Brave New World*

Literary texts, as I describe in the Introduction, can serve as thought experiments that illuminate the ramifications of philosophical ideas (Swirski, 4). This is especially true for novels that have already had wide-ranging effects on our understanding of ethical or political issues. As David Dunaway has pointed out, "The field of bioethics has already been conditioned by the mass reading of *Brave New World*" (176).[1] Aldous Huxley's *Brave New World* (1932) has taught us much about the possible ramifications of cloning, biological predestination, psychological conditioning, and state control. One aspect of the novel that has been little discussed also bears bioethical consideration: the fact that the Brave New World is, in W. B. Yeats's words, "no country for old men."

In Huxley's famous dystopia, the body's natural changes are one of the great enemies. The society keeps everyone youthful by giving them "gonadal hormones, transfusion of young blood, magnesium salts" (54). As a result, they stay strong and "young" into old age, or, to be more accurate, they do not age. In this society there is no place for human beings whose powers are declining. When people can no longer be rejuvenated, around age sixty, they are brought to Hospitals for the Dying, where their deaths proceed peacefully amid sensory distractions. The Brave New World makes literal what Hailee Gibbons describes as "compulsory youthfulness": the ideological mandate in our own culture "for people to remain youthful and able-bodied throughout the life course, including in old age" (71).[2] The novel thereby raises the question, of what value is old age? Or to frame the question in more bioethical terms, how ought we to value old people? Would it be better if there weren't any, if we conquered age to the extent that we enjoyed, as in the Brave New World, "youth almost unimpaired till sixty [or in our longer-lived society, say seventy-five or eighty], and then, crack! the end" (111)? Is the influential physician and bioethicist Ezekiel Emanuel right when he argues that it would be best to die at seventy-five, before one becomes "if not disabled, then faltering and declining"? Or is there value to the stage of life in which some of our cherished abilities wane?[3]

In this chapter I read *Brave New World* alongside contemporary discussions of the life span and the value of old age such as those by Emanuel, Gilbert Meilaender, and Alasdair MacIntyre. In the first section of the chapter, I lay out the relationship the fictional society has constructed between one's body and one's life span, arguing that the persistent youth embraced by the society robs life of its narrative arc and thereby of an important aspect of its meaning. In making this claim, I am relying on the idea of the life narrative as described by MacIntyre and others. In the remaining two sections, I raise the question of whether the sacrifice of life narratives might be considered worthwhile and show that the novel offers two reasons why it is not. First, by depicting the characters' mistreatment of Linda, the only person in the society who ages naturally, the text shows the loss of compassion that can result from knowing that one will never experience physical vulnerability or decline. Second, the novel exposes how the society's tight control of embodiment and its trivialization of bodily experience break apart the relationship between people's bodies and their emotions, a relationship ordinarily fostered not only by romantic love and the rearing of children, but also by the experience of bodily changes. While critics, and Huxley himself, view the novel as dystopian primarily because it portrays a totalitarian society where art, truth, and meaning are sacrificed to pleasure and distraction and where the ruled are programmed not to question the values of their rulers, the novel also makes clear that the excision of old age has significant political, moral, and emotional costs.

The question of how we ought to view our biological limitations runs throughout Gilbert Meilaender's study *Should We Live Forever?* He writes that we might think that since we are embodied beings, human flourishing will have to

include the aging and decline that characterize bodily organisms. Since, however, we are *rational* animals, our full potential may be realized only through our freedom to remake ourselves, transcending indefinitely the limits of the body. . . . Still more, when we notice that some of the more ambitious proposals for age-retardation seem rather like a desire to escape bodily existence itself, we may begin to wonder whether the aim is to transcend or to transgress the body's limits. (ix–x)

To transcend and to transgress bodily limitations amount to the same thing in *Brave New World*. Through the scientific production of embryos, the society is able not only to biologically and environmentally control the human beings who result, but also remove mothering and the family from their society altogether. With the exception of sexuality—which it turns into transient physical pleasure cordoned off from emotion—the society takes great pains to separate human beings from their embodiment. When Henry Foster, the assistant to the Director of Hatcheries and Conditioning, is explaining the production process to students, he "rubbed his hands. For of course, they didn't content themselves with merely hatching out embryos: any cow could do that" (13). By equating procreation with animality and differentiating human beings from both, the society transcends *and* transgresses embodiment, relegating natural births and natural aging to the uncivilized past.

Exploring the absence of old people as an aspect of *Brave New World*'s dystopia, this chapter brings together age studies and disability studies. Indeed, it suggests that age studies and disability studies ought to be put more fully in conversation, and both considered carefully in bioethical discussions.[4] Aging and disability are distinct, as are ageism and ableism, and it is reasonable that people who study either state are wary of folding it into the other. Moreover, disability studies scholars are rightly concerned, as Sally Chivers explains, by the tendency of gerontologists to attempt to cast age as less miserable by detaching it from disability in their celebrations of "healthy aging." Chivers objects to this move: "Equating disability with misery results in the denigration of disability (and disabled people) and is a woefully inaccurate understanding of what it can mean to have a disability" (21). As Stephen Katz suggests, however, the newer field of critical gerontology promises, among other things, to "historicize the ideological attributes of old age" (qtd. in Chivers, 15), making it more likely that age studies and disability studies can be brought together to study attitudes toward and representations of physical and mental ability and the life span.

When we approach aging and disability as cultural constructs, we find that beliefs about the value of human beings experiencing either aging or disability have much in common. Thomas Cole rightly argues that "the de-meaning of aging [is] rooted in modern culture's relentless hostility toward decay and dependency" (xxvi), characteristics that are not equivalent to but do bear cultural associations with disability. Emanuel's article claiming that he hopes to die at seventy-five is a good example of the ways ageism and ableism intertwine. Among the reasons he gives for not wanting to live after that age, the majority relate to a loss of productivity and creativity: a decline in abilities. Observing that "half of people 80 and over [have] ... functional limitations" and that "a third of people 85 and older ... [have] Alzheimer's," Emanuel writes:

> Even if we aren't demented, our mental functioning deteriorates as we grow older. Age-associated declines in mental-processing speed, working and long-term memory, and problem-solving are well established. Conversely, distractibility increases. We cannot focus and stay with a project as well as we could when we were young. As we move slower with age, we also think slower.
> It is not just mental slowing. We literally lose our creativity. (n.p.)

A central reason for devaluing old age, Emanuel's article makes clear, is that we are likely to become disabled, and that even if we are not technically disabled physically or mentally, our mental processes slow down and our creativity decreases—we are *less* able. For many of the same reasons Emanuel gives, Daniel Dennett proposes that we try to engineer sudden deaths for everyone via whole-body apoptosis (programmed cell death). Dennett goes further than Emanuel to denigrate old people, remarking that not many people will lament the loss of jobs "for end-of-life caregivers who now find their life's meaning in taking care of semi-comatose, incontinent, incommunicative old folks" (n.p.). Such views about old age are not unique to the present, of course. They were especially prevalent during the late nineteenth century and the eugenics period. These views motivate the euthanasia scheme in Anthony Trollope's late novel, *The Fixed Period* (1882), for example, which mandates euthanizing people after a "fixed period" of life so as to eliminate the "imbecility and weakness of human life when protracted beyond its fitting limits" (78).[5]

The emphasis on the contributions of a fit and productive citizenry marks one of the most significant commonalities between ageism and ableism in the eugenics period in which Huxley lived and in our own neoliberal society. In fact, a striking continuity is evidenced in the similarity of the chart Emanuel includes in his article to display the "Productivity [by Age] of People with High Creative Potential" to a chart created by the late nineteenth-century physician George Miller Beard entitled "The Relation of Age to Original Work" (1881). Both show the peak of creative output happening at age forty with a decline thereafter (Beard's chart is reproduced in T. Cole, 165). The clear suggestion is that once one is no longer likely to contribute original or creative work, one may as well make way for those who are. Like Emanuel, Beard thought it would be a good thing to die "before extreme old age" (qtd in T. Cole, 168). As Michael Brannigan points out, "Emanuel's posture represents a deep-rooted cultural symptom—our fixation on productivity. 'I produce, therefore I am of value.'"[6] In chapter 3 we will see that a similar attitude animates the belief held by Flannery O'Connor's character Rayber that his intellectually disabled son might as well never have been born. This attitude is prominent too in Dennett's blog post, where he describes life in terms of "diminishing returns," claiming that even if "we could arrange to live to be 100 (or 120!) we really have no right to use up so much more than our fair share of the world's resources and amenities" (n.p.).[7]

Attitudes about states of less than optimal ability and productivity are tightly intertwined with attitudes about the worth of human beings who are physically disabled, who think more slowly than average, or who are merely failing to contribute creative or scientific works to society in the first place. Ageism and ableism together marginalize "people with physical, sensory, and cognitive impairments . . . and people who are classified as elderly . . . because their physical and cognitive styles of performance differ from those of the socially dominant group, namely, youngish males" (Silvers, 205). Emanuel exposes how deep his ableism goes when he claims that if our children and grandchildren remember us "with memories framed not by our vivacity but by our frailty," that is "the ultimate tragedy" (n.p.). Dennett similarly values "the prospect of being able to live out your remaining days relatively confident that your survivors will not have to set aside memories of a pathetic decline in order to get to the memories of you that matter" (n.p.).

This misguided view of human frailty as pathetic is highlighted by the contrast offered in the epilogue to Paul Kalanithi's *When Breath Becomes Air*. There, Paul's wife, Lucy Kalanithi, describes how much she gained from loving her husband in his final year of life. She writes, "Indeed, the version of Paul I miss most, more even than the robust, dazzling version with whom I first fell in love, is the beautiful, focused man he was in his last year, the Paul who wrote this book—frail but never weak" (220). Emanuel's approach would deny people the opportunity to provide care and thereby, in many cases, recognize their own strengths and deepen their connections to loved ones. But more than that, we might question why aging people should judge their present worth by considering how their existence will affect others in the future. In her contribution to the *AgeCultureHumanities* special issue on aging, Jane Gallop suggests that old people take up Lee Edelman's queer "resistant logic" and refuse "to subordinate our present lives to the worship of the future" (n.p.).

Emanuel's influential article is a symptom of a larger consensus that a state of disability makes for a poor conclusion to a well-lived life—a consensus directly challenged by disability studies, which understands disability as consistent with a full and meaningful life at any stage.[8] In Huxley's dystopia the value placed on youth, able-bodiedness, and productivity is taken to its logical conclusion, so that people who are no longer physically strong and productive—Linda and everyone over the age of about sixty—are eliminated.

Stasis: Life Episodes

In *Brave New World* human biology is tightly controlled. Sexual promiscuity is mandated to prevent tension from building up among people with very little freedom.[9] Other aspects of embodiment, especially parturition and aging, are excised. The body is limited to serving as an instrument of physical pleasure, divorced from experiences that might generate strong emotions. This is purposeful, because strong emotions make for instability, and the Brave New World places a premium on social stability. The people's superficial happiness, not their actual flourishing, is a means to that end. In his foreword, written in 1946, Huxley explains that stability is the society's foremost goal: "The people who govern the Brave New World may not be sane . . . but they are not madmen, and their aim is not anarchy but social stability. It is in order to achieve stability that they carry out, by scientific means, the ultimate, personal, really revolutionary revolution" (9).[10]

This goal is carried out with such thoroughness that the rulers go beyond creating stability to produce stasis. Change is reduced to a bare minimum. Even thinking about change is dangerous, and so the leaders carefully control the people's access to historical knowledge. The Director tells the students that "most historical facts *are* unpleasant" (24), and when the Controller decides to tell the students about the past even though they're usually "taught no history," the Director becomes very nervous at what he might let slip (35). Henry Ford, who is revered almost as a god, is said to have contributed a "beautiful and inspiring saying": "history is bunk" (34). The Controller repeats this phrase solemnly to the students and explains that the creation of the new society was "accompanied by a campaign against the Past; by the closings of museums, the blowing up of historical monuments . . . ; by the suppression of all books published before A.F. [After Ford] 150" (51). Huxley elaborates upon this suppression in a handwritten (later canceled) addition to the typescript: "There is only *now*. The Past is unnecessary. We have abolished the Past" (Typescript, 1:38).[11] Theodor Adorno remarks that this refusal to acknowledge the past as giving rise to the present relegates "all continuity of life" to the "junkpile" (102).

In addition to history, serious art and the pursuit of science are prohibited because they too can lead to change. Toward the end of the novel, the Controller explains to John the Savage that art and science are incompatible with stability. There cannot be an *Othello* in their society

> because our world is not the same as Othello's world. You can't make flivvers without steel—and you can't make tragedies without social instability. The world's stable now. People are happy; they get what they want, and they never want what they can't get. They're well off; they're safe; they're never ill; they're not afraid of death; they're blissfully ignorant of passion and old age; they're plagued with no mothers or fathers; they've got no wives, or children, or lovers to feel strongly about; they're so conditioned that they practically can't help behaving as they ought to behave. And if anything should go wrong, there's [the mind-altering but hangover-free drug] *soma*. (220)

The loss of art and science, he concludes, is "the price we have to pay for stability. . . . We've sacrificed the high art. We have the feelies and the scent organ instead" (220). In his mention of old age, the Controller confirms that aging, living a whole life in one's changing body, is one of the things that would prompt strong feelings and thereby cause instability. Indeed, in the intertwining dialogues of chapter 3, through which the history of the society is presented, the statement that responds to "Stability was practically assured" is this: "It only remained to conquer old age" (54).

Aging can cause the strong feelings that lead to instability for many reasons: it can cause feelings of loss if one becomes unable to do what one is accustomed to doing; it can bring fear of the nothingness of death or hope for an afterlife; it can bring sadness about the impending separation from loved ones and all the other valued aspects of living. And it can be conceived of simply *as* loss due to our cultural propensity to read age as inexorable decline. Margaret Gullette points out that "bodily decrepitude in old age has been a powerful metaphor for loss in Western culture since Sophocles' *Oedipus at Colonus*" (176).[12]

The society of *Brave New World* also aims to preclude another emotional aspect of old age: reflection. The Controller, Mustapha Mond, tells the students that "old men in the bad old days used to renounce, retire, take to religion, spend their time reading, thinking—*thinking!*" (55). Now that there is no period of old age, "the old men work, the old men copulate, the old men have no time, no leisure from pleasure, not a moment to sit down and think—or if ever by some unlucky chance such a crevice of time should yawn in the solid substance of their distractions, there is always *soma*, delicious *soma*" (55). The rulers of the Brave New World cannot have old people reflecting, reading, valuing things other than pleasure, lest they then resist the sacrifice of art, meaning, and religion to stability.[13]

So the rulers promote stasis even at the level of the individual; as the Controller says, there is "no social stability without individual stability" (42). They do this both through the biological manipulation that ensures strength and youth for six decades and through social norms that prohibit close relationships. Relationships not only bring about strong feelings and can therefore be destabilizing, but they also change; they exist in time; they have beginnings, middles, and—if the relationship crumbles or when one party dies—ends. The Brave New World needs its citizens *not* to change. And it is not only their bodies that must remain the same: "Characters remain constant throughout a whole lifetime. Work, play—at sixty our powers and tastes are what they were at seventeen" (55). This degree of stasis, where one's character, tastes, and powers do not change over a lifetime, constitutes a radical redefinition of what it means to be a human being. After all, as Meilaender claims in *Neither Beast Nor God*, "Living things retain their individual existence over time only by *not* remaining what they are" (10).[14] In the Brave New World, instead of a life *span* made up of a trajectory or series of stages, one has more of a life *episode*—a single experience made up of various types of pleasure and distraction. The aging body is suppressed because it is the ultimate sign of change: it manifests the stages of life that are banished from this society.

We learn that aging is foreign to the society from the beginning of the novel, when we are introduced to the Director: "Old, young? Thirty? Fifty? Fifty-five? It was hard to say. And anyhow the question didn't arise; in this year of stability, A.F. 632, it didn't occur to you to ask it" (4). In the lower castes, this individual stability is taken even further through the Bokanovsky Process: "Making ninety-six human beings grow where only one grew before. Progress" (6).[15] The Director describes the process of dividing embryos to make ninety-six identical "twins" as "one of the major instruments of social stability! . . . The principle of mass production at last applied to biology" (7).[16] For these multiple human beings, the body is in effect a shared object. As Adorno describes it, identity in the novel "means the elimination of individual differences, standardization even down to biological constitution; stability, the end of all social dynamics" (99). This standardization begins the society's separation of human beings from their bodies, a separation also effected by the absence of aging.

When Bernard Marx and Lenina Crowne visit the Indian reservation— "an orientalist image of a chaotic space, an archaic state of nature beyond 'our' space and time" (Diken, 158)—they encounter a very old man whose role in the narrative is to demonstrate their shock at the mere fact of aging bodies. We see this again when we are introduced to Linda, a woman from the Brave New World who was accidentally left on the reservation twenty years before and who bore a son, John, fathered by the Director with whom she had traveled. In *Brave New World*, bodies in their natural (read: disabled) states are racialized. As Nirmala Erevelles notes about the "conditions of burgeoning capitalism," here too there is "a constitutive relationship of race and disability where racialized bodies became disabled and disabled bodies became racialized" (86).

The novel sets up a dichotomy between whiteness, cleanliness, civilization, and persistent youth on the one hand, and blackness, dirt, primitivism, and old age on the other:

> His face was profoundly wrinkled and black, like a mask of obsidian. The toothless mouth had fallen in. At the corners of the lips, and on each side of the chin, a few long bristles gleamed almost white against the dark skin. The long unbraided hair hung down in grey wisps round his face. His body was bent and emaciated to the bone, almost fleshless. . . .
>
> "What's the matter with him?" whispered Lenina. Her eyes were wide with horror and amazement.
>
> "He's old, that's all," Bernard answered as carelessly as he could. He too was startled, but he made an effort to seem unmoved. (110)

When Lenina protests that lots of people are old but do not look like that, Bernard explains their society's anti-aging program both to her and to readers. After detailing the chemical interventions that prevent aging, he adds that old people in their society "die long before they reach this old creature's age. Youth almost unimpaired till sixty, and then, crack! the end" (111). This key line both shows the many years of life lost across the population due to the limits of their rejuvenation capabilities and the Brave New World's insistence on youth and sums up the society's upbeat attitude toward deaths that come before any period of decline.

To maintain this positive attitude, the society handles death in a systematically sanitized way.[17] Once people are around sixty years old and rejuvenation can no longer succeed, they are removed to hospitals for the dying. As Peter Firchow has demonstrated, Huxley was influenced in his understanding of death by J. B. S. Haldane's *Daedalus*, which predicted that "the abolition of disease will make death a physiological event like sleep" (307). Since people in this society have no close relationships, it is rare for anyone to visit them at the hospitals, as John finds when he goes to visit his mother, Linda, and the nurse is surprised by his distress. "She was not accustomed to this kind of thing in visitors. (Not that there were many visitors anyhow; or any reason why there should be many visitors)" (199). They condition children not to fear death by bringing them regularly to the hospitals, where they play and eat sweets. Dr. Gaffney explains: "Death conditioning begins at eighteen months. Every tot spends two mornings a week in a Hospital for the Dying. All the best toys are kept there, and they get chocolate cream on death days. They learn to take dying as a matter of course" (164).[18]

The phrase "death days" is ambiguous, and indeed the novel does not make clear how the residents of these hospitals actually die. The phrase could simply mean days on which the children visit the hospitals, or it could indicate days on which groups of people are euthanized. The text contains evidence for both possibilities. When John is visiting Linda at Park Lane Hospital for the Dying, a nurse suggests that the patients die naturally when she says she must go because "'I've got my batch of children coming. Besides, there's Number 3.' She pointed up the ward. 'Might go off any minute now'" (200). In addition, we are told that the "moribund sexagenarians" (202) in the ward look like young girls; their "faces [are] still fresh and unwithered (for senility galloped so hard that it had no time to age the cheeks, only the heart and brain)" (199). This implies that the galloping senility makes short work of the patients' hearts and brains, and they die quickly and naturally.

On the other hand, there is no further explanation of what causes death in these people who can no longer be rejuvenated but are not allowed to age. Since Linda's death from the overuse of *soma* results in a rather grotesque asphyxiation, we can assume the others are not dying from the same cause. Euthanasia would explain how it is that there is no hope that anyone taken to one of these hospitals will ever return to society (199). The novel also suggests large-scale euthanasia when it describes a "convoy of gaily-coloured aerial hearses" that whir from the roof of the hospital, bound for the Slough Crematorium (198). Since it is unlikely that many people will die naturally on a single day, this detail suggests that the society kills its citizens before they can begin to decline. Further, when the Controller is telling Bernard and John that they are being banished, he says it is a good thing there are so many islands in the world to which to banish dissenters. "I don't know what we should do without them. Put you all in the lethal chamber, I suppose" (229). By saying "*the* lethal chamber" not "*a* lethal chamber," Mond implies there *is* one, and that perhaps this is how the citizens of the Brave New World are eliminated when they begin to threaten the compulsory youthfulness of the society.[19]

The ambiguity in the novel about how people die affirms a point Meilaender makes about deaths after "compressed morbidity." Meilaender notes that aging researchers are currently working toward a sudden end for all: "Live as long as we can at the peak of our powers—and then just fall off the cliff."[20] But he wonders how, then, we would die. "The idea is that we live a somewhat longer and (until the very end) disease-free life, and then we die suddenly. But we must ask: Die of what? . . . The answer cannot simply be: of old age. To be old is merely to be increasingly vulnerable to a variety of diseases. If one or another of these is to relieve us quickly of this mortal coil, we will still have had to age" (*Should We Live*, 12). If Huxley did not want to be clear about a large-scale euthanasia project, then, no wonder he had to leave this question open—it is not clear how people might die if they are *not* experiencing old age and its attendant vulnerabilities.[21]

While vague about the cause of the citizens' deaths, the novel describes the setting for them in detail. In the hospitals for the dying, the patients are distracted by televisions left running "from morning till night" and by scents that change every fifteen minutes. As the nurse explains to John, "we try to create a thoroughly pleasant atmosphere here, something between a first-class hotel and a feely-palace" (198–99). This setting, with each person alone amid a ward of people, constantly distracted from what is happening, prevents any emotion from attaching to the event. Even the deaths of the clones in *Never Let Me Go*, discussed in chapter 4, have more meaning than these. Jerome Meckier argues that Huxley scorns such distracted deaths: "Death is the all-important experience, Huxley insists; one should not miss it" ("On D. H. Lawrence and Death," 206). John represents this attitude when he squeezes Linda's hand to try to get her to "come back from [her] dream of ignoble pleasures . . . into the present . . . the awful reality—but sublime, but significant, but desperately important" (204).[22] In these hospitals for the dying, not only is the dying person not fully present, but there are no grieving loved ones to give meaning to the loss. These deaths are not linked in any meaningful way with individual lives, even less so since the value of individual lives is relentlessly subordinated to the value of the social body. The deaths, that is, cannot function as conclusions to life narratives.

The idea of life narratives provides a useful lens for thinking about the redefinition of human lives effected by the society depicted in *Brave New World*. In *After Virtue*, MacIntyre describes the centrality of narrative to human lives and selves. He notes that not only is narrative a basic way in which we understand our world (211), but our concept of ourselves depends on narrative unity. He describes an Aristotelian concept of self that still influences the way we think about our lives: "a concept of self whose unity resides in the unity of a narrative which links birth to life to death as narrative beginning to middle to end" (205). This "narrative concept of selfhood" means that "I am . . . in the course of living out a story that runs from my birth to my death; I am the *subject* of a history that is my own and no one else's, that has its own peculiar meaning" (217). It is clear that a life in the Brave New World cannot have "its own peculiar meaning" because of the unremittingly collective nature of the people's lives. But the problem is broader than that: the Brave New World precludes crafting a life narrative.

While not everyone agrees that lives should be thought of as narratives,[23] there is a fairly strong consensus that understanding our lives in these terms grants them shape and meaning. Helen Small writes, "The notion that . . . we intuitively view our lives as accruing meaning over time—and more specifically, that we see our lives as having the form of narratives, plots, or stories—commands considerable assent among philosophers of quite various kinds" (93).[24] We understand ourselves to be persons, to have unified selves, in part by connecting events that happen in our lives to each other in narrative sequences.[25] Marya Schechtman explains that "we should understand . . . unity not just in terms of relations between individual moments, but also in terms of the overall structure in which those moments play a role. A narrative is not merely certain kinds of connections between one event and the next; it is a structural whole that gives unity to the events within it" (103).[26]

This unity is unavailable to the citizens of the Brave New World. With unchanging bodies, characters, work, and pastimes, and no close relationships to create change, their lives have no structure and no shape.

Robert Combs describes the society as portraying "a falsely heroic utopian orientation toward the future, which is really no future, but a repetition of the past, the culture merely insisting on replicating itself" (163). The citizens' lives do have a beginning, in that they are bred in bottles into the caste for which they are destined; but once they reach maturity, the time for change is over. On the typescript Huxley handwrote further description of this stasis: "An adult has no particular age. Once grown up he remained grown up, almost unchangingly. You were either a child, growing and changing—or else an adult. . . . You lived, then you died" (Typescript 1:4).[27] The people's lives have no middle and no decline or denouement, no true conclusion—just a sudden stop detached from anything unique to that human being. As Meilaender points out in his discussion of contemporary efforts to "overcome the biological processes of aging," such efforts would "extend the maximum life span but would do so in a way that no longer seemed to leave place for stages of life" (*Should We Live*, 13). While the life span given in *Brave New World* isn't especially long (average life expectancy in 1932 was roughly sixty years old anyway ["Life Expectancy"]), the repeated rejuvenation in the novel, together with other aspects of their social mores, wholly removes stages from the people's lives.

One of the biggest factors that helps to preclude life stages and therefore narrative arcs is the elimination of childbearing and rearing. The Controller paints a fearsome portrait of what the "home" was like in the old days:

> Home, home—a few small rooms, stiflingly overinhabited by a man, by a periodically teeming woman, by a rabble of boys and girls of all ages. No air, no space; an understerilized prison; darkness, disease, and smells.
>
> And home was as squalid psychically as physically. Psychically, it was a rabbit hole, a midden, hot with the frictions of tightly packed life, reeking with emotion. What suffocating intimacies, what dangerous, insane, obscene relationships between the members of the family group! Maniacally, the mother brooded over her children (*her* children). (37)[28]

In the Brave New World the word "mother" has become an obscenity, occasioning fear or embarrassed giggles from the children. The intensity of the mother-child relationship was seen as threatening to the pleasure-seeking culture and needed to be eliminated to achieve the society's radical stability.[29]

But the removal of all family bonds means that the people miss the chance to experience stages of dependence on their parents and the gradual emergence from the world of their parents into their own lives. And they miss the chance to experience the stages of rearing children and fostering their gradual separation from themselves. Relationships between parents and children are the essence of change; they give shape to our lives. As Meilaender writes, "Once we begin to attend to the parent-child bond, or more generally to the relation between generations, we have begun to think not just of life but of a 'complete life'—a life marked in some way by stages and movement, a life that has shape and not just duration, a life whose moments are not identical but take their specific character from their place in the whole" (*Should We Live*, 15). This is not to say that a life in the absence of rearing children can have no shape; but the society's wholesale removal of intergenerational relations, its elimination of *having* parents and then of encouraging growth in younger generations, is a major factor in removing narrative trajectories from its citizens' lives.

The absence of life trajectories in turn contributes to the meaninglessness of the characters' deaths in the hospice/"feely palace." Meilaender suggests that "the decline that aging involves is, in a way, a gradual and (at least sometimes) gentle preparation for the cliff toward which we move. Even now we are especially distressed when someone dies at or near the peak of his powers" (*Should We Live*, 12). It seems to me that one reason we are especially distressed by this is our sense that the narrative of the person's life did not reach its conclusion—it stopped in what we take to be the middle, leaving no time for a denouement. In a denouement, on the contrary, the retrospection that allows us to see the shape of our lives becomes available to us. As Small argues in her discussion of what old age means for an Aristotelian view of the unity of lives, living in time can "pitch life towards old age as its culminatory stage: the point or place at which, if the life in question is a good life, we shall be able to see its achieved unity" (93).[30] While Meilaender stresses the need for human beings to realize that we cannot find all we seek in our mortal lives, but must trust in God, one does not have to accept a religious worldview to agree that there is something missing in a life that ends suddenly after "compressed morbidity": the completion of the narrative arc through which we typically understand our lives and know ourselves, as MacIntyre puts it, as the subjects of our own histories.

He Jests (or Shudders) at Scars

But perhaps, as the rulers of the Brave New World would argue, this sacrifice of life stages, the loss of a coherent life narrative with a meaningful conclusion, is worthwhile to avoid the stage of life when we feel ourselves to be in decline. The novel suggests two reasons why it is not a worthwhile sacrifice. The first is that the absence of bodily weakness in a society has moral and political consequences, making it less likely that people will have compassion for weak or dependent human beings or treat them justly. The characters' treatment of Linda, who elicits only disgust from everyone except her son, John, exemplifies the likely political outcome of excising the vulnerabilities of aging. The second reason the novel suggests that this sacrifice is too great is that the stasis necessary for human beings not to reflect, think, and *change* as they approach the end of their lives, for them *not* to experience life stages, requires the suppression of emotion from beginning to end. The excision of age is part of a larger excision of emotions—aside from pleasure—connected with the body. To maintain a life without change, one sacrifices not only a life narrative, but an emotional connection to an embodied life.

Linda represents for the novel and for the other characters bodiliness run amok. Her role as the society's monstrous body is the crux of the novel's misogyny. The text gestures toward feminism by depicting Bernard Marx as disturbed by Lenina's acceptance of herself as a "piece of meat" (93). But it focuses on the intellectual and political concerns of its male characters, while restricting the concerns of its female characters (Linda, Lenina, and Fanny) to men, sexuality, and items of clothing. We meet no women who are identified as belonging to the Alpha caste; we see the Controller and Director educating a group composed only of boys; and it is only the male characters—Bernard, Helmholtz, and John—who question the society's norms. As June Deery points out, men drive the helicopters, while women are depicted as lacking scientific knowledge (260–261, 264).[31] Linda is reduced to her body, then, not only by the society, but by the text itself.[32]

When we first meet her, on the reservation, in accord with the dichotomy described earlier, she is racialized by her association with nature, dirt, and the primitive as opposed to the ultra-sanitized civilization and youthfulness of the Brave New World: she's referred to as a "blond squaw" (118). When Lenina sees her, she is horrified:

> Lenina noticed with disgust that two of the front teeth were missing. And the colour of the ones that remained . . . She shuddered. It was worse than the old man. So fat. And all the lines in her face, the flabbiness, the wrinkles. And the sagging cheeks, with those purplish blotches. . . . And under the brown sack-shaped tunic those enormous breasts, the bulge of the stomach, the hips. Oh, much worse than the old man, much worse! (118–119)

As is revealed by the juxtaposition of the description of Linda's breasts and hips with Lenina's judgment that she is "much worse than the old man," the female body in a state of unruliness (she is fleshly; he is "almost fleshless") is understood as particularly frightening.

Being fat, aging naturally (and more quickly than she might have because of her excessive alcohol and drug use), and generally failing to adhere to norms of compulsory youthfulness, Linda serves as the threatening antithesis of Lenina. The text suggests that Lenina is especially shocked by Linda because of a disavowed and fearful identification with her. Lenina, for example, is repeatedly described as "pneumatic"; but while her full curves are under control and Linda's are depicted as excessive, Lenina does worry that Bernard might have found her "too plump" (94). Both women are promiscuous, though their promiscuity is viewed in opposing terms by their respective cultures. Linda visited the reservation with the Director, accidentally becoming stranded there; Lenina is now visiting with the Alpha Plus Bernard Marx. And Lenina, like her compatriots, regularly takes *soma* when she feels anxious or troubled, while Linda uses alcohol to assuage her distress.

Linda, for her part, views cleanliness and the body much as she was conditioned to do in "civilization." When John was young, she told him about the other world: "Everybody happy and no one ever sad or angry, and every one belonging to every one else, . . . and babies in lovely clean bottles—everything so clean, and no nasty smells, no dirt at all—and people never lonely, but living together and being so jolly and happy" (128). She has been pining for the other world all the years she has been on the reservation, doing her best to maintain its social norms by sleeping with multiple men and using alcohol and peyote. But because these drugs have side effects that *soma* does not, and because the Native Americans react to her promiscuity quite negatively (at one point three women whip her for having sex with "their men" in an incident that demonstrates Huxley's view of Native peoples as both traditional and brutal), she is worn out emotionally and physically.

Though Bernard professes to be critical of many of his society's maxims and norms, he shares a visceral horror of bodies that are ill or wounded. When John shows him a scar, "Bernard looked, and then quickly, with a little shudder, averted his eyes. His conditioning had made him not so much pitiful as profoundly squeamish. The mere suggestion of illness or wounds was to him not only horrifying, but even repulsive and rather disgusting. Like dirt, or deformity, or old age" (138). This linkage of dirt, deformity, and old age makes clear that the society's revulsion from old age is a horror of the body in any form other than youthful and able-bodied strength. Bernard's squeamishness is specifically contrasted with pity—it is not that he feels sympathy for the pain John must have experienced, but simply that he shudders at the sight of a body marked in any way by wounds or the more general stigmata of age.

When Linda and John are brought back to the Brave New World, its members react to Linda much as Lenina does. The narrator explains their aversion to her:

> To say one was a mother—that was past a joke: it was an obscenity. Moreover, she wasn't a real savage, had been hatched out of a bottle and conditioned like anyone else: so she couldn't have really quaint ideas. Finally—and this was by far the strongest reason for people's not wanting to see poor Linda—there was her appearance. Fat; having lost her youth; with bad teeth, and a blotched complexion, and that figure (Ford!)—you simply couldn't look at her without feeling sick, yes, positively sick. So the best people were quite determined *not* to see Linda. (153)

In contrast to her son John, who becomes a celebrity whose "quaint ideas" everyone wants to hear, Linda is even more of an outcast in the society of her birth than she was on the reservation. It is her bodily existence—having given birth, being fat, aging—that disgusts the "best people," demonstrating the society's near total intolerance for deviation from norms of compulsory able-bodiedness and compulsory youthfulness. Such disgust is an important reason that Martha Holstein, Mark Waymack, and Jennifer Parks critique anti-aging medicine. They write, "The widely shared premise behind the anti-aging movement is that aging is a place that we do not and should not want to go. To wind up old becomes a kind of failure. . . . Once we arrive there, we become a painful reminder, an embarrassment, a sort of obscenity that the rest of society would prefer not to see" (99).[33]

In the novel the people's revulsion from the "failure" and "obscenity" embodied in Linda is so stark that they see no point in her continued existence in their world. Rationalizing their visceral aversion by pointing out both that she cannot be rejuvenated and that she is not contributing anything to their society, they knowingly allow Linda to take enough *soma* that she will die within a month or two. Instead of rationing her *soma* as they do with everyone else, the doctors give her unlimited supplies. A Dr. Shaw comments on the fact that the *soma* will soon paralyze her respiratory center: "No more breathing. Finished. And a good thing, too. If we could rejuvenate, of course it would be different. But we can't" (154). This line demonstrates the extent to which compulsory youthfulness governs the people's ideas about human worth. The way they see it, if someone cannot be rejuvenated, then she may as well die; that is to say, old people have no value. Others are even surprised when John objects to the doctor's acquiescence to Linda's desires for more *soma*. For them, "on *soma*-holiday, Linda was most conveniently out of the way" (154). A scene like this exemplifies what disability activists against assisted suicide (such as the group Not Dead Yet) fear: they worry, with much justification, that while doctors will work to prevent people who meet certain socially valued criteria from killing themselves (will offer mental health counseling, antidepressants, or in the case of Linda, simply ration her *soma*), they will collaborate in the deaths of people who do not meet those criteria, as Dr. Shaw does in the novel.

The Brave New World's disregard for people who age is compounded by its utilitarian understanding of human contribution. "'Of course,' Dr. Shaw went on, 'you can't allow people to go popping off into eternity if they've got any serious work to do. But as she hasn't got any serious work . . .'" (155).[34] This idea that death should quickly succeed productivity recalls Emanuel's suggestion that to live past the age when one can make significant contributions is at best pointless and at worst burdensome to society and one's family. He writes that when he is seventy-five, he will have "lived a complete life. . . . I will have pursued my life's projects and made whatever contributions, important or not, I am going to make."[35] Once these contributions are finished, it is reasonable, he suggests, to make way for people who can contribute in their turn. This view not only values human beings only insofar as they contribute— values them instrumentally—but also takes a limited view of "contribution." As Michael Hiltzik writes in his response to Emanuel's article, "To narrow so drastically the range of contributions to life and society we define as worthy is to overlook the glorious richness of the mature mind" (n.p.). Correspondences such as these between the fictional society's biopolitical values and our own give credence to Bülent Diken's suggestion that "perhaps books like *Brave New World* deceive not by presenting what is fiction as true but by creating the illusion that what is true (biopolitics, inequalities, unfreedom) is fiction" (159).

Huxley's depiction of the society's treatment of Linda reveals the dangers of social norms that value only certain kinds of people and only for certain lengths of time. One point implied by this aspect of the novel's critique is that it is hard for people who know for certain that they will never experience being fat, being old, being in decline in any way, to empathize with someone who is. MacIntyre views the knowledge that one could be in another's place as a precursor to ethical treatment of that other: "Of the brain-damaged, of those almost incapable of movement, of the autistic, of all such we have to say: this could have been us. Their mischances could have been ours, our good fortune could have been theirs" (*Dependent*, 100–101). MacIntyre's assumption that none of his audience could be "brain-damaged," physically disabled, or autistic is ableist, and throughout *Dependent Rational Animals* he displays an arrogant separation from disabled people while reducing disability to dependence; but his point here is still worth considering. Our knowledge that it is by mere chance that we are not in another's shoes contributes importantly to our ability to have compassion for him or her.

Taking a universalizing view of dependence and disability, MacIntyre envisions "a form of political society in which it is taken for granted that disability and dependence on others are something that all of us experience at certain times in our lives and this to unpredictable degrees, and that consequently our interest in how the needs of the disabled are adequately voiced and met is not a special interest . . . but rather the interest of the whole political society, an interest that is integral to their conception of their common good" (*Dependent*, 130). Huxley's dystopian society demonstrates the opposite of this political vision, in that the people's knowledge that they will never experience physical vulnerabilities prevents them from sympathizing with or caring about Linda. Instead, they allow their disgust with her embodiment to override what ought to be their fellow feeling with her as a human being. Their lack of sympathy bears out Romeo's lament in *Romeo and Juliet*, "He jests at scars that never felt a wound."

It is certainly not impossible to empathize with someone whose state of being you will never experience—that is a key role of the imagination and a large part of the value of reading literature, which asks us to imagine ourselves in situations and embodiments that we are confident will never be ours. But such empathy is difficult for individuals to achieve and therefore less likely to govern a society. As Martha Nussbaum acknowledges, although it is not absolutely necessary, "the thought of similar vulnerability probably is, as Rousseau argues, an important avenue to compassionate response" (*Political*, 144).[36] And so MacIntyre's focus on chance and his universalizing understanding of dependence do shed light on the Brave New World's eliminationist cruelty toward Linda.

In her article on "Subjectivity as Responsivity," Kelly Oliver similarly focuses on universal human dependence as the root of ethical treatment of others. She writes, "Our dependence . . . brings with it ethical obligations. Insofar as we *are* by virtue of our environment and by virtue of relationships with other people, we have ethical obligations rooted in the very possibility of subjectivity itself" (330).[37] Huxley brings our attention to the idea of interdependence by repeatedly having the characters spout the "hypnopaedic proverb" that has been drummed into them during sleep from their infancy: "Every one belongs to every one else" (40). The novel's use of this line is both ironic and complex. It is ironic because the belief that everyone belongs to everyone else ought to serve the purpose of encouraging compassion for all, a sense of community that excludes no one; but instead the proverb is taken much more narrowly to mean that everyone should have sex with everyone else. As Fanny reminds Lenina, "You *ought* to be a little more promiscuous." When Lenina says she hasn't been feeling very keen on promiscuity, Fanny sympathizes but reminds her that she needs to make the effort, because "after all, every one belongs to every one else" (43).[38] As Diken remarks of this proverb, "The body becomes a networked common good, a public property" (154).[39] By applying this line so narrowly to sexuality, the citizens empty it of meaning and forestall the knowledge that everyone in any society is dependent on others for all kinds of practical and intersubjective goods.

The complexity of the proverb stems from its relation to the society's collectivist, pleasure-seeking brand of totalitarianism. If everyone belongs to everyone else, then everyone, the novel suggests, lacks freedom and self-determination. Adorno describes this principle as mandating "an absolute interchangeability that extinguishes man as an individual being" (104–105).[40] In this sense of the phrase, people do *not* belong to *themselves* and therefore ought not seek to satisfy any desires that run counter to the larger social good. Lenina, for example, ought not to stay with one lover even if she is so inclined, because deep personal relationships threaten the society's stability. Indeed, in accordance with their collectivist mindset, the citizens of the Brave New World take the proverb to mean not that an individual has an obligation to (care for) another individual, but that all individuals have obligations to the *society* ("every one else" naming a collective rather than a set of individuals)—obligations that serve to suppress the needs and interests of individuals. So the platitude is meant to seem dangerous, antagonistic to individual freedom. And yet what the novel demonstrates is that if it were taken differently, to stress interdependence and a sense of common humanity, it would encourage more ethical treatment of outsiders such as Linda. As it is, it serves to exclude Linda even further from consideration because "every one" clearly applies only to those in the Brave New World who are having sex with each other and who know they will never age. Those outsiders whose bodies do not meet their standards are treated as so much waste.

Embodiment and Emotion

In addition to undermining the potential for ethical treatment of outsiders, the novel, as I mention above, suggests a second reason that the sacrifice of life stages is not worthwhile: the suppression of emotion necessary to keep everyone living in an unchanging body in unchanging circumstances. In order to ensure that "characters remain constant throughout a whole lifetime" (55), the society has to prevent any serious reflection or emotional reaction that might prompt people to change their habits, their desires, or their goals—to grow. The people in this society thoroughly lack what bioethicists refer to as "open futures"; they cannot make choices about their own lives.[41] The novel demonstrates that their acquiescence to this lack depends both on their early conditioning and on the removal of life stages and their concomitant emotions.

We learn that the citizens are indoctrinated to find emotion threatening when Bernard tells Lenina he wants to feel strongly and she spouts one of the hypnopaedic lessons: "When the individual feels, the community reels" (94). This view of emotion as dangerous is also made explicit in the Controller's lecture to the schoolboys about the dangers of the old society's inclusion of "Mother, monogamy, romance," which he explains made everyone feel strongly. "And feeling strongly . . . how could they be stable?" (41). The Controller tells the boys how lucky they are never to have a significant gap between the formation of a desire and its satisfaction. "No pains," he tells them, "have been spared to make your lives emotionally easy—to preserve you, so far as that is possible, from having emotions at all" (44). The Brave New World's horror of strong emotion is demonstrated when the nurse views John's grief over Linda's death as a "disgusting outcry" (206). Emotions are among the "squalid" and "disgusting" things the society has overcome. Motherhood especially cannot be tolerated in this society because of the way it brings body and heart together, making embodiment meaningful instead of a source of trivial and passing pleasure.

The loss of strong emotion is clearly part of the loss of meaning Huxley is depicting. To avoid the angst of worrying about one's children, motherhood is removed from society. To avoid the passions and jealousies of unrequited or lost love, romantic love is removed. And to avoid the frustration that might accompany a period of non-able-bodiedness, aging is removed. But readers more readily see the loss caused by the removal of family and romantic relationships than the loss caused by the removal of aging. Indeed, as Meilaender points out and as Emanuel's essay demonstrates, in our society we seem to be aiming for just such an absence of old age—"compression of morbidity"—so that we may die suddenly without experiencing decline.[42] But reading *Brave New World* with the question of the value of old age and old people in mind, we can see that the novel criticizes the removal of aging as part of the loss of meaning in this society. The excision of age is the logical conclusion of the society's control and trivialization of human embodiment.

Controlling bodies is crucially important in the Brave New World, and it is Linda's inability to control hers that makes her so repugnant. The society's emphasis on control reflects our own less successful but no less desperate efforts to control bodies. Susan Wendell discusses the illusion that bodies are controllable: "A major obstacle to coming to terms with the full reality of bodily life is the widespread myth that the body can be controlled. . . . The essence of the myth of control is the belief that it is possible, by means of human actions, to have the bodies we want and to prevent illness, disability, and death" (93–94). In her contention that people embrace control to escape from what she calls "the rejected body," Wendell sheds light on the role of Linda in the novel: her presence makes visible the category of the abject for this society. She is what the society is always already keeping at bay. This is why her return is so destructive to the Director of Hatcheries and Conditioning, who can no longer maintain his post after she publicly embraces him. It is not only that she exposes him as a father, but that she exposes the fragility of the project he is so closely associated with, the project of controlling bodies.

Limiting bodies to markers of caste status and sites of transient physical pleasure, the society forecloses not only strong emotion but also any deeper connection to one's embodiment, a connection that aging (among other things) would have fostered. Aging reconnects us to bodies that we—to the extent that our bodies have fit into our social and built environments[43]—have tended to forget, as we become more aware not only that we *have* bodies, but that we *are* bodies, as our bodies "reclaim" us (Hamilton, 309). This process is impossible in Huxley's dystopia. Toward the end of the novel, the Controller, Mustapha Mond, discusses aging with John. Reading to him from Maine de Biran's discussion of Cardinal Newman, he links the absence of age with the loss of religion. Biran dismisses the claim that old men become religious because they are afraid of death. Instead, he says, they become religious because they are no longer distracted by the desires of able-bodied youth:

> My own experience has given me the conviction that, quite apart from any such terrors or imaginings, the religious sentiment tends to develop as we grow older; to develop because, as the passions grow calm, as the fancy and sensibilities are less excited and less excitable, our reason becomes less troubled in its working, less obscured by the images, desires and distractions, in which it used to be absorbed; whereupon God emerges as from behind a cloud. (233)[44]

Meckier asserts that Biran speaks for Huxley, who sought in his novels and nonfiction to "alert the reader to the possibilities for spiritual growth in being prepared for death" ("On D. H. Lawrence and Death," 212). Biran's view could also be Meilaender's, in that both thinkers understand old age as a period of reflection that leads to religious commitment. But the Controller goes on to explain that this view is not relevant in his society:

> "'You can only be independent of God while you've got youth and prosperity; independence won't take you safely to the end.' Well, we've now got youth and prosperity right up to the end. . . . 'The religious sentiment will compensate us for all our losses.' But there aren't any losses for us to compensate; religious sentiment is superfluous. And why should we go hunting for a substitute for youthful desires, when youthful desires never fail? A substitute for distractions, when we go on enjoying all the old fooleries to the very last?" (233–234)

John finds this reliance on "youthful desires" and "distractions" disturbing, believing that it "degrades" human beings to enjoy nothing but "pleasant vices" (236). He believes that there are far more meaningful things than the mere satisfaction of desire. Therefore, he believes that the ability to avoid old age and every other less-than-perfect aspect of life detracts from human dignity.

The debate between John and the Controller lasts for several pages, with John insisting that he doesn't want comfort—he wants real human experience: "I want God, I want poetry, I want real danger, I want freedom, I want goodness. I want sin" (240). Mond counters that he is claiming the right to be unhappy, and John concurs.[45] Then Mond continues: "'Not to mention the right to grow old and ugly and impotent; the right to have syphilis and cancer; the right to have too little to eat; . . . the right to be tortured by unspeakable pains of every kind.' There was a long silence. 'I claim them all,' said the Savage at last" (240). In John's view, it is impossible to achieve the highest human goods—truth, poetry, freedom—without opening oneself to the possibility of grief and pain.[46] The Controller believes that those goods are better sacrificed for stability and pleasure. This conversation brings readers' attention to aging as one of the elements being sacrificed in the society and to the losses attendant on that sacrifice.

Meckier describes the argument as "the novel's climactic dead end: instead of a revolution, two incomplete philosophies collide, neither able to defeat or accommodate the other" ("Aldous Huxley's Americanization," 450). Although the society depicted in the novel is dystopian, Huxley was not wholly critical of Mond. He was very interested in planned solutions to social problems (Bradshaw, 157), and named Mond after the industrialist Alfred Mond, whom he admired (Woiak, 117). Joanne Woiak notes that Huxley told a journalist that "he favored neither the conditioned stability of the World State nor the outsider John Savage's desire for 'freedom to be unhappy.' Instead, there had to be a workable compromise between the two extremes" (114).

Because of the dystopian aspects of the society, readers tend to align ourselves at least provisionally with John, protesting the absence of real meaning in the society. The novel may prompt us to sympathize with the view Meilaender espouses in opposition to transhumanism: "We might . . . wonder whether it would have been better to remain human . . . even if our capacities were fewer, our status (in some sense) lower, and our suffering greater" (Neither Beast, 22). It may induce us, too, to heed Nussbaum's call for "a society of citizens who admit that they are needy and vulnerable and who discard the grandiose demands for omnipotence and completeness" (Hiding, 17). We may hesitate over John's claim to being "old and ugly and impotent"; but we are brought to see, from the way the society so tightly manages bodies and emotions, that one cannot avoid *only* negative bodily states and emotions. The society has thrown the emotional baby out with the emotional and bodily bathwater; excising aging comes with high emotional and moral costs.

Brave New World suggests that there is positive value in aging—that one may become more knowledgeable, calm, courageous, compassionate, and most importantly, reflective. But even more so, it demonstrates that aging is a necessary part of having a body that experiences the world and all the myriad emotions that stem from those experiences. Old age contributes to our life narratives a denouement, a conclusion from whose vantage we can see the shape of our lives, see our lives *as* meaningful narratives. David Carr describes aging as a process of gradually shifting from "the *vita activa* to the *vita contemplativa*" (184). Thomas Rentsch argues that aging is a "task of interpretation," of achieving "clarification about life as a whole" (353, 348).[47] And insofar as our curiosity about future stages of our lives helps drive our desire to continue to live, Peter Brooks's suggestion that literary plot is driven by the "*anticipation of retrospection*" (23) can also be applied to human lives. If we anticipate living to old age, we are anticipating (among other things) retrospection (the *vita contemplativa*), an anticipation that, as with reading a novel, propels us forward with interest and engagement, making for rich and full lives.

To assert the value of the stage of life that is old age for any given individual is distinct from asserting that we should value old people; but they are related, in that the intrinsic value of the stage of life to an elderly person must also be of concern in making bioethical judgments. In his discussion of the moral significance of age in bioethical decision-making and policy, John Harris accepts that in most cases, if person A wants to go on living, no matter how long she has left, then her time is equally precious to her as person B's time is to him, even if person B has longer to live (90). That is, the intrinsic value of older people's lives is generally not less than the intrinsic value of younger people's lives.[48] Moreover, Harris's discussion calls our attention to another aspect of the Brave New World's policy of killing, or letting die, everyone at around age sixty. He writes that "an almost necessary condition for valuing life is its open-endedness. The fact that we do not normally know how long we have to live liberates the present" (100).[49] The Brave

New society's fear of and revulsion from aging bodies, its insistence on removing any reminders of bodily weakness or vulnerability, means it also forecloses life's open-endedness. Instead of liberating the present, this fear imprisons it.

Returning to *Brave New World* from the joint perspective of age and disability studies enables us to see more clearly our own culture's fear and revulsion surrounding aging bodies, our own compulsion to try both to transcend and transgress, as Meilaender puts it, our embodiment.[50] Reading the novel in these terms works against the cultural tendency to judge old people's lives as expendable, to think that it would be best for everyone to die before reaching that stage of life that would allow us to create meaningful denouements to the narratives of our lives.

3

Disabled Lives

O'Connor's *The Violent Bear It Away*

Philosophical thought experiments are microfictions that seek to isolate particular factors for analysis. With their stipulations, for example, that we know only one characteristic of the players in a scenario or that "all other things" are equal, thought experiments can be flattening, providing less rich material than literary narrative for thinking through normative questions.[1] Their technique of isolating individual factors becomes especially problematic in discussions of intellectual disability in mainstream bioethics. Narratively removing an intellectually disabled person from his or her social context, isolating his or her disability as the only relevant factor in a case study, can work to objectify the imagined person in a narrative analogy to the freak show. For example, when Jeff McMahan discusses a "congenitally severely retarded human being," he stipulates that this person has "cognitive capacities comparable to those of a dog" and suggests that such a life, while fine for a dog, is very unfortunate for a human being (*Ethics*, 146 and passim). There is no information about this person's family, social environment, or sources of pleasure and joy.[2] Nor is there evidence that there *are* human beings whose cognitive capacities are comparable to those of dogs, or even what that would mean, given that dogs' superior sensory capacities make up such a large part of their cognitive world.[3] There is not meant to be any such information, of course, because this is simply a thought experiment.[4]

Because of their complexities, however, literary narratives conjure imaginary people and events that can form the basis for more fully contextualized ethical thought experiments. As James Terry and Peter Williams point out, "Philosophic understanding of a given moral problem can be enriched by a literary account that places issues in a context of the lives and activities of particular characters" (1). And literature can aid ethical reasoning in another way as well: because most complex narratives are made up of competing voices or points of view, they can, more fruitfully than a typical thought experiment, be read against their grain. In his discussion of the role of literature in bioethics, Tod Chambers quotes John Fowles, who compared writing to a fixed fight in boxing: the writer "positions 'conflicting wants into the ring and then describes the fight, letting that want he himself favours win'" (81). Readers, however, can catch the writer out in this process of fixing the fight; we can root for the other fighter, even as we see that he will lose. Such resistant readings have long been common practice in feminist and antiracist criticism and are often crucial to other endeavors, such as disability studies, that dispute conventional understandings of literary texts.[5]

When we read a novel such as Flannery O'Connor's *The Violent Bear It Away* (1960), for example, we need to look carefully at the way the ethical fight is fixed. In this novel, the murder and simultaneous baptism of a young, intellectually disabled boy, Bishop Rayber, by his fourteen-year-old cousin, Francis Tarwater, forms the climax of a text that foregrounds a series of judgments about Bishop's worth. The boys' great-uncle, Mason Tarwater, who raised young Tarwater, sees Bishop as protected and valued by God and in need of baptism; Francis Tarwater sees his young cousin merely as a tool with which to control his future; and Bishop's father, George Rayber, sees his son as "useless" and tries to resist the love he feels for him. By presenting their disparate views, O'Connor sets up a three-way fight, dramatizing debates parallel to those being carried out in bioethical literature from a range of mainstream and disability studies orientations about the value of different kinds of human lives. Bishop himself is not a participant in this fight; while those around him argue about his value, he is excluded from the ring. As I demonstrate below, O'Connor fixes the fight in favor of young Francis Tarwater, the murderer. And yet her artistry—along with her successful efforts to give the atheist character Rayber "his due" and her professed commitment to the views of old Mason Tarwater—enables readers to see the ways in which her narrative (and not just young Tarwater) has devalued and dehumanized Bishop, making his life seem expendable. It enables us to crip the narrative.

The Violent Bear It Away engages readers in questions of Bishop's worth that are directly relevant to contemporary bioethical considerations—for example, issues surrounding selective abortion, euthanasia, and assisted suicide for disabled people. The views of George Rayber bear comparison to the most objectionable views of Princeton philosopher Peter Singer, who holds that if we reject the metaphysical notion of the "sanctity of human life," it follows that we ought to judge disabled human lives as worth less than nondisabled human lives. That is to say, Singer believes there are only two possible methods to judge human worth: a (religious) method that sees all human life as sacred and a (secular) method that understands value as stemming from a being's capacities.[6] His rejection of the former method, then, leads him to argue that parents ought to be able to have babies with severe disabilities "humanely" killed to make way for nondisabled babies they can reasonably hope to give birth to subsequently.[7] In this chapter I consider points of view about the worth of intellectually disabled human beings expressed by O'Connor's fictional characters alongside those expressed by Singer and other bioethicists and demonstrate a revealing convergence of views held by the intensely secular Singer and the fervently Catholic O'Connor. Although O'Connor died in 1964, before the first "test-tube baby" was born and well before the age of the human genome, the underlying question of value remains central to how we think about bioethical questions.

It is clear that O'Connor agrees in principle with Mason Tarwater that Bishop's soul is valuable to God and detests the views of Rayber, who thinks about human beings in instrumental terms. The Church holds that every human soul is equally valuable and objects to eugenics on the grounds that human beings must not, as a result of judging souls by human criteria, interfere with God's dominion over matters of reproduction. But as Christine Rosen points out, even in the 1930 papal decree about Christian marriage in which Pope Pius XI condemned eugenic *methods*, he did not clearly critique eugenic *aims* (159). In fact, the pope conceded that "procuring the strength and health of the future child" is "not contrary to right reason" and did not question the idea that some offspring may be "defective" (qtd. in Rosen, 158). O'Connor's representation of Bishop displays a similar complexity. Even though she attests to the value of Bishop's soul, her narrative ultimately implies a disturbingly eugenic view about disabled lives. Much as Singer does explicitly, the novel implicitly distinguishes the *moral worth* of a human being from the worth or value of that person's *life*, ultimately presenting Bishop's life as worth less than the lives of those with unimpaired intellects. That is, in staging debates about Bishop's worth in a rationalistic world, O'Connor accepts eugenic positions she purports to critique.[8]

This is the case even though O'Connor herself used crutches because of her lupus, of which she rightly expected to die young (Gooch 185, 192–195, 232). While several O'Connor critics assume that her own disability gave her what we might now call a "disability consciousness,"[9] ableism is as easily internalized as sexism or racism. Garland-Thomson reminds us that "having been acculturated similarly to everyone else, disabled people also often avoid and stereotype one another in attempting to normalize their own social identities" (*Extraordinary Bodies*, 15). Even had O'Connor had a sort of disability pride, it is highly unlikely that it would extend from physical to intellectual disability. As Joseph Valente demonstrates, even writers who value certain forms of mental disability (most often madness) tend to denigrate intellectual disability. In his discussion of Rebecca West's *The Return of the Solider* as representative, he asserts: "The contrast is stark: a mental disability can be transvalued as a psycho-spiritual difference superior to and critical of the sociocultural status quo, unless it smacks of cognitive deficiency or mental retardation, at which point the hell of the most infernal war ever imagined is decisively preferable" (396).[10] As becomes clear in what follows, O'Connor joins the writers Valente discusses in casting her intellectually disabled character's life as expendable in ways that other lives are not.

While Bishop is a fictional character, the contention undergirding this study is that fictional representations are part of our thinking about bioethical questions. They help form our views about human value. In *The Secret Life of Stories*, Michael Bérubé discusses the overlap between our understandings of fictional characters and our sense of ethics in judging human beings. He notes that "no matter how formalist I try to be in my reading of literary works dealing with intellectual disability, it remains impossible to bracket out entirely the question of justice" (190). He maintains that "the stakes are always high when the subject is intellectual disability, because the stakes are ultimately about who is and who is not determined to be 'fully human' and what is to be done with those who (purportedly) fail to meet the prevailing performance criteria for being human" (192). When we think about Bishop's worth, then, we are also necessarily thinking, at least in general terms, about the worth of living people with intellectual disabilities.

Rosemarie Garland-Thomson makes a compelling case for "conserving disability," and other scholars such as Alison Kafer explore ways we can imagine futures *with* disability. Philosophers such as Martha Nussbaum, Eva Kittay, and Licia Carlson and political scientists such as Stacy Clifford Simplican join, from different angles, in defending the rights and dignity of people with intellectual disabilities.[11] This body of work constitutes a crucial rebuttal to attitudes, such as those described below, that place intellectually disabled people "at the margins of personhood and moral consideration" (Carlson, 16). Here I take it as a given that excluding people from moral consideration on the basis of disability is unethical, and analyze the devaluation of intellectually disabled people even within views that claim to accept "the sanctity of human life." That this devaluation underlies such a wide range of political and religious views demonstrates an unsettling continuity between earlier eugenic judgments that some people are weeds, who should be plucked for the racial garden to flourish, and our current acceptance of a "curative imaginary" (Kafer, 27) that aims to cure or eliminate those anomalous human beings we find unfit for a future.[12]

Debating Bishop's Worth

The Violent Bear It Away opens with Francis Tarwater failing to bury his great-uncle, old Mason Tarwater. Old Tarwater has died without fulfilling an obligation he talked about repeatedly to young Tarwater: baptizing Bishop Rayber, the son of his atheist nephew, George Rayber. Mason told Francis that if he died without baptizing him, the obligation would pass to him. The novel's central subject is the struggle within Francis Tarwater whether to accept or reject his great-uncle's religious views and his own calling as a prophet. Francis Tarwater has begun hearing the voice of a "stranger" (a devil-figure) who goads him into various sacrilegious ideas and actions, such as not to bother giving Mason a Christian burial. After his great-uncle's death, Tarwater leaves the homestead for the city, moving in with Rayber and Bishop. By representing Tarwater's life with Rayber and regularly flashing back to his former life with Mason Tarwater, O'Connor is able to present the other characters' distinct points of view about Bishop's value.[13]

Throughout the novel Bishop is used as what David Mitchell and Sharon Snyder call a "narrative prosthesis"—a crutch to prop up the novel's plot and concerns. Not only do the other characters regularly express opinions about his worth as a human being, but he also serves as a symbol of the pull of religious faith, of young Tarwater's calling as a prophet. This symbolism has decisive results: it is in trying to resist his calling that Tarwater drowns Bishop, but his "accidental" baptism of Bishop confirms the calling. Bishop's use as a narrative prosthesis thus crucially informs the novel's plot. O'Connor acknowledged Bishop's strategic value when she wrote to Cecil Dawkins in 1958, "I suppose my novel too will be called another Southern Gothic. I have an idiot in it. I wish I could do it without the idiot but the idiot is necessary. In any case it's a very nice unobjectionable idiot" (*Habit*, 300). Her offhand defense of "the idiot" as "very nice [and] unobjectionable" is also an admission that Bishop is not quite a character in his own right—that he serves instead as a symbolic device. This dismissive attitude is compounded by her use of the pronoun "it" instead of "he" to refer to Bishop.

Within the novel, the self-styled prophet Mason Tarwater's view of Bishop is bound up with his belief in an immortal human soul. For Mason, all human souls are valuable to God, and so all human beings must be baptized to prepare them to go to God. He recounts how he tried to convince Rayber that his son needed to be baptized: "'That boy cries out for his baptism,' the old man said. 'Precious in the sight of the Lord even an idiot!'" (33). Mason's view about the equal worth of all souls accords with the stance of the Catholic Church. A prominent American priest named John Augustine Ryan (1869–1945), for example, "questioned whether a society was 'justified in instituting a comparison between quality and quantity in respect of beings endowed with human souls, each of which has consequently an intrinsic and, in a sense, an infinite value'" (qtd. in Rosen, 141–142). And yet Ryan was a longtime member of the American Eugenics Society (Rosen, 141ff.)—a contradictory stance that echoes the novel's devaluation of Bishop in spite of O'Connor's religious commitment to the equality of souls.

Mason Tarwater believes that God made Bishop "dim-witted" specifically to protect him from his virulently atheistic father: "And the Lord, the old man said, had preserved the one child he had got out of [his then-wife] from being corrupted by such parents. He had preserved him in the only possible way: the child was dim-witted" (9). Mason frequently "brood[s] on the schoolteacher's child" musing that "the Lord gave him one he couldn't corrupt" (77). In O'Connor's short story "The Lame Shall Enter First," whose characters are variations on those of *The Violent Bear It Away*, this assumption is inverted in that the father, Sheppard, thinks that his young son, Norton, though not intellectually disabled, is "not bright enough to be damaged much" by the religious talk of the fourteen-year-old Rufus Johnson (*Complete*, 463).[14] Susan Srigley explains why, in Mason Tarwater's view, Bishop needs to be baptized even though he is portrayed as incorruptible: "Old Tarwater . . . sees [Bishop] as already saved from Rayber because his limited rational capabilities protect him from Rayber's rationalistic view of the world. The rite [of baptism] is the recognition and proclamation of Bishop's spiritual worth and dignity before and by God" (112).[15]

Mason disdains the achievement-oriented view of human beings to which Rayber clings. He tells Tarwater about a time when Rayber wanted to raise him: "'Then he turned his mind to raising you. Said he was going to give you every advantage, every advantage.' The old man snorted. 'You have me to thank for saving you from those advantages'" (66). His different view of true advantages prepares readers to see the flaws, from O'Connor's perspective, in Rayber's outlook.[16] In differentiating himself from Rayber, Mason opposes spiritual riches to material wealth, spiritual knowledge to a destructive intellectualism: "He could never take action. He could only get everything inside his head and grind it to nothing. But I acted. And because I acted, you sit here in freedom, you sit here a rich man, knowing the Truth, in the freedom of the Lord Jesus Christ" (76–77).

O'Connor explicitly endorsed Mason's view that human value is intrinsic and that, therefore, Bishop's soul is "precious in the sight of the Lord." In a letter to Elizabeth Hester in 1955, she affirmed, "I believe and the church teaches that God is as present in the idiot boy as in the genius" (*Habit*, 99). Linda Haranjo-Huebl claims that O'Connor accepted the "concept of the sanctity of all human life, an absolutely egalitarian life ethic that uses as its barometer the treatment of those who lack the power to demand and/or seize full recognition of their personhood and right to life" (73). Such a view is displayed in exaggerated form within the novel by the woman working in the motel where Tarwater ultimately murders Bishop. When she hears Tarwater speak rudely to Bishop, she responds sternly: "'Mind how you talk to one of them there, you boy!' the woman hissed. . . . 'Them there what?' he murmured. 'That there kind,' she said, looking at him fiercely as if he had profaned the holy'" (155). While the woman's reverence goes beyond O'Connor's assertion of spiritual equality, it is not completely mocked by the novel. The same woman, after all, presciently warns Tarwater, "Whatever devil's work you mean to do, don't do it here" (156). Her presence in the novel adds a voice to Mason Tarwater's side of the argument, staged throughout the novel, about Bishop's worth and contributes to the symbolism that associates Bishop with the call to prophecy.

The second point of view about Bishop is Francis Tarwater's. He sees Bishop as a symbol of his own calling. Tarwater wants desperately to resist the obligation to baptize Bishop placed on him by Mason Tarwater and, the novel suggests, by God.[17] But he is drawn inexorably to perform the rite. Tarwater's sense that Bishop represents God's summons is confirmed by the imagery through which the novel represents Bishop. Our first introduction to Bishop focuses on his eyes: "The little boy somewhat resembled old Tarwater except for his eyes which were grey like the old man's but clear, as if the other side of them went down and down into two pools of light" (23). We soon get a similar set of descriptors from Francis Tarwater's point of view: "A small pink-faced boy stood in [the door]. . . . He wore steel-rimmed spectacles and had pale silver eyes like the old man's except that they were clear and empty. He was gnawing on a brown apple core" (32). Bishop's name, his similarity to the prophet-figure Mason, his clear eyes resembling pools of light, and his association with the apple core hint at his linkage both with holiness and with humanity's fallen state.[18] Bishop is used as a metaphor for humanity's dual spiritual and embodied condition and by implication, therefore, for Tarwater's obligation to baptize.

Two other descriptions of Bishop fill out the portrait of him as symbolic of human spiritual existence. First, he carries around a trashbasket with a rock in it (101). If we understand the rock as symbolizing the Church (Matthew 16:18) and yet note its location in a trashbasket, we might see Bishop as carrying both human sin and redemption. Indeed, given O'Connor's contemptuous references to "the idiot" in this novel and "the idiot daughter" in "The Life You Save May Be Your Own" (*Habit*, 301, 85, 174, 186), this rock-in-trashbasket may be intended to serve as an objective correlative to O'Connor's statement that God's spirit (the rock) can be found as much in the "idiot" (the trashbasket) as in the "genius." This implied comparison between Bishop and a trashbasket makes O'Connor's statement look less like an affirmation of the value of all souls and more like an affirmation of the presence of God in every living substance, no matter how insignificant.

Second, Rayber comments that "Bishop looked like the old man grown backwards to the lowest form of innocence" (111). With this observation he links Bishop with the origin of humankind. The words "backwards," "lowest," and "innocence" signal an understanding of disabled people common in the eugenics period and lingering through the succeeding decades. As I mention in chapter 1, Douglas Baynton demonstrates that both nonwhite and "defective" people were understood as "evolutionary laggards or throwbacks." Baynton quotes a late nineteenth-century writer asserting that "to use sign language with deaf children would 'push them back in the world's history to the infancy of our race'" (*Defectives*, 67). The similarity of this rhetoric to Rayber's description of Bishop demonstrates Rayber clinging to what he sees as a scientific view of human populations—a view founded on racist understandings of fitness and unfitness. Indeed, the stranger/devil's warning to Tarwater reinforces a eugenic association between disabled and nonwhite people: "If you baptize once, you'll be doing it the rest of your life. If it's an idiot this time, the next time it's liable to be a nigger" (166).

The association between Bishop and a state of primitive or animal innocence is given colorful expression when young Tarwater compares Bishop alternately to a dog and a hog. When Rayber teases Tarwater for being afraid to look at Bishop, he retorts that he'd "as soon be afraid to look at a dog" (143). When the three of them are at a restaurant, Tarwater tells Rayber that Bishop "'eats like a hog and he don't think no more than a hog and when he dies, he'll rot like a hog. Me and you too,' he said, looking back at the schoolteacher's mottled face, 'will rot like hogs. The only difference between me and you and a hog is me and you can calculate, but there ain't any difference between him and one'" (116–

117). By dismissing Bishop, Tarwater flaunts his (temporary) dismissal of the Christian belief in the immortal soul. His equation of Bishop with the hog parallels Peter Singer's judgment that some mentally disabled human beings are less worthy of consideration than some nonhuman animals. But while Tarwater uses the ability to calculate as his *sine qua non*, Singer uses criteria such as "rational and self-conscious . . . aware of themselves as distinct entities with a past and a future" (*Practical Ethics*, 94). Tarwater, then, understands Bishop as the very crux of his dilemma: an embodiment of the question whether human beings have immortal souls, which would imply that he ought to baptize as many people as he can, or are no different, existentially, from other mammals.

As much as Tarwater disavows a kinship with Bishop, the novel makes clear that he sees his fate as dependent on his relationship to him. Failing to recognize Bishop as a subject in his own right, he sees him alternately as part of himself and part of Rayber. His feeling that Bishop is part of him contributes to the text's use of Bishop not only as narrative prosthesis but also as a metaphor for a sort of heart of darkness, the primitive within the civilized person. For example, when Tarwater first encounters Bishop after his great-uncle has died, it is his breathing he hears first. Having heard the same breathing on the telephone before arriving at Rayber's house, he recognizes it: he hears the "faint familiar sound of heavy breathing. It was closer to him than the beating of his own heart. His eyes widened and an inner door in them opened in preparation for some inevitable vision" (90–91). This suggestion that the "lowest form of innocence" embodied by Bishop also exists within Tarwater is reinforced by a description of Tarwater himself that links him both to Christianity and to ancientness: "His cheekbones protruded, narrow and thin like the arms of a cross, and the hollows under them had an ancient look as if the child's skeleton beneath were as old as the world" (48).

Tarwater also sees Bishop as a part of his father, Rayber: "The boy had a vision of the schoolteacher and his child as inseparably joined. The schoolteacher's face was red and pained. The child might have been a deformed part of himself that had been accidentally revealed" (93). The narrator later confirms this suggestion in the description of Rayber's reaction to Bishop's death: his hearing aids "made the sounds [of Bishop's bellow as he struggles against drowning] seem to come from inside him as if something in him were tearing itself free" (202). Bishop serves here as a rejected part of Rayber's self. These metaphorical representations of Bishop underscore the text's use of him as a tug-of-war rope between God and the devil for Tarwater's soul.

When Tarwater experiences a "certainty, sunk in despair" that he *is* intended by God to baptize Bishop, he rages against what he sees as a pointless task: "The Lord out of dust had created him, had made him blood and nerve and mind, had made him to bleed and weep and think, and set him in a world of loss and fire all to baptize one idiot child that He need not have created in the first place and to cry out a gospel just as foolish" (91–92). Here we see his sense of superiority to Bishop in his ascribing only to himself "blood and nerve and mind" and the ability to "bleed and weep and think." These triplicate phrases conjure the trinity, infusing holiness into Tarwater's description of himself. His claim that God need not have created Bishop replicates Rayber's earlier protest to Mason, when he shouts at him, "Ask the Lord why He made him an idiot in the first place, uncle. Tell him I want to know why!" (33–34). His association of Bishop with a "foolish" gospel echoes Rayber's sarcastic comment that Bishop was "formed in the image and likeness of God" (113). As much as he claims to be ignoring Rayber, then, Tarwater's views of Bishop are heavily influenced by his. As Srigley points out, Tarwater carries out the murder only after Rayber details his own previous attempt to drown his son. Srigley writes: "The stranger proposes that Tarwater take the matter of his divine election into his own hands by drowning Bishop as an act of defiance; the suggestion comes from the voice, but the idea, along with the devaluation of Bishop's worth is Rayber's" (126).

The third point of view about Bishop presented by the novel is Rayber's, whose primary way of understanding his son is instrumental. For Rayber, people are valuable insofar as they can be mentally independent, self-sufficient, and useful to society. In his view, accordingly, an intellectually disabled boy is useless and without a future. When Mason tells Rayber that either he or young Tarwater will baptize Bishop, Rayber replies, "You could slosh water on him for the rest of his life and he'd still be an idiot. Five years old for all eternity, useless forever" (34).[19] When he takes in Tarwater, he focuses on making him into the "useful" man that he believes Bishop will never be. He tells him, "It's not too late for me to make a man of you!" (90). Tarwater instinctively resists this version of what it means to be a man. But Rayber assures him that he can still "develop into a useful man" and adds: "'All the things that I would do for him—if it were any use—I'll do for you,' he said. 'Now do you see why I'm so glad to have you here?'" (92).

Rayber links this idea of usefulness not only to masculinity but to the possibility of a future. This can be seen both in his claim that Bishop will be "five years old for all eternity" and his disappointment when he finds he will not be able to rehabilitate Tarwater: "He thought of his foolish emotions the night the boy had come, thought of himself sitting by the side of the bed, thinking that at last he had a son with a future" (201). The notion that Bishop has no future because of his disability exemplifies Michael Davidson's claim that for racial others, disabled people, and those understood as "inverts," the eugenic mindset envisioned "no future. They represented the past, the ill formed, the animal that needed to be expunged for the 'right' future to be possible" ("Pregnant Men," 211).[20] Or as Alison Kafer puts it in her discussion of crip temporality, "Ideas about disability and disabled minds/bodies animate many of our collective evocations of the future; in these imaginings, disability too often serves as the agreed-upon limit of our projected futures" (27).

Rayber thinks of his son as futureless because he is certain that only accomplishment can create a future (and here his view is similar to that of Ezekiel Emanuel, discussed in the previous chapter). As Kafer demonstrates in her trenchant analysis of the case of Ashley X—the intellectually disabled girl whose parents and doctors concocted a "treatment" to prevent her from entering puberty or growing to an adult size—"disability is often understood as a kind of disruption in the temporal field" (48). The idea of the "eternal" child appears in many descriptions of Ashley X: "From the beginning of the case, she has been represented as temporally disjointed, as an eternal child" (49). This idea is included in the description of Bishop as "dim and ancient, like a child who had been a child for centuries" (91). In the representation of Bishop, then, are combined ideas of ancientness (evolutionary reversal), futurelessness, and childishness: a sense of being outside of time.

Because he sees him as without a future, Rayber finds his love for Bishop itself useless and "horrifying." "He was not afraid of love in general. He knew the value of it and how it could be used. . . . None of this had the least bearing on his situation. The love that would overcome him was of a different order entirely. It was love without reason, love for something futureless, love that appeared to exist only to be itself" (113). As is clear from this passage, Rayber views even love in instrumental terms. For him, the right kind of love can manifest itself in guiding a child to achievement or success. But he fears loving "without reason," without that love resulting in tangible outcomes. While Rayber's attitude, baldly expressed, seems patently absurd and dangerous, the idea that raising children is fundamentally a matter of promoting their material success is common in mainstream bioethics.

We see this assumption that love is an instrument, for example, in a comment by bioethicist R. Alta Charo about a deaf lesbian couple who chose a deaf sperm donor to conceive their two children. Charo is quoted as saying, "The question is whether the parents have violated the sacred duty of parenthood, which is to maximize to some reasonable degree the advantages available to their children" (qtd. in Mundy, 24). The idea that our highest, even "sacred," duty is to maximize our children's advantages implies a capitalistic mindset where a life's value is measured by achievement. Moreover, the word "advantages" is a relative one, implying a view of life as a competition in which one tries to give one's own children a head start.

Similarly, discussions of genetic enhancement and selective abortion often focus on giving a child "the best possible start in life" (Singer, "Shopping," 312).[21] In his essay "Shopping at the Genetic Supermarket," Singer uses this phrase multiple times, relying on its prima facie reasonableness to argue that selective abortion is itself reasonable. He writes:

> Now think about a couple who are told that the child the woman is carrying will have a disability, let's say, Down's syndrome. Like most parents, the couple thinks it important to give their child the best possible start in life, and they do not believe that having Down's syndrome is the best possible start in life. . . . They may also accept—as I do—that people with Down's syndrome often are loving, warm people who live happy lives. But they may still think that this is not the best they can do for their child. Perhaps they just want to have a child who will, eventually, come to be their intellectual equal, someone with whom they can have good conversations, someone whom they can expect to give them grandchildren, and to help them in their old age. Those are not unreasonable desires for parents to have. (313–314)

Singer is not calling parental love for children with intellectual disabilities "horrifying" as Rayber might. But he *is* expressing a common, unstated understanding of parental love as that which produces results. The goal of doing the best for one's child, in this microfictional scenario, is disingenuous because it means *not having that child*, but having *another* child instead, one whom they can, "with reasonable confidence, expect to have later, under more auspicious circumstances" (313). An underlying premise of this discussion is that it is more reasonable to love a child "with a future," as Rayber would put it, who can become one's "intellectual equal" and have his or her own children, than to love one who cannot do those things.[22]

Singer points out that the desire to give a child "the best possible start in life" "sells millions of books telling parents how to help their child achieve her or his potential; it causes couples to move out to suburbs where the schools are better, even though they then have to spend time in daily commuting; and it stimulates saving so that later the child will be able to go to a good college" (312). Parental love, then, is regularly understood in instrumental terms not entirely dissimilar to Rayber's.[23] O'Connor's stark representation of Rayber's and Tarwater's insistence on usefulness, their inability to understand the value of Bishop's life, and their denial of his future enables readers to more clearly see the prejudices against disabled lives that undergird discussions such as Singer's. And this in turn sheds light upon Tarwater's comment when the woman at the motel saves Bishop from falling off the dock: "It wouldn't have been no great loss if he had drowned" (168). As Judith Butler writes in *Frames of War*, some populations are "'lose-able' or can be forfeited, precisely because they are framed as being already lost or forfeited" (31): they always already have no future.

Rayber deludes himself into thinking that his devaluation of Bishop is a matter of mercy. When he sees a child preacher and believes she is being exploited, he sympathizes with all the exploited children he has seen: "himself when he was a child, Tarwater exploited by the old man, this child exploited by parents, Bishop exploited by the very fact that he was alive" (131). His account of the time he tried to drown Bishop indicates that he believed he was trying to save Bishop from the injustice that was his own life. "He had taken him to the beach, two hundred miles away, intending to effect the accident as quickly as possible and return bereaved" (141). When he panics at the last moment and calls for help, it is because he suddenly "envision[s] his life without the child" (142). Without Bishop there, his "terrifying" love would not be "contained," but might overflow (141). As he thinks later, "He could control his terrifying love as long as it had its focus in Bishop, but if anything happened to the child, he would have to face it in itself. Then the whole world would become his idiot child" (182). All of this suggests that Rayber sees his son's life as a burden to them both, useful only insofar as it contains his irrational love. Rayber believes this love is a form of madness instilled by Mason. In a more rational world, he thinks, there would be no purpose to a person like Bishop at all: "In a hundred years people may have learned enough to put them to sleep when they're born" (169).

Here again Rayber's views coincide with those of Peter Singer. Singer is notorious for his argument that disabled newborns should be allowed to be killed if the parents do not want them to live and if the family's doctor agrees that their disabilities would negatively affect their quality of life. "When the death of a disabled infant will lead to the birth of another infant with better prospects of a happy life, the total amount of happiness will be greater if the disabled infant is killed" (*Practical Ethics*, 163). It's important to note that Singer would probably not condone Tarwater's killing of Bishop, because Bishop, at the age of about five or six, likely has enough mental capacity to conceive of himself as a living being, to want to live; in spite of his intellectual disability, he is not an un-self-aware newborn; he has interests.[24]

In "Shopping," Singer writes contradictorily that "the moral worth of individuals is not dependent on their abilities, except where they have very limited intellectual capacities" (315). In this way Singer separates intellectual disability from other disabilities, depoliticizing it and removing it from the realm of the social. Assuming that Bishop's intellectual capacities are not *as* limited as Singer intends in this alarming statement, he would have to view Bishop's moral worth as equal to others'—a point to which I will return below. But like Rayber, he believes that killing disabled newborns such as Bishop once was would be a more rational way to go about providing for the greater good. Such beliefs bolster Janet Lyon's claim that intellectual disability has been treated historically as the "site of disposability" ("Modernism, Debility"). Underlying this belief is not just a rejection of the "sanctity of human life" but also a view of newborn human beings as interchangeable, replaceable (until they are self-aware) with "better" versions.[25] Michael Sandel counters this view by stressing that all understandings of "the sacred" (even secular versions that use the word loosely) "insist that we value nature and the living beings within it as more than mere instruments" (94).

Mechanical Man

O'Connor clearly finds Rayber's ideas reprehensible. As Christina Lake writes, O'Connor believed that "to view any individual life primarily instrumentally is to destroy that life as a unique gift" (27). In fact, O'Connor said that she had a hard time depicting Rayber because of his intense secularism: "Rayber, of course, was always the stumbling block. I had a version of this book about a year ago in which Rayber was really no more than a caricature. He may have been better that way but the book as a whole was not. It may just be a matter of giving the devil his due" (*Habit*, 352–353). She further noted that she could not treat Rayber the same way she treated Tarwater because "the Devil who prompts Rayber speaks a language I can't get down, an idiom I just can't reproduce—maybe because it's so dull I can't sustain any interest in it" (*Habit*, 367).

Within the novel, O'Connor indicates her distaste for Rayber's views by using another disability, deafness, as a metaphor for Rayber's godlessness, and by extension, his status as not quite human. On the surface, O'Connor uses Rayber's deafness in a stereotypical way as a symbol for—as John Desmond puts it without noting the ableism of the symbol—the inability to hear the "'good news' from beyond the world" (141). This equation of deafness with spiritual obtuseness is included in the novel. When Rayber follows Tarwater to the chapel and pities the child preacher, she uses him to dramatize her testimony: "His ear is deaf to the Holy Word!" (134).

But O'Connor goes further than this, using Rayber's reliance on his hearing aid as a way of diminishing his humanness. Through her representations of Rayber's hearing aids, she portrays Rayber as a sort of mechanical man with a false sense of control over his world.[26] She introduces this aspect of the characterization when Tarwater arrives at Rayber's house in the middle of the night. Rayber tells him, "Wait here, deaf," and goes to get his hearing aid. "He came back almost at once, plugging something into his ear. He had thrust on the black-rimmed glasses and he was sticking a metal box into the waist-band of his paja-mas. This was joined by a cord to the plug in his ear. For an instant the boy had the thought that his head ran by electricity" (87). Here Tarwa-ter's lack of familiarity with hearing aids gives O'Connor the opportunity to suggest that Rayber's head does, in a sense, run by electricity, that there is something robotic in his refusal of spirituality.

The motif of the electric man continues throughout the novel. Tarwater asks Rayber, "'Do you think in the box,' he asked, 'or do you think in your head?'" (105), and later, "Why don't you pull that plug out of your ear and turn yourself off?" (175). To the truck driver who picks him up after he kills Bishop, Tarwater describes Rayber: "He's got this wired head. There's an electric cord runs into his ear. He can read your mind" (212). The woman at the motel participates in representing Rayber in mechanistic terms: "His eyes had a peculiar look—like something human trapped in a switch box" (154). And the motif of the electric man also runs through the narrator's descriptions of Rayber. One night, as he lies "watching the window darken, he felt that all his nerves were stretched through him like high-tension wire" (117). When Tarwater leaves the house and Rayber follows him to the storefront chapel, he catches his own "bloodless wired reflection in the glass of a shoe shop" (123).

While it is the hearing aid that provides the particular imagery of electricity, deafness itself is associated with a wooden inhumanity in the novel. When Tarwater does not show any interest in Rayber's tour of the city, the narrator comments that "the boy for all the interest he showed might have been the one who was deaf" (108). And after Ray-ber is mocked by the child preacher and Tarwater runs into him, the narrator reports that "Rayber's face had the wooden look it wore when his hearing aid was off" (135). These comments represent deafness as a condition of being cut off from human emotion. In *Enforcing Normalcy*, Lennard Davis quotes several lines from Joseph Conrad that similarly equate deafness with emotional incapacity: "He was made blind and deaf and without pity," for example, and he was "unmoved like a deaf man" (44). Rayber also shares this woodenness with Carson McCull-ers's deaf character, John Singer, who is emotionally detached to what McCullers described as a "psychopathic degree" (qtd. in Evans, 197).[27]

During the scene of the drowning, when Rayber waits in their cabin, imagery that casts Rayber as fundamentally machine-like intensifies. Here the hearing aid also symbolizes Rayber's false sense of control over the world—as he can turn the sounds of the world off and on, he thinks he can turn off his knowledge of the word of God. As he waits for the boys to return from their boating excursion, Rayber turns "the hearing aid on and at once his head buzzed with the steady drone of crickets and treefrogs. . . . He waited expectantly. Then an instant before the cataclysm, he grabbed the metal box of the hearing aid as if he were clawing his heart" (202). The metallic heart reappears when he intuits what has happened:

> What had happened was as plain to him as if he had been in the water with the boy and the two of them together had taken the child and held him under until he ceased to struggle. . . . He knew with an instinct sure as the dull mechanical beat of his heart that he had baptized the child even as he drowned him, that he was headed for everything the old man had prepared him for, that he moved off now through the black forest toward a violent encounter with his fate. (203)

Here Rayber acknowledges his complicity in the murder, and his instinct is described as "sure" precisely because it is a machine powered by the "dull mechanical beat of his heart." He then waits for the "raging pain, the intolerable hurt" to begin, but because he is more machine than human, it does not come. Rayber's deafness serves to convey his mechanistic refusal of emotion and spirituality.

Spirituality and emotion, for their parts, are equated with idiocy. The text is peppered with metaphoric uses of intellectual disability, usually when Rayber's armor seems at risk of being penetrated. For example, the narrator describes Rayber's "irrational" love for Bishop: "If, without thinking, he lent himself to it, he would feel suddenly a morbid surge of love that terrified him—powerful enough to throw him to the ground in an act of idiot praise" (113). And when Rayber yells at Mason for instilling the faith he views as madness in him, he uses language of both infection and mental disability: "You infected me with your idiot hopes, your foolish violence" (73). Rayber several times refers to young Tarwater as "a goddam backwoods imbecile" or a "freak" when he seems compelled to baptize Bishop (147, 170, 173). Combined with Bishop's name and the rock he carries around, these associations of religious feeling with idiocy indicate O'Connor's attempt to affirm that, as I quote above, "God is as present in the idiot boy as in the genius" (*Habit*, 99).

A "Dead Whole Character"

Though emphasizing that Bishop's soul is "precious" to God, the novel does not value his *life* equally to other lives.[28] In fact, O'Connor comes surprisingly close to Peter Singer's views in her implicit separation of the value of Bishop's soul (or as Singer would have it, "moral worth") from the value of his life. Singer distinguishes between one's moral worth and the value of one's life, leaving open the possibility that murdering an intellectually disabled person is not as bad as murdering someone else. In his discussion of an argument by philosopher and legal scholar Ani Satz, he claims that "we should distinguish two different kinds of judgment that are in danger of being conflated . . . : judgments about 'the moral worth of disabled individuals' and judgments about the general quality of life, or even the *value of life*, with a given disability" ("Shopping," 315, emphasis added).

Singer next quotes philosopher Allen Buchanan, who argues that "there is nothing incoherent or disingenuous in our saying that we devalue the disabilities and wish to reduce their incidence and that we value all existing persons with disabilities—and value them equally to those who are not disabled." Singer objects to this last clause. In his own microfiction (thought experiment), he writes,

> Suppose that there are two infants in the neonatal intensive care unit, and we have the resources to save only one of them. We know nothing about either of them, or their families, except that one infant has no disabilities, and the other has one of the disabilities that Buchanan mentions—a disability that will limit the child's "welfare and opportunities." [Note the common move of isolating disability as the only relevant factor in a life.] In these circumstances, it seems rational, for precisely the reasons Buchanan gives, to save the life of the child without disabilities but this shows that there is a clear sense in which we do not value both children equally. ("Shopping," 316)

Singer argues, then, that while someone's "moral worth" may be equal to someone else's, the value of his life may not.[29]

This judgment is shared by other philosophers, notably McMahan, whose book *The Ethics of Killing* distinguishes between persons and nonpersons on the basis of certain capacities, arguing that it is less bad to kill a nonperson than a person. For personhood, one must have "a mental life of a certain order of complexity and sophistication" (*Ethics*, 6). Eva Kittay—who recounts an appalling debate with McMahan and Singer at a conference during which Kittay was asked to justify the value of her daughter's life—notes that McMahan believes that certain capacities "should determine whether an individual is due justice and whether it is as bad to kill that individual as it is to 'kill one of us.'" Kittay's severely intellectually disabled daughter, Sesha, "according to this reasoning, has no grounds to claim justice, and it is less bad to kill her than to kill 'one of us'" ("Personal," 395).[30] This suggestion that someone's life can be less valuable than someone else's, and that therefore to murder that person is less wrong than to murder someone who has greater capacities, *empties the concept of equal moral worth of its practical meaning.*

This highly objectionable view, which on its face O'Connor would surely find repugnant, nevertheless animates her representation of events in *The Violent Bear It Away*. The first piece of evidence for this claim is the murder-baptism itself. When Tarwater drowns Bishop, he "accidentally" baptizes him as well. This conjunction invites readers to be less horrified by or even to accept the murder because it is at the same moment redemption. The novel here dovetails with the claim made by O'Connor's famous killer The Misfit, who justifies his murder of the grandmother in "A Good Man Is Hard to Find" by suggesting that he provided the opportunity for redemption: she "would of been a good woman . . . if it had been somebody there to shoot her every minute of her life" (*Complete*, 133).

Ruth Vande Kieft is one of the critics most troubled by the murder of Bishop (several don't mention it at all, and a few join Tarwater in dismissing its importance), but she nevertheless justifies it: "It is difficult to accept, humanly, the positive spiritual meaning to the innocent child of this grotesquely horrible murder–baptism. . . . Yet the implication is that divine grace may work through or despite a murderous obsession" (352). As Carol Shloss comments, citing Vande Kieft, "For an author to maneuver her subject so that his end can be viewed positively only if the reader can accept self-defeat as victory, death as mercy, sacrament as blasphemy, and murder as inconsequential, is a notable fictional achievement, but also a puzzling one" (98–99). In my view, the cause of this puzzling state of affairs in which the murder can be viewed as "inconsequential" is the ableism of the text and many of its readers. We are trained culturally and by the text itself not to value Bishop as much as we value other people or characters, not to identify with him, not, indeed, to see him as a subject.

The idea that Bishop's murder is the reader's "self-defeat" is echoed in Patricia Yaeger's reading of the murder. She writes:

> The fiercest example [of "an unbearable space of discomfort for the reader"] occurs in *The Violent Bear It Away*, when the narrator asks us to accept the drowning of a Down's syndrome child, dreadful, profane act though it is, as the sacred moment of his baptism. The primal bellow welling up in the text when Bishop's small body goes under I take to be not only the idiot Bishop's cry but also the idiot reader's cry of pain at the wound that suddenly opens between signified and signifier, at the impossibility of collapsing these opposites into narrative coherence. (196)[31]

This description of the murder takes it more seriously than most; and it is one of the very few to express pain arising from reading about Bishop's death. But in her compassion for Bishop, Yaeger overlooks the ways the novel discourages us from identifying with him and the ways it excludes him, except as object, from the moral drama playing out in the novel.

The most basic way the novel discourages readers from identifying with Bishop is by not offering his point of view. We move from young Tarwater's perspective to Rayber's, and hear many of Mason's long stories through Tarwater's vivid memories. But O'Connor does not give us any thoughts or impressions from Bishop's perspective. In withholding his perspective from us, O'Connor "inhibit[s] imaginative access to the stigmatized position" (Nussbaum, *Not for Profit*, 109). Such inhibition of our access to fictional disabled minds is common in modern literature. As Janet Lyon remarks in her discussion of Virginia Woolf's encounter with physically disabled characters in "Street Haunting," "The aesthetic experiment . . . gradually extends modernist subjectivism to its limit point, beyond which Woolf's narrative sentience does not go" ("Asylum Road," 563).[32] This is even more fully the case with intellectually disabled characters such as Albert, the "village idiot" in Woolf's *Between the Acts* and young Guido in Djuna Barnes's *Nightwood*; the tendency to absent disabled minds from modernism explains why Faulkner's representation of Benjamin Compson's consciousness has such disruptive potential.

A second way *The Violent Bear It Away* prevents readers from taking Bishop seriously as a subject is by comparing him, not only through Tarwater's insults, but also through textual imagery, to a nonhuman animal—especially a domesticated dog. For example, when Rayber asks, "Who wants to go for a ride?" "Bishop jumped off the bed and was at his side in an instant" (177). When they are in the car, "Bishop was hanging out the window, his mouth open, letting the air dry his tongue" (179–180). Bishop "gallops" rather than runs (145) and wears his pajama straps up over his neck like a "harness" (91). When Tarwater tells him to get off his bed, the narrator comments, "He might have been commanding a small animal he was successfully training" (189). When Rayber considers the possibility that Tarwater's aim is to control Bishop, he is annoyed that "Bishop would be at his command like a faithful dog" (197).[33]

This motif participates in a long history of using animal comparisons to dehumanize intellectually disabled people. A major source of this comparison was the idea, mentioned above, that disability was atavistic and would eventually be eradicated through evolution or eugenics. Darwin, for example, compared "idiots" to animals in explaining intellectual disability as evolutionarily backward (*Expression*, 244). Baynton contextualizes this type of belief, writing that "in the context of an assumption that the normal tendency of the human race was to improve steadily, to advance ever further from its animal origins . . . abnormality was [understood as] a retarding or atavistic force with the potential to slow or even reverse progress" (*Defectives*, 67). The text's representation of Bishop as dog-like evokes the threat of evolutionary backwardness and tames it at the same time.

The third and most important way the novel ousts Bishop from subjecthood is by depicting him as outside the spiritual drama animating the story as a whole. Throughout the novel, Tarwater grapples with the calling to be a prophet. Even Rayber is placed firmly within this spiritual drama in that he uses his intellect to forcibly suppress his love for humanity, which if he allowed it, would turn "the whole world" into his "idiot child" (182). There is always surrounding Rayber a sense that the "madness" of faith will overtake him the minute he lets down his guard. But Bishop is not part of this drama because he is not understood to have any spiritual capacity. When Mason asserts that God saved Bishop from the intellectualism of his parents by making him "dim-witted," he establishes Bishop's exclusion from the complexities of faith. O'Connor wrote revealingly to a friend, "I am one, of course, who believes that man is created in the image and likeness of God. I believe that all creation is good *but that what has free choice is more completely God's image than what does not have it*" (*Habit*, 104, emphasis added). Since Bishop is represented as lacking free choice, in O'Connor's view his innocence is not a credit to him. From this perspective, Bishop is not as much in God's image as Tarwater is, even though Tarwater commits murder.

Richard Giannone discusses a related irony. He says of Tarwater, Hazel Motes in *Wise Blood*, and The Misfit in "A Good Man Is Hard to Find" that they are "not clean of hands. They are killers. Strikingly, they are also seekers. As seekers, they draw God's compassion. On the immense poverty of their unbelief O'Connor founds the immensity of hope" (105). Being a seeker, for O'Connor, brings a character to life. In *Mystery and Manners* she writes (using more disability imagery) that "the writer can choose what he writes about but he cannot choose what he is able to make live, and so far as he is concerned, a living deformed character is acceptable and a dead whole one is not" (27). In these terms, Tarwater is a "living deformed character." What brings him alive is the dynamic struggle within him between the stranger/devil and God's will. His ravenous hunger, detailed throughout the novel and only satisfied at the end when he has accepted his vocation, dramatizes this living, unfinished quality. Giannone writes, "In the marrow of his adolescent bones [Tarwater] learns that he has been seeking a god limited by his own limitations. But he has at least been seeking. Again, knowing that he is a sinner puts him in the acknowledged need of clemency" (113). This explanation helps contextualize O'Connor's affirmation to Hester that "in his place I would have done everything he did. Tarwater is made up out of my saying: what would I do here? I don't think he's a caricature" (*Habit*, 358).

All of this suggests that while O'Connor believes Bishop's soul matters to God, she does not believe his life matters as much as other lives; being outside the drama of good and evil, he is more akin to a "dead whole" character than to a "living deformed character." In another letter to Hester, she describes Tarwater's likely career after the events of the novel end: "Tarwater's mission might only be to baptize a few more idiots. The prophets in the Bible are only the great ones but there is doubtless unwritten sacred history like uncanonized saints" (*Habit*, 342–343). Here she makes clear that for her, baptizing those who can struggle and decide for themselves whether to accept the word of God is of greater value than baptizing those who are (she believes) incapable of such struggle, even though both tasks must be completed.

The most devastating revelation of the degree to which O'Connor devalues Bishop comes further along in the same letter, where she tells Hester that Tarwater will not go to a reformatory, because "that murder is forgotten by God and of no interest to society" (*Habit*, 343). This stark admission that Bishop's life was expendable strikes at the foundations of O'Connor's assertion that God is present in the "idiot boy." It demonstrates that she not only values Bishop's life less than another life in human terms ("of no interest to society"), but does not fully believe the distinction she drew to assert that from a God's-eye view, Bishop is worth as much as anyone else. Instead of condemning Tarwater for the murder, instead of asking him "What hast thou done? The voice of thy brother's blood crieth to me from the earth" (Genesis 4:10),[34] God in O'Connor's version of events "forgets" the murder even though Tarwater feels no remorse. To use Judith Butler's term, O'Connor does not represent Bishop's life as "grievable" (*Precarious*, 20).

This view is unaccountably echoed by Lorine Getz, who goes so far as to assert that "the murder of Bishop seems of little consequence in moral terms" (108fn.). And it is expanded by Ronald Grimes, who asks, "Even morally, can we be so sure that Tarwater did the wrong thing? Was it murder? Could it have been euthanasia? No court is convened in the story. If there had been a court, it probably would not have cared" (17). Euthanasia can be defined in multiple ways, but in democratic societies it is generally undertaken to halt unbearable and incurable suffering. Bishop is not suffering—he is portrayed as a happy and loving boy. Grimes's question supports Sonya Loftis's incisive claim that "the death of a cognitively disabled person may be read through the lens of euthanasia regardless of circumstance" (476). The only definition of euthanasia that could fit this murder would be a Nazi one, aimed at removing the burden on society to support a "useless eater" or a "life unworthy of life."[35]

Although her worldview is dramatically different from that of Peter Singer or Jeff McMahan, O'Connor's assumptions about intellectual disability bring her into uncomfortable proximity to their more blunt admissions that they do not value people with intellectual disabilities as highly as they value "one of us." Each has certain capacities that he or she believes are necessary for full personhood.[36] For O'Connor, the necessary capacity, the novel demonstrates, is to be able to wrestle with God as Jacob wrestled with the angel. Kittay, on the contrary, sharply questions this sort of requirement. She writes, "My point of contention is with the very idea of a list of attributes as the basis of moral personhood." As she told Singer and McMahan at the conference she describes, she rejects the idea that we can "base moral standing on a list of cognitive capacities, or psychological capacities, or any kind of capacities. Because what it is to be human is not a bundle of capacities" ("Personal," 408).[37] For O'Connor, certainly, to be human is to have an immortal soul. But to be *most fully human*, one needs the capacity of free choice in spiritual matters, which requires a certain level of intellectual ability. Because Bishop is represented as lacking that ability and is therefore excluded by the novel from moral and spiritual subjectivity, we can see that for the novel as a whole, and not just for Tarwater, his drowning is "no great loss."

In fact, the murder-baptism can be understood as a violent form of cure. As I describe in chapter 1, citing Kafer and Clare, the ideology of cure is closely related to ideologies of elimination.[38] By eliminating Bishop, Tarwater has cured the condition in which he was "exploited by the very fact that he was alive," as Rayber put it (131). He has eliminated intellectual disability from the world of the novel. And he has also cured the other condition that the novel suggests has afflicted Bishop: the condition of living outside the realm of spiritual struggle. By baptizing him, Tarwater has made for Bishop a decision he believes Bishop could not make for himself. Tarwater simultaneously brings Bishop into a spiritual community and eradicates him from the world. The novel's dangerously ableist suggestion that something has been righted by the murder may explain the absence of outrage or grief over Bishop's loss in most discussions of the novel, even those that express such feelings about other events, especially the rape of Tarwater.[39]

The indifference of author, characters, and most critics to the murder of an intellectually disabled boy demonstrates a common prejudice across this wide spectrum of religious and secular thinkers: the belief that disabled human lives are worth less than nondisabled human lives. If, as Nussbaum argues, it is "as readers of novels that we should approach the social choices before us" ("Literary Imagination," 907), then we need to read this novel against its grain and (like Yaeger but unlike Getz and Grimes) allow ourselves to feel the pain of Bishop's murder even as his father waits in vain for it to come. And we need to realize that his absence from the fictional world O'Connor has created is not only a great loss, but a threat to a diverse and (to use Garland-Thomson's phrase) habitable world. Resistant readings of *The Violent Bear It Away* help us "evaluate and oppose the conditions under which certain human lives . . . are more grievable than others" (Butler, *Precarious*, 30).

Reading against the Grain

While O'Connor has fixed the fight in favor of the murderer, the rich texture of her novel not only makes visible some of the ways the fight is fixed, but also provides material for resistant, or crip, readings. Because of her novelistic skill, she can hardly help but give life to her characters, including Bishop. This liveliness means that his subjectivity, though elided by the text, lurks in its details. For example, the first time Tarwater meets Bishop, he lashes out at him, smacking his hand away and screaming "Git!"

> [Bishop] clambered up his father's leg, pulling himself up by the school-teacher's pajama coat until he was almost on his shoulder.
> "All right, all right," the school teacher said, "there there, shut up, it's all right, he didn't mean to hit you," and he righted the child on his back and tried to slide him off but the little boy hung on, thrusting his head against his father's neck and never taking his eyes off Tarwater. (93)

Tarwater certainly did mean to hit Bishop; Rayber's comfort is perfunctory at best; and the chapter ends by highlighting Tarwater's determination to have nothing to do with Bishop (that is, not to accept his calling by baptizing him). But the description of Bishop clamoring up his father's body, burying his face in his father's neck, and staring at

Tarwater, is so vivid, so perfectly true to young children's behavior, that readers who are not already inclined to dismiss his humanity may have their attention drawn not to the drama playing out between Tarwater and the spirit of old Mason Tarwater ("his silent adversary")—the drama foregrounded by the text—but to the scared child instead.

Although Bishop is animalized, he is also portrayed as similar to other young children, excited about a fountain, adoring his older cousin (after that initial encounter), affectionate toward his father. Even in the midst of descriptions that compare Bishop to an animal, for example, resisting readers can find glimmers of sympathy for him. When he sees a fountain, he is described only as "the dim-witted boy," his run is called a "gallop," and his shout is described as a "whoop." And yet even in the objectifying description of him "flapping his arms like something released from a cage" (164), we see his human exuberance and understand his father's dry protectiveness as entrapment. When Bishop stands "grinning in the pool, lifting his feet slowly up and down as if he liked the feel of the wet seeping into his shoes," the "as if" indicates that Tarwater, who is focalizing this description, doesn't actually ascribe emotion to Bishop. Nevertheless, readers may ignore the "as if" and revel in the image of a young boy, wet and refreshed on a hot day, enjoying his squishy shoes.[40]

In both versions of the fountain scene (one from the point of view of the narrator and one from Tarwater's point of view as he remembers the outing shortly thereafter), Rayber grabs Bishop out of the fountain to prevent Tarwater from baptizing him. Bishop naturally cries at having his romp so abruptly halted. In the first version of the scene, Bishop first howls and then "stopped howling and was crying quietly, his face red and hideously distorted. Rayber turned his eyes away" (147). In the second, the child "split[s] the silence with his bellow" and then lies on the ground "roaring from a red distorted face" (165). In spite of the fact that Bishop is crying, both of these descriptions seem to work against readers' sympathy for him by emphasizing the unappealing redness and distortion of his face. But resisting readers can find in ourselves sympathy for the young boy whose joy has just been sharply curtailed for no reason he can discern.

Another complexity in the novel's politics is O'Connor's unsympathetic portrait of Rayber. When he turns his eyes away from his crying child because he finds his face "red and hideously distorted," readers are meant to disapprove of his shallow callousness. O'Connor, that is, uses Rayber's treatment of Bishop to help demonstrate his lack of spiritual depth. The text does not invite readers to treat Bishop much better: he is a symbol of faith, a "dead whole" character. Still, his father's lack of sympathy for him when he cries may induce some readers to try to make up for Rayber's callousness, as it were, by lavishing our readerly sympathies upon Bishop.

Moreover, readers tuned into disability as a political category may well view the fountain scene as an example of the ways disabled people are used as tug-of-war ropes between others whose agendas have nothing to do with them. Rayber is annoyed that his child has gotten wet, but yanks him out of the fountain only when he observes Tarwater approaching Bishop as if "blindly" and realizes he is about to baptize him. At first he does not know why Tarwater is moving toward Bishop, and feels "that something was being enacted before him and that if he could understand it, he would have the key to the boy's future." "The boy" here is Tarwater, the only boy understood to *have* a future. Rayber's concern is what Tarwater's approach means *for Tarwater*.

When he "snatche[s] the child out of the water," he feels "that he had just saved the boy from committing some enormous indignity" (the indignity of trying to baptize anyone, but perhaps especially "an idiot") (146). He pulls Bishop out of the water not to protect Bishop, then, but to protect Tarwater. Bishop's body is the object with which Rayber and Tarwater are enacting their spiritual struggle. In his remembered version, Tarwater is temporarily released from his compulsion to carry out the baptism and silently tells Rayber, "I wasn't going to baptize him . . . I'd drown him first" (165). Readers who keep Bishop's personhood in mind, and who therefore observe the ways he is being objectified in this scene, are likely to feel a sense of outrage on his behalf rather than either relief or chagrin about the fact that he was not baptized. Such grist for the mill of resistant readings is what makes fiction so fruitful for bioethical analysis.

By revealing the commonality between O'Connor and Singer—otherwise diametrically opposed thinkers living in periods of quite different technological proficiency—this chapter exposes the pervasive and enduring devaluation of intellectually disabled people, which must be confronted and overcome as we develop the capabilities to take more and more matters of life and death into our own hands. *The Violent Bear It Away* is instructive both in its critique of rationalistic views of human beings such as Rayber's, and in its collusion, in spite of itself, with those views.

4

Cloned Lives

Ishiguro's *Never Let Me Go*

Kazuo Ishiguro's sixth novel, *Never Let Me Go* (2005), is set in an alternative recent past: in 1990s Britain, the government runs a program to raise cloned human beings who will become organ donors in their young adulthood. The government raises the clones mostly in "vast government homes," but a few philanthropists have developed boarding school-like facilities to raise the clones in good conditions, educate them, and encourage them to engage in sports and creative expression. The novel takes place largely at one such home, Hailsham, a place initially very little distinguishable from an ordinary boarding school. Its narrator, Kathy H., describes her time growing up at Hailsham with her friends Tommy and Ruth and the post-school stages of living in "the Cottages" while awaiting training, becoming a "carer" for other clones who are undergoing organ harvesting, and finally, anticipating her own transformation from carer to "donor." Because the clones are being raised as biological material to benefit others at the cost of their own lives, the scenario offers a strong parallel with animal farming.

As is the case for the novels discussed in previous chapters, Ishiguro's novel invites readers to read bioethically, to rethink our assumptions about humanness. From Wells's *Moreau* to Ishiguro's *Never Let Me Go* roughly a hundred years later, we can trace a scientific and cultural arc in explorations of how humanness can be manipulated, an arc running from surgical to genetic interventions. Ishiguro remarks in a *Guardian* column that using clones is a way to return to fundamental questions such as "What does it mean to be human?"—it's a "futuristic way of going ancient" ("Future Imperfect"). As Gabriele Griffin suggests, the novel participates in a tradition of "critical science fiction," "comment[ing] critically on the history of the present" (653). It asks us to consider carefully what is "humanly responsible behaviour towards those *or that* which we deem or designate potentially non-human" (Griffin, 656). Ishiguro had had his student characters in mind for many years, knowing that "some strange fate hung over [them]" before a radio program about advances in biotechnology prompted him to draw the contours of that fate (Ishiguro, "Future Imperfect"). While the narrative may not be particularly plausible—we will certainly grow organs in nonhuman animals or far preferably in labs rather than growing entire human beings from whom to harvest organs[1]—it offers important insights into the ways certain beings can be excluded from moral consideration, while showing how unstable and in constant need of shoring up that exclusion can be.[2]

Ishiguro's clones are genetically, intellectually, and emotionally human beings.[3] As Martha Nussbaum writes, "The sheer fact of cloning does not seem to pose any threat to human dignity as I conceive it, since the basis of dignity is the person's strivings, or basic capabilities, and clones have these as much as the clonees" ("Human Dignity and Political Entitlements," 375). The donation program is therefore indisputably unethical. But the government homes where the cloned human beings live in "deplorable conditions" (261) suggest factory farms, while Hailsham and its like evoke humane, organic farms. These parallels raise issues of animal ethics. The novel itself establishes a clear association between the cloned characters and nonhuman animals in its descriptions of the animals Tommy draws in his notebooks. Although Tommy's animals sometimes look "copied" and have parts that look mechanical, representing the engineered aspect of the human clones, they are vulnerable, and Tommy cares about their imaginary lives.[4] Through this parallel, along with others discussed below, *Never Let Me Go* raises questions about what it means to provide humane treatment to beings who are only valued instrumentally, and more broadly, about the ethics of humane farming.

Is it enough to have, as influential food writer Michael Pollan believes, a good life and a respectful death (328, 332, passim) even if that life is dramatically shortened?[5] Confronting the horror of a system in which human beings are raised to have good lives and respectful but early deaths to benefit others may spur readers to consider why we think such a system for nonhuman animals is acceptable (assuming we agree that *factory* farming is shamefully unjust). In exploring how the fictional society handles its knowledge of the donation program, the novel provokes further questions about our society's ability to suppress our knowledge of the suffering of the animals we eat, animals we acknowledge to be complex emotional beings. Most generally, it prompts questions about how societies make certain beings "killable" (Haraway, 78)—that is, how it becomes possible to kill without committing murder.

Giorgio Agamben has discussed ways in which people can be made killable by being reduced to *zoë*, or "bare life."[6] This category is opposed to *bios*, which refers to "the form or way of living proper to an individual or a group"—that is, life in a social context (*Homo*, 1). In his exploration of the ancient Roman category of the *homo sacer*, Agamben aligns this class of criminal, who is cast out from the community and who can be killed by anyone but not ritually sacrificed, with life that is bare of social meaning, seen as mere biological material. He compares this figure to the victims of Nazi concentration camps, arguing that the Nazis made their victims killable by first reducing them to bare life. It is initially tempting to think that the clones of *Never Let Me Go* are reduced to *zoë*. Shameem Black takes this approach, arguing that the clones are akin to Agamben's conception of *homo sacer* and that the space of Hailsham evokes "Nazi-era incarceration" (789).[7] Arne De Boever takes up Black's use of Agamben and more directly compares Hailsham to a concentration camp. But what is so interesting about Hailsham is the way in which it does *not* reduce the clones to bare life but rather encourages them to enrich their lives by reading and studying, forming close relationships, developing their physical strength, and engaging in artistic pursuits. It is far from a "state of exception," where anything can be done to the students; it is a place of ordinariness, a typical English boarding school in most ways. It is all the more surprising, then, that the students are nevertheless killable within Ishiguro's fictional world. It is because of this puzzling state of affairs that the novel is so illuminating about our relationship to nonhuman animals.

After all, if the clones are valuable enough to deserve good lives, as the Hailsham movement proposes, how is it that their lives are permitted to be drastically shortened for the good of others? To put the question another way, what grounds their right to *good* lives that somehow does not ground their right to *stay alive*? Tommy questions the value of good treatment for a being who will soon be killed when he argues with Kathy about the difference a carer can make in a donor's life: "Okay, it's really nice to have a good carer. But in the end, is it really so important? The donors will all donate, just the same, and then they'll complete"—that is, die. In her reply, Kathy defends the system in which she is participating as a carer, arguing quite rightly that "a good carer makes a big difference to what a donor's life's actually like" (282). But Tommy's question lingers, hinting at an incoherent belief system in which a being is held to deserve a good life up until the point at which her death can benefit others; she is not held to deserve a life *span* or the right to determine her life's course.

In what follows I first discuss general issues of animal ethics raised by the novel; next I consider the ways both the clones and nonhuman animals are made killable by mechanisms that suppress people's care for them, and explore the ways clone welfare and animal welfare are understood. Then I turn to Agamben's discussion of *homo sacer*: I argue that instead of being reduced to *zoë*, the Hailsham clones are more closely associated with *bios*. And yet once one's *bios* is recognized, one has a social role and is no longer killable. This discussion highlights the cognitive dissonance inherent in the fictional scenario—a dissonance ultimately fatal to the Hailsham experiment—and illuminates the ethical and logical contradictions of the humane meat movement.

Animalized Human Clones

The first thing to note about the killability of the clones is that it is bolstered by a thoroughgoing speciesism that allows the "normals" to think about the clones as a sort of animal in spite of their genetic identity as members of the species *Homo sapiens*. When the noncloned humans are forced to think about the clones, they justify their status by believing that they do not have souls.[8] When the protagonist Kathy and her by-then-lover, Tommy, meet with their former Guardians late in the novel, the Guardians reveal that the reason they used to take away the children's artwork was to try to prove to the outside society that the clones had souls: "We took away your art because we thought it would reveal your souls. Or to put it more finely, we did it to *prove that you had souls at all*" (260). Despite their efforts, the idea that the clones have souls is "still not a notion universally held" (260). Martha Nussbaum comments that "humans frequently deny compassion to the suffering of animals on account of this irrational splitting of the world of nature" into animal bodies and human souls (*Political*, 159). The belief that only human beings have immortal souls—the religious version of human exceptionalism—is of course the most common distinction used in Judeo-Christian cultures to justify the exploitation of animals.[9]

Even while ostensibly setting out to demonstrate the existence of their souls, the Guardians, like the rest of their society, think of the children as non- or subhuman. Madame, one of the school's founders, twice calls Kathy and Tommy "poor creatures" when they visit her and Miss Emily at the end of the novel (254, 272). When, as children, Kathy and her friends test Madame's feelings toward them by sauntering close to her in a group,

> she just froze and waited for us to pass by. . . . I can still see it now, the shudder she seemed to be suppressing, the real dread that one of us would accidentally brush against her. Ruth had been right: Madame *was* afraid of us. But she was afraid of us in the same way someone might be afraid of spiders. We hadn't been ready for that. It had never occurred to us to wonder how *we* would feel, being seen like that, being the spiders. (35)

Even Miss Emily, the school's headmistress (and as is suggested at the end of the novel, Madame's lesbian partner), admits that "we're *all* afraid of you. I myself had to fight back my dread of you all almost every day I was at Hailsham. There were times I'd look down at you all from my study window and I'd feel such revulsion" (269).[10] This revulsion seems to be a form of proteophobia, sparked by the clones' liminal status as neither quite human nor quite animal.[11] This fear is a realistic touch within the speculative novel; as Susan Squier points out, "as the impact of biotechnology grows, the variety of liminal figures to which we need to develop a response grows even greater" (5).

Because of the society's deep speciesism (another realistic feature of the scenario), the demotion of the clones to non- or semihuman status is an apparently sufficient precursor to making them killable. Miss Emily tells Kathy and Tommy, "For a long time you were kept in the shadows, and people did their best not to think about you. And if they did, they tried to convince themselves you weren't really like us. That you were less than human, so it didn't matter" (263). Such a refusal to recognize others' full humanness is of course at the heart of slavery, genocidal programs, and instances of racist medical abuse such as the Tuskegee syphilis experiments. In the case of Ishiguro's clones, it puts them in the position of nonhuman animals whose own rights and needs are eclipsed by the use-value they have for normative human beings. As Rebecca Walkowitz points out, *Never Let Me Go* critiques "the idea that it is ethical or acceptable to sacrifice non-human animals to the needs and desires of human life. At many points in the text, we are asked to notice that an unquestioned hierarchy, in which humans are distinguished from animals, makes the donation system possible" (224).[12]

Like nonhuman animals, the clones are objectified as bodies that matter only as a means to someone else's end. Each clone is essentially divided in two: a body that matters, and a subjectivity that does not. They are reduced to body in the sense described by Rae Langton in her discussion of feminist philosophy. Langton quotes Catharine MacKinnon, who writes that "To be sexually objectified means having a social meaning imposed on your being that defines you as to be sexually used . . . and then using you that way" (Langton, 243). In a parallel way, to be medically objectified, as the clones are, is having a social meaning imposed on your being that defines you as *to be medically used*, and then using you that way.

In the case of animals, their objectification—their purpose—consists in their to-be-eaten or to-be-experimented-upon state; that is, we override their subjectivity and make over their lives' purposes to meet our own desires. Brian Luke reports that a veterinarian giving him a tour of a vivisection facility "pointed to a group of beagle puppies in a cage and said, 'Beautiful, aren't they? At least this way they have a purpose'" (144). Like animals being used for meat or research, the clones exist to serve a function, their own interests and desires, their very lives, superseded by the interests and desires of others. The Guardian Miss Lucy, later fired for giving the students too much information, ominously tells the students, "You were brought into this world for a purpose, and your futures, all of them, have been decided" (81).

Carol Adams describes the animal subjects who are erased by their use as meat as "absent referents." Crediting Margaret Homans for the term, Adams writes that "behind every meal of meat is an absence: the death of the animal whose place the meat takes. The 'absent referent' is that which separates the meat eater from the animal and the animal from the end product. The function of the absent referent is to keep our 'meat' separated from the idea that she or he was once an animal . . . to keep *something* from being seen as having been someone" (xxiv). The clones too become absent referents as their subjectivities are obliterated by their medical function and they are reduced to organ sources. Adams explains that one of the ways animals are turned into absent referents is by the language we use to talk about them: we don't say we are eating a calf, but that we are eating veal; we don't say that we are eating a pig, but that we are eating pork. Jonathan Safran Foer similarly remarks that language about farmed animals can "misdirect and camouflage. . . . Some words, like *veal*, help us forget what we are actually talking about. Some, like *free-range*, can mislead those whose consciences seek clarification. Some, like *happy*, mean the opposite of what they would seem. And some, like *natural*, mean next to nothing" (45).

The donation program similarly uses euphemisms and outright lies to describe its processes. The word "donor" is willfully inaccurate since it implies a free choice, whereas the clones have no such choice. As Nathan Snaza notes, "These 'donors' have their organs taken from them. Calling such a taking a 'donation' is a cruel misnomer" (224). The clones "give donations" and then "complete." In the mythology of the donation program, the clones' deaths are reframed as the completion of their purpose: they do not die, they complete. The word "die" is used only once in the novel to refer to the end of the clones' lives: Kathy comes out with it in her distress at learning there can be no reprieve for her and Tommy. Further, the organs being harvested are never named; instead the donations are labeled by the number of operations the donor has experienced: first donation, second donation. This terminology obscures the harrowing fact that particular parts of their bodies are being extracted. Even the word "clone" is only used in the novel twice, once in the phrase "clone model" and once when Miss Emily gives their history, saying that "all clones—or students, as we preferred to call you—existed only to supply medical science" (261). The clones are instead labeled by their social functions: students, then carers, then donors, much as cattle are described as dairy cattle or beef cattle, or chickens labeled as laying hens or broilers.

Like the clones lucky enough to be raised at Hailsham, animals on organic farms have more freedom and autonomy than on factory farms, but they are still ultimately means to someone else's end. Many writers on animal rights have pointed out the abuses to which animals are subject even on most humane farms: castration, branding, tail-docking, debeaking, and other physical alterations usually without anesthesia;[13] artificial insemination;[14] being prevented from rearing young.[15] And of course even the best-treated animals on humane organic farms are allowed to live out only a fraction of their natural lives. Ishiguro's novel reimagines such an organic farm for humans, offering several parallels to the lives of humanely reared animals.

First, the students have "some form of medical almost every week" (13). The doctors', nurses', and Guardians' concern for the health of the clones is insidious because it gives the impression that they care about the students' health for their own sake; but in reality they care only about keeping their bodies vigorous so that they can donate healthy organs to others. As Eva Kittay writes in her discussion of relations of care, "When we care for someone for the individual's own sake we do so because we presume that the individual has a sake for which to care" ("At the Margins," 109). Kittay is talking about whether someone needs to be able to be conscious of her egoistic concern or be able to articulate it in order to be said to *have* egoistic concern. Her point about attributing a "sake" to someone is relevant here: the Guardians and medical professionals do not presume the cloned human beings have a "sake for which to care," in spite of the fact that the clones *are* conscious of their egoistic concerns. This is one of the ways the clones, who are "severely able-bodied"—as Rosemarie Garland-Thomson describes them using Paul Longmore's famous phrase ("Eugenic World Building," 135)—are nevertheless, like disabled people in our ableist society, pushed to the margins of personhood.

The Guardians stress that the students must keep their bodies healthy, telling them for example that they mustn't smoke, and that the importance of this near-taboo (Kathy even turns the picture on her favorite cassette tape inside out because it shows a woman smoking) is far greater for them than for the "normals." As Miss Lucy says, "For you, all of you, it's much, much worse to smoke than it ever was for me" (68). When the Guardians start teaching the students about sex, they similarly "tended to run [the lectures] together with talk about the donations." After all, as Kathy acknowledges, if the Guardians were "telling us how we'd have to be very careful to avoid diseases when we had sex, it would have been odd not to mention how much more important this was for us than for normal people outside" (83). And when Tommy injures his elbow and other students tease him that the wound might "unzip," Tommy asks Kathy for help, because "we should never take chances with our health" (86). This emphasis on the students' physical health for the sake of others offers a parallel to the concern of farmers with the health of their stock for the sake of profits. As an ad reproduced in Sunaura Taylor's *Beasts of Burden* reminds farmers, "ONE Bruise is ONE Too Many . . . IT COSTS YOU MONEY! So . . . It's Good Business to Remember . . . When Handling Livestock. . . . 'Easy Does It'" (35).

In a rough correspondence to the removal of farm animals' young, and thereby the thwarting of their strong desires to suckle and rear them, the clones are engineered to be sterile.[16] This fact causes Kathy significant emotional pain, as we can see in her interpretation of the fictional song "Never Let Me Go" from which the novel takes its title. When Kathy hears the song's chorus, "Baby, baby, never let me go," she imagines "a woman who'd been told she couldn't have babies, who'd really really wanted them all her life. Then there's a sort of miracle and she has a baby, and she holds this baby very close to her and walks around singing: 'Baby, never let me go . . .' partly because she's so happy, but also because she's so afraid something will happen, that the baby will get ill or be taken away from her" (70). This song is emphasized not only by its use for the novel's title but also by the text's focus on Kathy's loss of her tape and the search for a replacement tape in Norfolk with Tommy. Indeed, when Kathy first loses the tape, her "main thought was that I mustn't give away how panicked I was" (74). Like many of Ishiguro's other characters who cannot face their deepest desires or fears—such as Stevens in *The Remains of the Day*, Christopher Banks in *When We Were Orphans*, and Axl in *The Buried Giant*—Kathy cannot let her friends or even herself know how much she cares that she will never be able to have a baby.

The physical alterations most farm animals undergo, as well as the fear and pain they experience in being transported to slaughter and in being slaughtered (even in "humane slaughterhouses") are suggested by the multiple surgeries of the donation process. The clones do receive anesthesia for their surgeries. But they still endure a significant amount of pain, weakness, immobilization, and confinement in their recoveries from each surgery and preceding their deaths.[17] We get a sense of fragility when Tommy is recovering from his third donation, and the first time he and Kathy have sex, they are cautious because they have "stiches to worry about" (238). When Ruth is dying after her second donation, Kathy recognizes the look on her face, "which I'd seen on donors often enough before. It was like she was willing her eyes to see right inside herself, so she could patrol and marshal all the better the separate areas of pain in her body" (236). The fact of anesthesia, even accompanied by analgesics afterward, does not entirely remove the pain, weakness, and fear that result from major surgery. Even on organic farms (for human beings or animals), being used as physical material for others' needs entails significant pain and suffering.

Moreover, like farm animals, the clones often die prematurely even by the standards of the donation program. About factory-farmed hens, Pollan writes: "The ten percent or so of hens that can't endure it and simply die is built into the cost of production" (318). The novel's donation program is meant to proceed over the course of four operations, but many times people die after the first or second operation. When Kathy, Tommy, and Ruth are discussing the death ("completion") of their former housemate, Chrissie, after her second donation, Ruth asserts that "it happens much more than they ever tell us" (225). When Kathy objects that it doesn't happen that often, Ruth repeats her claim: "'I bet it happens much more than they tell us,' Ruth said again. 'That's one reason why they keep moving us around between donations'" (226). Her own death after her second donation later confirms her suspicion.

And of course even when the cloned people do live until their fourth donations, their life spans, like those of farm animals, are dramatically truncated. As Jeff McMahan notes, "Although humane rearing, when practiced scrupulously, does not cause animals to suffer, it does involve killing them quite early in their lives. Beef cattle have a natural life span of about thirty to thirty-five years, but they are normally killed at about three years of age. Pigs can live about fifteen years, but they tend to be killed at about six months, while chickens can live about eight years but are killed less than a year after birth" ("Comparative Badness," 65). In *Never Let Me Go*, Miss Lucy explains to the children: "You'll become adults, then before you're old, before you're even middle-aged, you'll start to donate your vital organs" (81). Kathy is thirty-one in the present of the narrative and will begin her donations at the end of the year; she has outlived her friends because she has remained a carer (for unknown reasons—perhaps there has not been a demand for organs with her blood or tissue type) for an unusually long time: eleven years. This means that many clones begin their donations in their early twenties, and Kathy, the oldest cloned person we hear about, will live to be about thirty-two or thirty-three.

The injustice of this limited lifespan is clear to readers, but the people in the fictional society find it acceptable. In his contribution to *The Feminist Care Tradition in Animal Ethics*, Luke argues that it's not that most people do not care about animals, but that we spend enormous energy deflecting that care so that we can eat them. Many of our rituals help assuage this guilt. Luke proposes shifting the question

> from [Tom] Regan's and [Peter] Singer's "How can we get people to oppose animal exploitation, given that they don't care?" to "How does animal exploitation continue, given that people do care?" The answer I would give to this latter question is that animal exploitation continues with great difficulty. Enormous amounts of social energy are expended to forestall, undermine, and override our sympathies for animals, so that vivisection, animal farming, and hunting can continue. (136)

If this were not the case, Luke suggests, then "there would be no need for mechanisms that make killing somewhat more bearable—the exploitation of animals would be as straightforward as, say, drinking water or breathing air" (136). Even Pollan, who advocates eating humanely raised and slaughtered animals, notes that our "rituals governing slaughter" and habits such as "saying grace before the meal" are designed to resolve "whatever spiritual or moral dilemmas the killing and eating of animals posed" (305).

Suppressing Care

Assuming they do or could potentially care, what mechanisms allow the "normals" in the society of *Never Let Me Go* to submerge or suppress their care for the cloned human beings? The simplest mechanism, as quoted above, is that people in the society try not to think about them at all. The program is well designed to encourage this: the homes where the clones are raised and the Cottages where they await their training as carers are situated in remote locations, and only a few delivery or maintenance men ever interact with them. As Miss Emily tells Kathy and Tommy, "The world didn't want to be reminded how the donation programme really worked. They didn't want to think about you students, or about the conditions you were brought up in. In other words, my dears, they wanted you back in the shadows" (264–265). This willed ignorance, or "act of national forgetting" (Teo, 127), is similar to how most people handle their relationship to meat.[18] Modern slaughterhouses, like Hailsham and the Cottages, are located away from cities and population centers.[19] As Pollan writes, "Most of us would simply rather not be reminded of exactly what meat is or what it takes to bring it to our plates" (305). The physical distance in both relationships enables this ignorance. Pollan continues: "We tolerate this schizophrenia [of giving Christmas presents to dogs but eating ham for Christmas dinner] because the life of the pig has moved out of view; when's the last time you saw a pig in person?" (306).[20] About the factory farm, Pollan asserts, "Industrial animal agriculture depends on a suspension of disbelief on the part of the people who operate it and a willingness to avert one's eyes on the part of everyone else" (317). This also applies to organic farming: without looking into the particular conditions of rearing, transportation, and slaughter, people assume that animals on organic farms do not suffer.

We can think about the nonrecognition of the clones' humanity—the refusal to register them as subjects—through the terms offered by Judith Butler in *Frames of War*. Butler uses the metaphor of the frame to discuss the ways we recognize only some living beings as having *lives*. The frames organize our perceptions of groups of living beings, seeking to "contain, convey, and determine what is seen" (*Frames,* 10). They serve as norms that "operate to produce certain subjects as 'recognizable' persons and to make others decidedly more difficult to recognize" (*Frames,* 6). The fictional society's frames discourage citizens from seeing clones as beings whose lives matter; they understand that they are living, but do not count their lives *as* lives.

Another mechanism that operates for the people "outside" in *Never Let Me Go* is the idea that the cloned people are satisfied to devote their lives—and deaths—to the welfare of others. The Guardians continually tell the students they are "special" and that they have a purpose. As Tiffany Tsao argues, their purpose is exactly what closes down their autonomy: "Ishiguro's novel asserts . . . that the purpose-driven life is terrifyingly reductive and devoid of freedom" (223). But because the Guardians are successful in indoctrinating the cloned people to feel as though their predetermined path in life is fitting, there is no rebellion (beyond Tommy's rages, only at the end of the novel consciously directed at their fate); and this absence of rebellion is taken for consent.[21]

Many advocates of "humane meat" similarly assume a form of consent by farm animals, positing a kind of social contract between them and us. Taylor describes this point of view: "These theorists [Pollan, Hugh Fearnley-Whittingstall, and others] say that if we look at matters in evolutionary terms, domesticated animals are doing remarkably well." But Taylor persuasively rebuts this argument. She points out that it is factory farming, condemned by both Pollan and Fearnley-Whittingstall as a *breach* of the "co-evolutionary contract," that has created the high numbers of animals they are calling a boon to domesticated species, and "these animals live in the most oppressive of environments from the day of their birth until the day of their slaughter." Taylor therefore calls claims that our farming systems are a "boon" to domesticated animals a "ludicrous misuse of the concept of evolutionary success" (*Beasts*, 168–169).[22]

The issue of consent comes up in terms of individual animals as well. Luke cites a National Public Radio reporter who toured a slaughterhouse and could "see in the terrified animals' eyes that they would willingly go to slaughter if they understood the human purpose being served" (Luke, 145). Pollan tells a story about a man who came to farmer Joel Salatin because he believed that he ought to kill his own chicken if he wanted to eat it. Pollan describes the scene: "'He slit the bird's throat and watched it die,' Joel recalled. 'He saw that the animal did not look at him accusingly. . . . He saw that the animal had been treated with respect while it was alive and that it could have a respectful death—that it wasn't being treated like a pile of protoplasm'" (332).[23] The absence of an accusing look returns us to the scene of Ruth's death in the novel, where her vision turns inward to "marshal" the different areas of pain. A being *in extremis* may very well lack the resources to accuse his or her murderer, but this does not mean he or she has consented to be killed. The idea that it is permissible to kill a being who has had a decent, if short, life and who is being killed in a "respectful" way redounds upon the scenario of *Never Let Me Go*: this is exactly the situation of the clones, and it is manifestly immoral. Below I will return to the question of the difference between such deaths for nonhuman animals and for human ones.

A third way that the society manages to accept the donation program is by viewing it as pure science, as apolitical. The program began quietly as scientific breakthroughs abounded.

> After the war, in the early fifties, when the great breakthroughs in science followed one after the other so rapidly, there wasn't time to take stock, to ask the sensible questions. Suddenly there were all these new possibilities laid before us, all these ways to cure so many previously incurable conditions. This was what the world noticed the most, wanted the most. And for a long time, people preferred to believe these organs appeared from nowhere, or at most that they grew in a kind of vacuum. (262–263)

The strength of the "curative imaginary" (Kafer, 27) means that when a medical breakthrough arrives, most of society immediately accepts it. Ethical inquiry comes late, if at all. By cordoning off science as apolitical, as outside the scope of ethics, the fictional society found itself faced with a program that was clearly within the scope of ethics and politics, but without a way to intervene. In the case of animals, "improvements" in technology and medical interventions have gradually increased the suffering of farmed animals in ways that seemed commonsensical—more efficient—within the capitalist mindset until we reached the state of intensive factory farming we now have. As historian Yuval Harari writes in the *Guardian*, "Once modern science had deciphered the secrets of birds, viruses and antibiotics, humans could begin to subject animals to extreme living conditions. With the help of vaccinations, medications, hormones, pesticides, central air-conditioning systems and automatic feeders, it is now possible to cram tens of thousands of chickens into tiny coops, and produce meat and eggs with unprecedented efficiency" (n.p.).[24]

Further, the donation program has enormous benefits, creating a strong motivation to accept it and requiring great moral courage to resist it. Miss Emily tells Kathy and Tommy that by the time people thought to ask questions, there was no way to reverse the process. How can you ask a world that has come to regard cancer as curable, how can you ask such a world to put away that cure, to go back to the dark days? There was no going back. However uncomfortable people were about your existence, their overwhelming concern was that their own children, their spouses, their parents, their friends, did not die from cancer, motor neurone disease, heart disease. (263)

These benefits are dramatically more significant than those we derive from eating meat, and yet many people find the scenario of *Never Let Me Go* implausible because it is so obviously unethical. But the novel asks us to consider what we might allow to happen to someone else if it would extend the lives of those we love. As Earl Ingersoll writes, "Horrible as the option of accepting the transplant of a Kathy H. might seem at first, few would long resist the cynical impulse to say, 'Well, she's just a clone, that's what she was made for, and she really wants to help me save my child'" (54). In our society, even without benefits of this order, the social structures and norms that bolster the meat industries are so strong that many people conclude that there is "no way to reverse the process."

And finally, the program has a governmental imprimatur, something that contributes to the people's willingness to accept that it is morally permissible. One of the best and creepiest elements of Mark Romanek's film version of the novel is a van driving around with a National Donor Programme logo on its side—just another part of the government infrastructure. In a similar way, we tend to assume (incorrectly) that there is sufficient government oversight of animal farming and slaughter and that someone else—our political leaders—will make sure nothing unethical is happening.[25]

Clone Welfare

The role of Hailsham in this scenario is complex.[26] It exists to improve the welfare of cloned human beings, much as a humane farm exists to improve the welfare of animals until they become meat. Of course, as Kelly Rich describes it, Hailsham's care for the students is "merely palliative, delivered in advance of the wounds administered by the state" (635). At the same time, the institution works to convince the people inside that it is right and natural for them to be sacrificed and to convince the people outside that the clones are free and well treated. In the preface to the tenth anniversary edition of *The Sexual Politics of Meat*, Carol Adams writes, "We believe both that we are being kind to the animals and that they like how we are treating them. . . . To paraphrase Rousseau, everywhere animals are in chains, but we image them as free" (xxix). Hailsham images the clones as free to the extent that the clones themselves almost believe it: they choose the time to start their training as carers (190, 197, 202); Ruth says that it felt right to stop being a carer and become a donor, which is "the kind of thing you hear donors say to each other all the time" (227); Kathy thinks there is something "ridiculous, reprehensible even, about the way we were now thinking and planning" to try to get a deferral for her first and Tommy's final donation (242).[27] The "sham" of Hailsham is not only of health ("hale"), but of ordinariness and especially of freedom.

Such a sham freedom implies an equally false autonomy. In her discussion of objectification, Langton describes "a false vision of autonomy" as "among the most potent enemies of autonomy" (253). What does it mean to "choose" to start one's training as a carer when one has no other options for one's life? One can only delay that "decision" to a small extent, not make any other. But Langton also argues that "objectification sometimes *depends* on affirmation of autonomy" (245). Langton is talking about pornography and rape; in some cases, she points out, objectification is strengthened by a rapist's acknowledgment of someone's autonomy, her desire *not* to be in the situation she's in, and his violation of that autonomy. In other words, a rapist can disbelieve in the autonomy of his victim, or he can believe it in and derive pleasure from overriding it.

In the case of the Hailsham clones, their objectification proceeds through the larger society's ambivalent acknowledgment of their autonomy. Much as the man who came to Salatin to kill his own chicken acknowledged the chicken's autonomy when he searched for a reproachful look, but overrode that presumed autonomy by killing the chicken, the society simultaneously acknowledges the clones' autonomy by taking the trouble to indoctrinate them at places like Hailsham to accept their purpose as organ donors and overrides it through that same indoctrination. Being trained to think of themselves as mere bodies effects their objectification, as medically necessary but subjectless.[28]

The Hailsham scenario brings out additional aspects of the ethics of humane farming. The ideal of the humane meat movement is a small farm where the farmer knows his animals well and gives them a certain amount of freedom and autonomy before slaughtering them as painlessly as possible. But as Taylor claims, when such a relationship is established between the farmer and the animals, the slaughter is "actually a deep breach of trust between the interdependent beings who are mutually supporting each other" ("Beasts," 210).[29] Such a breach of trust is suggested toward the end of *Never Let Me Go*, where it is hinted that Miss Emily is preparing to receive an organ from a cloned "donor." When Kathy and Tommy visit her, they find that Miss Emily is now using a wheelchair. She tells them, "You both look rather shocked at the sight of me. I've not been well recently, but I'm hoping this contraption isn't a permanent fixture" (257). Since we know that many of the old diseases are now curable by organ transplantation, readers gather from this remark that Emily will soon become an organ recipient.

If she is willing to accept an organ, possibly from a cloned person she helped raise and knew well, is this hypocrisy? Or is it consistent with the clone-welfare rather than clone-rights position she has all along taken? The aim of Hailsham, after all, is to improve the lives of clone donors, not to eradicate the donation program. As Nathan Snaza points out, the label "Guardian" indicates the teachers' protective role, but what they really aim to protect are not the cloned human beings themselves, but the donations (224). Similarly the aim of humane farming is obviously not to eliminate meat-eating, but to give animals better lives until they are usable for meat.[30] And yet we may have a sense that the very intimacy nurtured by such humane rearing (in both cases) renders the final killing/eating/organ-receiving even greater violations. In his discussion of "backyard butchery," James McWilliams points out the "moral disengagement from the food that backyard slaughterers insist that we do everything possible to get to know." He argues that people who take the local food movement to this extreme are "burying ["the omnivore's contradiction"] in layers of denial" (102). The apparent relationships of care in the cases of slaughtered animals and "completed" clones are in reality relationships of exploitation.

In both Hailsham and a humane farm, moreover, the good life is good relative to the factory farms, but not without avoidable loss, pain, fear, coercion, and of course death. One unsettling correspondence between animal slaughter and the novel's depiction of the clones' deaths is the question of when a being becomes unconscious in the process of being killed. Pollan writes that he was disturbed by Temple Grandin's description of a slaughterhouse she had designed because there were always times that stunning was not effective and cows would be hung upside down to have their throats slit while still conscious. As Pollan says, this is "troubling, because I can't help dwelling on all those times 'you've got a live one on the rail.' Mistakes are inevitable on an assembly line that is slaughtering four hundred head of cattle every hour. (McDonald's tolerates a 5 percent 'error rate')" (330). Even in humane slaughterhouses, stunning is not always effective. According to a report by the General Accounting Office about the Humane Methods of Slaughter Act, "The most prevalent noncompliance documented was the ineffective stunning of animals, in many cases resulting in a conscious animal reaching slaughter" (17).[31]

The worry that something similar might happen to them lingers in the minds of the cloned human beings in the novel. Tommy tells Kathy that the reason "everyone worries so much about their fourth" donation is that "they're not sure they'll really complete. If you knew for certain you'd complete, it would be easier. But they never tell us for sure." Addressing her readers as though we are in a similar position as donors (a narrative tactic Ishiguro also uses in *The Remains of the Day*), Kathy explains further, suggesting that this fear is widespread:

> You'll have heard the same talk. How maybe, after a fourth donation, even if you've technically completed, you're still conscious in some sort of way; how then you find there are more donations, plenty of them, on the other side of that line; how there are no more recovery centres, no carers, no friends; how there's nothing to do except watch your remaining donations until they switch you off. It's horror movie stuff, and most of the time people don't want to think about it. (279)

The correlation between this fear of being conscious while one's body is taken apart and the fact of conscious animals being slaughtered is one of the ways the novel questions the ethics of killing, of using the bodies of sentient beings for others' good.

The parallels between Hailsham and humane farms lead us to question whether even scrupulously humane farming is acceptable for animals, given that it is so patently unacceptable for cloned human beings. Pollan writes that "[w]hat's wrong with eating animals is the practice, not the principle. // What this suggests to me is that people who care about animals should be working to ensure that the ones they eat don't suffer, and that their deaths are swift and painless—for animal welfare, in other words, rather than rights" (328). This is what Hailsham is about: working for clone welfare rather than clone rights. The wrongness of this system even when the clones are reared in humane conditions shows that there is something in principle wrong with using human beings as involuntary organ donors. And this returns us to the central question of animal rights debates: whether there is anything about human beings that legitimately makes it wrong to use us, to put it in Kantian terms, as means only, while some characteristic or lack of nonhuman animals makes it acceptable to use them that way.

Animal Welfare

While most philosophers believe it is wrong to use human beings as means only, to objectify us, to reduce us to bodies, many give reasons why it is not wrong to do the same to nonhuman animals, reasons mostly relating to their alleged inability to think rationally, use language, and/or project themselves into the future.[32] They believe that human lives are objectively valuable and worthy of respect in ways that animal lives are not. In his argument against what he dubs the "human superiority thesis," Mark Bernstein exposes a logical leap in common accounts of why animal lives matter less, morally, than human lives. Many accounts of the superior value of human lives rest on the idea that death harms human beings more than it harms animals, because of our self-conscious desires to stay alive, our complex visions of our futures, our plans and projects, all of which death forecloses. But Bernstein points out that the *subjective* harm of death for a being living a certain kind of life does not necessarily entail that that life has greater *objective* value. He writes, "We cannot conclude that one kind of life is more (objectively) valuable than another kind from the fact that members of one kind of life lose more in death than another kind" (139). Such a connection would have to be argued;

but it is simply assumed in most accounts of the "disvalue of death" for human beings relative to animals.

Much within animal rights discussions hinges on matters of fact that we cannot determine or have not yet determined, such as the degree of psychological connectedness, or sense of identity through time, experienced by animals such as cows, pigs, and chickens. Christopher Belshaw goes so far to deny psychological connectedness to animals that he views every moment for an animal as, in effect, a separate life, and then argues that taking away some of the future lives of an animal is no different from not allowing an animal to come into existence in the first place—and therefore morally neutral (43). This view of animal consciousness seems highly likely to be disprovable. As Mel Chen writes, we should question

> nonhuman animals' simplistic or templatic *exclusion* from such capacities, since even at the level of scientific research there are increasing numbers of ways in which, as these capacities are refigured away from previous, implicitly anthropocentric constructions, nonhuman animals come to share with humans certain territories of sense, percept, cognition, feeling, and, indeed, language. (124–125)[33]

But what if human beings do imagine our futures in much greater detail and further into the future than do nonhuman animals?

In *Never Let Me Go*, Ishiguro touches on the question of psychological connectedness and projection into the future when he has his character Ruth long to work in an office with an open floor plan and "smart" colleagues (140, 144, 158, 229–230). Her emphasis on the open plan invokes the very thing she lacks—an open future, a future she could plan—making her longing all the more affecting. (It is also possible that this is meant to conjure the common reference to office cubicles as "veal-fattening pens."[34]) The fact that Ruth can envision a future that she is being deprived of makes her death more poignant. But does it make it more *wrong*? Wouldn't she have the same right to a future even if she could not, for whatever reason, envision it? Certainly it doesn't seem that her death is more of a crime than the death of Tommy, who had no such dreams about a future precisely because he knew they would be unattainable.

Even if animals do project themselves into the future more than we suppose, it is possible to grant a view such as Belshaw's and still argue for the wrongness of killing animals. Ben Bradley, for example, uses the deprivation account of the badness of death to demonstrate that even if one accepts that cows have momentary well-being but not lifetime well-being (that is, if one accepts the premise that they cannot evaluate or even experience the cumulative or overall well-being of their lives), it is still a loss to the cow if it has no more moments of well-being.[35] Moreover, Bradley argues that a sort of lifetime well-being can accumulate even in a being who cannot "care about the aggregate well-being in its life" (62).[36] He concludes, therefore, that not only pain, but a painless death is bad for a cow, depriving it of both momentary and aggregate well-being.

After all, if the well-being of an animal matters, then its being alive, necessary to its having well-being, has to matter too. McMahan points out that "some defenders of humane omnivorism" assume that "the painless killing of an animal that has been humanely reared requires no moral justification at all. But presumably that could be true only if the well-being or happiness of animals does not matter at all" ("Comparative Badness," 69). Even if we grant to animals only a lower moral status that tells us they should not be made to suffer unnecessarily—a degree of moral status defenders of humane omnivorism do grant—then, as McMahan points out, "it seems that their happiness should matter as well" ("Comparative Badness," 69). Pollan and his followers are outraged by the abuses of factory farming because they cause animals to suffer. This stance entails that animals' well-being matters morally. But he and others in the humane meat movement believe it is morally permissible to kill animals—at a fraction of their natural lifespans—without caring that animals' well-being is cut off completely by their deaths.

The deprivation of death is emphasized in Tom Regan's discussion of animal welfare. As an advocate of animal rights, not just animal welfare, he explains the serious problem with the view that suffering is the only harm we can cause animals: "It overlooks . . . the harm done by deprivation. And an untimely death is a deprivation of a quite fundamental and irreversible kind." Even though some things are worse than death, death is a "fundamental" harm because it "forecloses all possibilities of finding satisfaction" (100). Further, since in his account animals do have "psychophysical identity over time," an untimely death cuts an animal's life short "in the sense that a particular psychological being ceases to be" (101). In discussing the possibility of painless killing, he argues that in addition to attempting to reduce animal suffering, "it is essential that we recognize that not all harms hurt" (117).

Although Nussbaum takes a capabilities rather than a rights-based approach, she agrees with Regan about the wrongness of killing animals, even painlessly. She argues that animals have "entitlements based on justice"—that they are entitled to conditions under which they can flourish. The first condition, or capability, is necessarily that they remain alive. "In the capabilities approach, all animals are entitled to continue their lives, whether or not they have a conscious interest, unless and until pain and decrepitude make death no longer a harm" (*Frontiers*, 393).[37]

The idea that animals' flourishing or well-being matters morally is further supported by Christine Korsgaard's argument that even though Kant did not see animals as ends in themselves (because, as he thought, they could not reason), his arguments can be understood to demonstrate that all sensate beings should be treated as ends in themselves. Korsgaard identifies an ambiguity in Kant's explanation of where our moral value comes from, asking "Do we presuppose our value only insofar as we are beings who are capable of willing our principles as laws? Or do [we] presuppose our value as beings *for whom* things can be good or bad? In fact, Kant's argument actually shows that we presuppose our value as beings for whom things can be good or bad—or, as we might put it for short, as beings who have interests" (161). I will not reproduce the intricacies of Korsgaard's reading of Kant here, but for current purposes it is enough to seriously consider her conclusion: since nonhuman animals also have interests—they can "like and dislike things, be happy, or suffer" (162)—then they, "as beings with interests . . . are ends in themselves" (163).[38]

Finally, it may not matter just what capacities animals have when we consider justice toward them. As I discuss in the introduction, Cora Diamond repurposes Simone Weil's view of justice as opposed to rights to consider our treatment of animals. Whether or not animals can be said to have *rights*, Diamond argues, they should be treated justly.[39] As human beings who expect or believe that we deserve good, we should be "brought up short" by harmful treatment of other beings, especially vulnerable ones. Applying Leo Tolstoy's argument about the limitations of our compassion for those we exploit to the context of animals, Diamond writes: "In terms of Tolstoy's images, we might say that the welfarist view is essentially that we should ease the burdens we impose on animals without getting off their backs, without ceasing to impose burdens on them, burdens that we impose because we can, because they are in general helpless" (141). This shows, she points out, a "kind of pitilessness at the heart of welfarism" (141). Justice, on the other hand, requires compassion for the vulnerable rather than continued subjection of them to our will (142).

Even though the clones have what the humane meat movement aspires to for animals—good lives and respectful deaths—the Hailsham scenario suggests that using sentient beings as means only is unethical. Perhaps killing a being who cannot reason, conceive of itself as a living being, or imagine its future is not *as* wrong as killing one who can (although I am at all not sure of that, since such an argument uses performance criteria to determine moral value, a tactic disability scholars such as Kittay and Taylor have persuasively critiqued[40]). But the ability to reason (or other capacities) cannot on its own make such a moral difference that it is horribly wrong to kill Kathy, Tommy, and Ruth, but *not at all* wrong to kill a cow at a fraction of her natural life span, even if she has experienced a couple of nice years in a sunny pasture.[41]

Making Killable

For human beings, well-being is usually related to, though not necessarily the result of, the social context of one's life—one's life's meaning, to oneself and/or to others. Agamben's *homo sacer* is a fascinating figure because his life lacks value to the extent that even his death cannot have meaning: this is what it means that he cannot be ritually sacrificed. He can be killed by anyone without that person committing a crime. Quoting from Pompeius Festus, Agamben notes that "it is not permitted to sacrifice this man, yet he who kills him will not be condemned for homicide" (*Homo*, 71). Setting out to understand the meaning of violence that "is classifiable neither as sacrifice nor as homicide, neither as the execution of a condemnation to death nor as sacrilege," Agamben concludes that "*the sovereign sphere is the sphere in which it is permitted*

*to kill without committing homicide and without celebrating a sacrifice,
and sacred life—that is, life that may be killed but not sacrificed—is the life
that has been captured in this sphere*" (*Homo* 82, 83). Exploring Ishiguro's
clones in terms of Agamben's discussion of this figure helps illuminate
their sociopolitical position.

In a very limited sense, the clones are reduced to bare life in that
they are treated merely as bodies. Black argues that the "regulated and
automated sense of personhood in the novel evokes Giorgio Agamben's
theory of *homo sacer*" and suggests that "*Never Let Me Go* can be read as
a meditation on a world shaped by the eugenic fantasies of Nazi-era incarceration" (789). De Boever builds upon Black's assertions to focus on
the "logic of existence" in Hailsham that he argues is similar to the logic
of a concentration camp. There are serious factual and ethical problems
with De Boever's argument. Discussing the scene where Miss Lucy mentions "soldiers in World War II being kept in prison camps" (78), De
Boever claims that Lucy has compared "Hailsham to a concentration
camp" and refers to this as the "concentration camp episode" (65). But
prison camps for soldiers were very different places from concentration
camps.[42] De Boever also questions why the clones do not resist their
exploitation without analyzing the ways the society builds psychological fences around Hailsham (66).[43] He then goes on to ask facilely why
the victims of the Nazis said "yes" when asked to get on trains and leave
their homes—again without looking at the various brutal ways Nazis
enforced their vision of a *Judenrein* Europe. And finally, De Boever mis-
represents Stanley Milgram's experiments exploring "the human being's
will to obey" as though they applied primarily to the victims, rather than
the perpetrators of Nazi crimes (67). All of this has the effect of placing
blame on the victims of fictional and, worse, real atrocities.

But Agamben's theories about bare life and the camps do help us understand the politics of *Never Let Me Go*'s fictional culture. The cloned
human beings are reduced to their bodies in ways that to a limited extent resemble the bare life of the *homo sacer*. They themselves matter
only insofar as they can take care of their bodies until they donate their
organs. This reduction to body is especially pernicious because, as I
mention above, they are taught to feel as though *they* matter, they are
"special," when it is only really their bodies that matter. But instead of
describing this as a reduction to *zoë*, it would be more accurate to say

they are reduced to body, that their bodies are rendered objects. Nussbaum discusses what is involved in treating someone as an object, and includes seven notions, including instrumentality, denial of autonomy, fungibility, violability, and denial of subjectivity ("Objectification," 257).[44] The clones are certainly objectified in those ways. They are valued instrumentally as organ donors; their autonomy is disregarded; they are considered interchangeable except to the degree that their blood and tissue types differ; their bodies are not only violable but intended for violation; and their subjectivity is, if not denied, much trivialized. This differs, however, from being reduced to bare life because in *zoë* one's life is merely biological, without any cultural/social role or significance, whereas the clones' lives and particularly deaths have great significance, as they make it possible for others to live.

So in a larger way, the clones are reduced not to *zoë*, but to *bios*. In a fascinating reversal, their lives matter socially, but not intrinsically. They have social meaning and purpose. (Indeed, their sense of purpose, instilled in them at Hailsham, is the greatest part of what keeps them compliant.) If anyone killed a clone outside of the donation process, that person *would* be committing a crime—a crime, though, not against the clone himself or herself, but against the state, which has taken to itself the right to ownership of the clones' bodies. This question of whom a crime harms arose in the history of definitions of rape; for a long time rape was understood as a crime against the man whose property the raped woman was thought to be: her father or her husband (Freedman, 4). Her autonomy was not thought to have been violated because she was not understood to *have* autonomy. Similarly, the clones do not own their own bodies, and so to violate their bodies is, legally, to harm not them but their owners, the British government.[45]

The state's relationship to the clones is, moreover, interestingly different from the Nazi state's relationship to the bodies of those it killed without seeing itself as murdering or sacrificing them. In his chapter entitled "Life That Does Not Deserve to Live," Agamben discusses the Nazi concept of "life unworthy of life" and the ways that this category of living being "corresponds exactly—even if in an apparently different direction—to the bare life of *homo sacer*" (*Homo*, 139). The Nazi state killed people whose lives and bodies it did not value; the state in Ishiguro's novel kills people whose *lives* it does not value but whose *bodies* it values highly. The clones are not seen as inferior forms of life; rather, they are cultivated to be exceptionally fit and healthy. As Agamben points out, the idea of life that does not deserve to live has as its correlate life that does deserve to live (*Homo*, 137): in *Never Let Me Go*, the lives of aging or ill noncloned human beings. Here is a vital example of Eli Clare's assertion that cure, as an ideology, "prioritizes some lives over others" (xvi).

Garland-Thomson discusses the irony of sacrificing the ultra-fit bodies of the clones for the sake of the ill and disabled "normals"—what she calls a "disability reversal." She writes, "Perhaps the most perplexing and therefore arresting of the story's strange inversions is that the uber-fit and healthy young Hailsham donor clones Kathy, Ruth, and Tommy . . . are biologically fiercely able-bodied but socioculturally disabled in the disordered world of the story. In other words, they paradoxically possess normate embodiment and disabled status" ("Eugenic World Building," 138).[46] The clones are required to transfer their fitness to live to bodies with more cultural capital, capital gained by having received two sets of chromosomes from separate germ cells at conception.

Further, unlike the *homo sacer*, the clones can be and are *sacrificed*; that is, their deaths do have meaning.[47] The donation process has ritual qualities. First, one goes through stages, such as leaving school, starting one's training to become a carer, working as a carer, and receiving notice to become a donor. Once one is a donor, a carer is assigned, and one enters the next four stages, or operations, interspersed with recovery periods, with (if the person has not died before this) the fourth operation the fatal one. Before one's final donation, one is granted elevated status; for example at the recovery centers, "most donors . . . get their own room after third donation" (237). As one heads into the fourth donation, one is met by congratulations from other donors as well as from medical staff: "Even the doctors and nurses play up to this: a donor on a fourth will go in for a check and be greeted by whitecoats smiling and shaking their hand" (276). These ritual elements stress the meaning of the clones' deaths—they are marked with significance that the *homo sacer*'s death, or even the deaths in *Brave New World*, completely lack. Moreover, the deaths are sacrifices in that they provide life to others— the clones are sacrificed *for* the "normals" rather than merely dying "as cattle" (Owen, 12).

The Fatal Paradox of the Hailsham Experiment

Agamben's discussion of bare life is also helpful in understanding the demise of Hailsham, which has closed by the present of the narrative. Thinking about the clones' status as *bios* explains why Hailsham could not last: its philosophy was internally contradictory. Clones in factory farms, who *were* reduced to bare life, would be more easily killable, although given that they go through the same ritualized deaths, their deaths would retain meaning. But cloned people in an almost ordinary boarding school, people who are cultured, creative, and intelligent—how could they remain killable? Since they are enmeshed in a web of social relations, it is impossible to reduce them sufficiently to *zoë*. (This is another way of understanding the contradiction involved in viewing a being as worthy of a good life but not worthy of a lifespan.)

The founders of Hailsham were fighting for rights for clones, but not for an end to the donation program. "Here was the world, requiring students to donate. While that remained the case, there would always be a barrier against seeing you as properly human. Well, we fought that battle for many years, and what we won for you, at least, were many improvements, though of course, you were only a select few" (263). This project is incoherent: if the world did come to see the clones as "properly human," they would no longer be able to sacrifice them for the good of others. This incoherence began to be visible to the fictional British society as a result of a scandal involving the work of a scientist named James Morningdale. Morningdale worked in "a remote part of Scotland" to create "enhanced" children he planned to offer to ordinary families (263–264). The public's recoil from Morningdale's work was the impetus for financial backers to withdraw their support from Hailsham and its like. "It reminded them of a fear they'd always had. It's one thing to create students, such as yourselves, for the donation programme. But a generation of created children who'd take their place in society? Children demonstrably *superior* to the rest of us? Oh no. That frightened people" (264).

Treating the clones well, educating them so they had the chance to become "as sensitive and intelligent as any ordinary human being" (261), increased the cognitive dissonance in which the society was already engaging to enable themselves to accept cloned organs for themselves and their loved ones. Imagining clones (the genetically enhanced children Morningdale was creating) as full-fledged members of society made it impossible for the "normals" to pretend that the donation system was permissible, and so they had to reject Morningdale's work. When Kathy and Tommy ask Miss Emily why people would want students treated so badly, she explains, as I quote above, that it's more that people "preferred to believe these organs appeared from nowhere, or at most that they grew in a kind of vacuum" (262). To create that vacuum, the society raised the clones in the "vast government homes" that are still working in the narrative present: "even if they're somewhat better than they once were, let me tell you, my dears, you'd not sleep for days if you saw what still goes on in some of those places" (265). That is, the society was trying to reduce the clones to bare life, to keep them killable. Hailsham's resistance to that effort, Hailsham's success at rendering the clones' lives *bios*, meant that Hailsham had to go. The public's unease with Morningdale demonstrates the instability of the clones' exclusion from moral personhood. The reason people do not want to be reminded of "how the donation programme really worked" is that the clones' suppressed moral personhood—their intrinsic value—keeps threatening to rise to the surface and override their use value.

Giving the clones good childhoods, while certainly more ethical than giving them bad ones, also increased the cognitive dissonance of the clones themselves, who were taught that they were valuable and "special" until as teenagers and young adults they began to realize the radically limited extent to which that was true.[48] When Kathy learns that the purpose of taking their artwork was to demonstrate to the world that the cloned children had souls, she is confused: "Did someone think we didn't have souls?" Miss Emily answers: "It's touching, Kathy, to see you so taken aback. It demonstrates, in a way, that we did our job well" (260). Their job, then, was to make the children feel valued, feel themselves to be beings who matter, whose humanness—whose souls—were taken for granted. Ishiguro is quoted in the *Guardian* describing Hailsham as "a physical manifestation of what we have to do to all children," since "all children have to be deceived if they are to grow up without trauma" (T. Adams). But these same Guardians who supposedly took their value for granted, who spared them from trauma, were at the same time training them to think of themselves as sacrifices.[49] They were peddling, as Wilfred Owen put it, "the old Lie" (29) with a new twist.[50] They were teaching the children to be careful with their bodies and keep themselves healthy only so that they would be more valuable later as donors; this returns us to the widespread assertion in marketing for organic farms that well-treated animals will *taste better.*

Madame highlights this irony when she says, "Poor creatures. What did we do to you? With all our schemes and plans?" (254). Giving the cloned human beings the opportunity to become educated, cultured, and socially connected increases their pain at realizing they are valued purely instrumentally. Repeatedly using the word "creatures" for beings whose souls Madame and Miss Emily purport to believe in brings out the pathos of the Guardians' false position. While their work on the organic farm of Hailsham affirmed basic rights of cloned human beings for a limited period of time, their own dread of them partook of the system that viewed them as spiders, if extraordinarily useful spiders.

The cognitive dissonance involved in treating the cloned human beings as *bios* and yet maintaining their killability exposes a similar contradiction at the heart of humane farming. Taylor and others are rightly concerned that the humane farming movement's focus on animal welfare leaves the larger structures of animal exploitation intact (easing their burdens without getting off their backs, as Diamond puts it), and this claim applies to the cloned people in Ishiguro's novel as well. Taylor writes, "Although recognizing animal suffering is crucial to improving how we treat them, focusing only on suffering leads us to ignore that animals may in fact value living itself" (*Beasts*, 147). As McWilliams points out, there is a false consciousness or denial involved when a farmer slaughters animals whom he has come to know and become fond of, and for whom he has tried to provide good lives—while at the same time treating them as "commodit[ies] with a 'use by' date" (116–117). This false consciousness is visible in statements such as this tagline for a feature story about Purdue University's Department of Animal Sciences: "Faculty in the Department of Animal Sciences study every stage of the life cycle to optimize animal health, well-being, and product quality" (Mickelbart, n.p.). As Anne Whitehead points out, *Never Let Me Go* asks us to consider the relations "between our society and the dystopic England that Ishiguro depicts" (75). One such relation, detailed here, is the willingness in the humane meat movement to ignore the contradictions inherent in affirming an animal's right to a good life ("well-being") and then appropriating that life when we judge the animal's body to be useful to us ("product quality"). The horror of turning the clones' lives into instruments does not disappear in the case of nonhuman animals.

In *Never Let Me Go*, Kathy attempts to counter the killability of her fellow clones by writing her story, narrating her own and her friends' lives. In doing so, she places value on their lives, making space to grieve for them in a culture that works assiduously to foreclose that possibility.[51] In a discussion of the ways global violence makes many lives precarious, Butler asks, "Who counts as human? Whose lives count as lives? And, finally, *what makes for a grievable life*?" (*Precarious*, 20). Lives that can be grieved are lives that matter, and Kathy's narrative works against the systematic erasure of her friends' value. It serves as a life narrative as discussed in chapter 2, a narrative that helps Kathy discern and solidify the shape of her life and her friends' lives. It attempts to stave off the knowledge of an "abyss beneath our illusory sense of connection with the world" ("Nobel Prize in Literature"). Her relationship to her friends is important because it signals the social meaning the Hailsham clones are granted, their *bios*. The clones' *bios* operates in extreme tension with their status as killable; but this tension is suppressed at Hailsham, much as the tension between safeguarding animals' welfare and killing those animals is suppressed on an organic farm. Kathy's poignant narrative— and the mere fact that she has a story to tell—reveals that tension, showcasing the cultural suppression of knowledge that continually threatens to reemerge.

Epilogue

Revaluing Lives

In the foregoing chapters I've described some of the ways that four fictional texts, ranging from the turn of the twentieth century to the turn of the twenty-first, exhibit, rely on, and interrogate a few key ideologies. We see how human exceptionalism leads to torturous animal experimentation in *Moreau* and the use of cloned human beings as involuntary organ donors in *Never Let Me Go*, as well as to a curative imaginary that, in both scenarios, abandons beholding for molding and commits great violence in service to the quest for cure. We see a form of ageism—animated by ableism and emerging from a capitalist mindset—that suggests that only people who are contributing to their society at a sufficient rate and level of originality should continue to live. This leads not only to an untold number of lost life years in *Brave New World* but also to the people's failure to accept the frailties of others or to forge emotional connections to their bodies. In *The Violent Bear It Away* we see a related ableism that valorizes certain kinds of intelligence ("one tendency in human thought" as J. M. Coetzee's Elizabeth Costello puts it) to the degree that it denigrates lives with intellectual disability and excludes intellectually disabled human beings from the category of the "fully human."[1] These ideologies, while changing in some ways over the course of the twentieth century, retain their strength to a surprising degree in the early twenty-first, with important real-world effects. In what follows I briefly outline some of these effects, which in the case of disability lead me into a discussion of twentieth-century eugenics and the new, "liberal eugenics"—efforts to intervene in human evolution that necessarily make judgments about the value of different kinds of lives.

Because of the continued dominance of human exceptionalist ideologies, nonhuman animals continue to be exploited, abused, experimented upon (in ways that often amount to torture), and killed at a fraction of their natural life spans. While some protections have been added for a minority of lab animals, and while a few countries and individual US states have mandated less miserable conditions for farm animals, for the most part animal suffering has *increased* with the intensification of industrial farming. "Whereas the number of animals used in research in the United States is, at about twenty-five million, roughly equal to the population of Texas, the number of birds and mammals killed for food each year—again, in the U.S. alone—is around ten billion" (Singer, "Preface" x). The overwhelming majority of farm animals are raised in factory farms,[2] known to anyone who cares to look into them as bastions of suffering and abuse. While my chapters in this study focus on the more complex issues of animal experimentation and humane farming, factory farms are the obvious place to start to reduce the unconscionable suffering we visit on our fellow creatures.

Contemptuous attitudes about people who are frail or disabled and/ or no longer productive within capitalist frameworks contribute to the widespread phenomena of elder abuse and neglect. Strides have been made to combat such abuse, but even with the "passage of legislation in every state, education of practitioners, formation of multidisciplinary teams, and the development of innovative techniques for intervention," elder mistreatment continues and "remains hidden" (Quinn and Tomita, 3). A congressional report found that "over 30% of nursing homes [in the United States] had been cited for abuse violations between 1999 and 2001" (Bozarro, Boldt, and Schweda, 233). And the National Council on Aging estimates that one in every ten adults aged sixty and older has "experienced some form of elder abuse," though only a small minority of cases are reported ("Elder Abuse Facts").

The healthy aging movement does not cause the devaluation of older people, but it does stem from and exacerbate such devaluation: it separates old people into those who can be dismissed (those who are not aging healthily) and those who can be celebrated (those who are sufficiently similar to younger, nondisabled people). While encouraging many older people to keep active and look after themselves, the healthy aging movement also casts many people's old age as pathetic, thereby contributing to the isolation and exclusion of those older adults who do not meet the criteria for healthy aging.[3]

Descriptions of the increase in older populations across the developed world are often couched in inflammatory rhetoric unlikely to contribute to esteem for older adults. A 2010 *Economist* editorial entitled "The Silver Tsunami" quotes Martin Amis's xenophobic comparison of "the growing army of the elderly to 'an invasion of terrible immigrants, stinking out the restaurants and cafés and shops.'" Amis and his fellow novelist Christopher Buckley have both "touted the benefits of mass euthanasia" ("Silver"), with Amis provocatively calling for euthanasia booths where elderly people could go out with "a martini and a medal" (qtd. in Davies, n.p.). Amis's suggestion takes Ezekiel Emanuel's more measured statements to an extreme, but the logic is similar: there is no reason to outlive the decline of one's powers. This attitude applies especially to mental powers. Amis claims that "novelists tend to go off at about 70" (qtd. in Davies, n.p.). While "silver tsunami" is Amis's phrase, Andrea Charise cites a study finding that the *Economist*, a representative mainstream publication, consistently uses apocalyptic language to talk about the aging of the population (3n9).[4] Both the toxic humor of the "martini and a medal" suggestion and the anxious language used to talk about aging populations add to the sense that older people consume resources that ought to belong to those who are younger, more productive, and more "fit."

Disabled people continue to be devalued, incarcerated, and in many cases still sterilized. As the movement for deinstitutionalization (which gained traction in the 1970s) encouraged the closure of large mental and custodial institutions, more intellectually and psychiatrically disabled people have been sent instead to prison. Liat Ben-Moshe, Chris Chapman, and Allison Carey note that "in 2005, more than half of all prison and jail inmates were reported to have a mental health problem" (13). As Angela Davis points out in the preface to their collection, *Disability Incarcerated*, "The three largest contemporary psychiatric facilities, this volume dramatically reveals, are jails: Cook County Jail in Chicago, L. A. County Jail, and Rikers Island in New York" (viii). Given the high incidence of mentally disabled people in prisons, we should understand contemporary sterilizations of inmates as outgrowths of earlier eugenic programs. Nearly a hundred and fifty women in California prisons were illegally sterilized between 2006 and 2010, with "perhaps 100 more dating back to the late 1990s" (C. Johnson). Those targeted were chosen because the prison doctors and psychiatrists thought them likely to be repeat offenders; but since the doctors were not willing to speak to investigators, it is not clear what nonnormative behaviors led them to that assumption.

In Tennessee, prison officials have been offering (small) reductions in prison terms to people who are willing to undergo vasectomies, if they are men, or the implantation of Nexaplon—a contraceptive device that prevents pregnancy for four years—if they are women (Holloway). As the state ACLU director Hedy Weinberg has written, "Such a choice violates the fundamental constitutional right to reproductive autonomy and bodily integrity by interfering with the intimate decision of whether and when to have a child, imposing an intrusive medical procedure on individuals who are not in a position to reject it" (qtd. in Holloway). This program, very much like earlier eugenics programs, targets "unfit" people, re-linking criminality, poverty, and disability in an attempt to improve society by intervening in reproduction.

In *Fit to be Tied: Sterilization and Reproductive Rights in America, 1950–1980*, Rebecca Kluchin details other modern, non-state-sponsored sterilization projects. For example, she notes that in 1978 the American Cyanamid Company gave women workers the "choice" between moving to low-paid positions away from lead exposure or being sterilized and continuing to work in higher-paid jobs in the area of the plant that exposed them to lead (214). She explains that American Cyanamid's "policy was not unique. In the late 1970s and early 1980s, companies like General Motors, Allied Chemicals, St. Joe's Minerals, Olin, and B. F. Goodrich adopted similar policies that banned all women of childbearing potential (defined by General Motors as fertile women between the ages of fifteen and fifty) from jobs that involved toxic chemicals, with the exception of those women surgically sterilized" (214–215). Such policies target working-class women to gain control of reproduction, to "reproduce citizens and a society that reflected the values and power of the dominant group" (215).

In her discussion of the evolution of the Association for Voluntary Sterilization, Kluchin traces how it retained its eugenic attitude toward sterilization of people with mental disabilities:

The AVS did not abandon its support for the compulsory sterilization of individuals with mental disabilities as it eased into its voluntary sterilization agenda, although it did temper its approach. In its eugenic phase, the AVS argued for the compulsory sterilization of people with mental disabilities on the grounds of racial hygiene. In its neo-eugenic phase, the AVS separated its support for the voluntary sterilization of the poor from its support of nonvoluntary sterilization of people with disabilities in order to legitimize contraceptive sterilization for "healthy" Americans and to persuade public health officials to include the surgery in their programs. (31)

Much as the parents of Ashley X argue in the early twenty-first century,[5] the leaders of the AVS argued in the 1950s and 1960s that sterilization protects mentally disabled people themselves by helping to keep them out of institutions and prevent unwanted pregnancies (Kluchin, 31). This neo-eugenic attitude pretends to a benevolence that only thinly covers the judgment that "unfit" women should not reproduce.[6]

The eugenics movements of the early twentieth century aimed to improve the human species by using various methods to encourage the fertility of "fit" citizens and "limit and discourage the over-fertility of the mentally and physically defective," as eugenicist and birth control advocate Margaret Sanger put it (25). This movement was in the mainstream of science, public policy, and—after the 1927 Supreme Court *Buck v. Bell* decision upheld forced sterilization—law in the United States. Michael Sandel reminds us that "the crusade to rid the nation of defective protoplasm was no marginal movement of racists and cranks. . . . By the 1920s, eugenics courses were offered at 350 of the nation's colleges and universities" (64, 65). As scholars of the period have pointed out, Nazis learned from American racial and eugenics laws, and American eugenicists praised Nazi eugenic policies (Larson 146–147; Whitman). While many assume that eugenics was finished both as an ideology and as a set of practices after the Nazi era, and certainly the movement's credibility was badly damaged, the number of eugenic sterilizations in some areas of the Unites States was highest *after* the Second World War (Murphy, 138; Larson, 155–159).

Eugenic ideologies have now been revised and resuscitated, not just in prisons, but within the academic sphere. As we get closer to being able to genetically engineer our offspring, many philosophers believe we must intervene in the biology of the human species, usually with a primary or secondary goal of eradicating disability. In a sentence that could have been written a hundred years earlier, Ronald M. Green (whose approach to genetic engineering is neither cavalier nor rash), proclaims: "In this new era we will take the direction of our evolution into our own hands" (2). The new "liberal eugenicists" believe that eugenics was harmful insofar as it was dictated by the state and, depending on the type of eugenics discussed, resulted in coerced sterilizations, incarceration, or murder. They, on the contrary, advocate for individual parents making decisions for their own children.

Nicholas Agar, who coined the term "liberal eugenics," contrasts it with the old eugenics on the basis of reproductive freedom: "Twentieth-century eugenicists thought that bettering humanity would require the strict regulation of reproduction. The eugenics defended here differs in being primarily concerned with the protection and extension of reproductive freedom" (*Liberal Eugenics*, vi). Peter Singer, for his part, casts the difference in terms of its practical outcomes: "No state is ordering anyone's death; no one who wants to go on living is being murdered; no children whose parents want them to survive are being killed" (note the ominous qualification about the children) ("Shopping," 317).[7] The new eugenicists therefore believe that a liberal eugenics—possibly, as Robert Nozick suggests, a "genetic supermarket" approach to human genetic enhancement—will avoid the moral pitfalls of the old eugenics.[8]

But the lack of state control over, for example, involuntary sterilizations does not necessarily mean different outcomes from the old eugenics. For example, poor women of color continue to be sterilized at much higher rates than middle- or upper-class white women, and an unknown number of these surgeries result from racially tinged pressure exerted by medical professionals or from outright unethical procedures. Beverly Horsburgh explains some aspects of contemporary sterilization politics:

Although *Relf v. Weinberger* [1974] prohibited the practice of threatening welfare mothers with the cancellation of their benefits unless they agreed to sterilization as well as the use of federal monies for involuntary sterilization, there is little in the way of monitoring to ensure compliance with federal regulations or that a truly informed consent was obtained. For example, a recent study reported that physicians tend to diagnose white

women as suffering from endometriosis, treatable with the new reproductive technology. In contrast, Black women are diagnosed with pelvic
inflammatory disease which is "cured" by sterilization. (557)

In many cases of court-ordered sterilization for mentally disabled
women, Horsburgh further points out, "women's rights to voluntary
procreative choice [are] used against them to justify involuntary procedures. Any eugenic thinking underlying these decisions disingenuously
remains unstated" (571). Phenomena like these demonstrate the ease
with which abusive eugenic practices can continue outside of state-
sponsored eugenic programs.

Indeed, many parents of intellectually disabled children and young
adults either wish to have them sterilized or do manage to use the legal
system to have them sterilized. "A 2003 study in the journal *Mental Retardation and Developmental Disabilities Research Reviews* about the
ethics of involuntary sterilizations of mentally handicapped people ex-
amined surveys from the 1980s and 1990s and found that roughly half
of all parents with mentally disabled children have considered or would
consider sterilizing their child" (Kamenev).[9] Individual decisions for the
alleged good of sterilized people often turn out to be the same types of
decisions made by the U.S. states in the eugenics period. Such individual
decisions have broad social relevance. As Merryn Ekberg asserts, "Individual decisions invariably affect others, and the cumulative effect of
many individual decisions must ultimately have social consequences. . . .
Indeed, the recent interest in promoting genetic screening programmes
to enhance public genetic health signals a revival of the collective ethos
of the old eugenics" (587).

Most important, there is a similar flaw in the arguments of old and
new eugenicists. This flaw was identified by G. K. Chesterton in his 1922
book, *Eugenics and Other Evils.* Analyzing the thinking of those who say
that the birth rate among the poor ought to be controlled, Chesterton
quotes a man who has written to a major newspaper: "When people
have large families and small wages, not only is there a high infantile
death-rate, but often those who do live to grow up are stunted and weak-
ened by having had to share the family income for a time with those who
died early. There would be less unhappiness if there were no unwanted
children." Chesterton comments:

You will observe that he tacitly takes it for granted that the small wages and the income, desperately shared, are the fixed points, like day and night, the conditions of human life. Compared with them marriage and maternity are luxuries, things to be modified to suit the wage-market. There are unwanted children; but unwanted by whom? This man does not really mean that the parents do not want to have them. He means that the employers do not want to pay them properly. Doubtless, if you said to him directly, "Are you in favour of low wages?" he would say, "No." (138)

While Chesterton's objections to eugenics arise out of his religious commitments, his astute analysis uncovers the extent to which eugenicists unreflectively viewed some conditions as unchangeable constants and others as malleable material, intervention in which could ground social change.

The same logical flaw justifies current eugenic practices, such as selective abortion and genetic enhancement, that aim to improve the human species biologically. These practices take social problems to be "fixed points" and therefore approach them with biomedical tools. Such approaches stem from the "strong drive to medicalize—to describe features of life in biological terms wherever possible, so that their problematic aspects become things best dealt with biomedically" (Scully, *Disability Bioethics* 4). Liberal eugenicists would be encouraged, for example, by reports that births of babies with Down syndrome in Iceland have hit a record low, at only two babies per year, as well as by the report that of pregnant women whose fetuses are diagnosed with Down syndrome in Iceland, close to 100 percent decide to abort the fetus (Quinones and Lajka).[10] But in their assumptions that by preventing people with Down syndrome from being born, we are reducing suffering and increasing the overall happiness of the human species, these new eugenicists are making the same type of mistake Chesterton's letter writer makes. They are taking a complex social situation (that disabled people are "worse off" in some contexts and environments) as a hard and fast "condition of human life." They are ignoring the great extent to which the suffering of disabled people has its origins not in their bodies or minds, but in the social and environmental exclusion they experience.

Melinda Hall makes a similar point about genetic enhancement. She writes that enhancement is "framed as inevitably a matter of bodily intervention. We should reconsider enhancement in terms of political and social intervention. This is particularly urgent given that the problems outlined in enhancement literature are political and social, yet the causes of these problems are reduced to biological factors" (xi). When philosophers such as Julian Savulescu argue for the moral obligation to select "the best" embryos for implantation (Savulescu calls this the "principle of procreative beneficence"), they are assuming that biological factors can be mapped straightforwardly onto social flourishing for the resulting human being.[11] His confidence that genetic science can determine the "best" embryos is an example of the fantasies Ellen Samuels explores in *Fantasies of Identification*. As she notes, "The very fact that genetics is comparatively reliable science seems to provoke even more extreme and expansive fantasies about it" (186).

Indeed, as Joseph Stramondo points out, Savulescu is defining "best" narrowly, in accordance with typical species functioning. Stramondo counters that there is not "a rational, objective standard of what sorts of traits we should think of as 'best'" (494). In line with this understanding of disability's relation to human flourishing, Elizabeth Barnes argues that "disability is *neutral* with respect to well-being" (54). Ensuring that a person is biologically "normal" (even if we could agree what that is) will not substantially increase that person's chances of a good life: "There are too many variables" (H. Johnson, 511).

Just as the hypothetical employer Chesterton discusses could pay higher wages, we could accommodate rather than eliminate the variety of bodies and minds born into the human family and, by so doing, not only remove or dramatically decrease the suffering that makes disabled people "worse off," but also make it acceptable and satisfying for parents to raise disabled children. We could dramatically reduce both the stigma and the disablement of impairment, turning myriad kinds of "bad-difference" into "mere-difference."[12] We could work for a world, as Johnson describes it, "in which killing [or selective abortion] won't be such an appealing solution to the 'problem' of disability" (517). We could approach social problems with social solutions.

Justice for Sentient Beings

In writing about genetic enhancement, cautious philosophers warn that we might engineer ourselves right out of our humanness. As I quote in chapter 2, Gilbert Meilaender writes that "we might . . . wonder whether it would have been better to remain human . . . even if our capacities were fewer, our status (in some sense) lower, and our suffering greater" (*Neither Beast*, 22). Even Agar, in *Truly Human Enhancement* (2013), while still promoting many types of enhancement, argues against what he calls "radical enhancement" so as not to threaten our human identity. To these concerns about preserving humanness we might reasonably respond that humanness is already wildly overvalued; that our adherence to human exceptionalism is the cause of overwhelming harm to nonhuman animals and to the natural world; that we should discard the golden calf and good riddance.

But as Octavia Butler makes clear in her speculative novel *Dawn* (1987), our humanness can hardly help but be dear to us. The novel underscores our deep emotional connection to our humanness, putting the brakes on claims that humanness ought not to matter at all. In the novel, an alien species called Oankali must merge their DNA with that of humans in order to survive. In the process, they are changing human beings to counteract our tendencies to hierarchy and domination that have already led to nuclear devastation. As we see in the second book of the trilogy, *Adulthood Rites* (1988), the mixed human-Oankali children have sensory and mental abilities far beyond what human children have. Nevertheless, many human characters agree with Meilaender: they wish to remain human, even with fewer capacities. In *Dawn*, some react with violence to the imminent adulteration of humanness. And even the protagonist Lilith, who loves some of the Oankali and sympathizes with their situation and their view of human beings, is still dismayed to be carrying a baby who isn't—and there's that qualification again—fully human. On the final page of *Dawn* she says of the children she and others will have, "But they won't be human. . . . That's what matters. You can't understand, but that *is* what matters" (248). While it would be easy—and in many ways just—to dismiss Lilith's feelings as chauvinism, the novel asks us to consider, indeed to accept, our unavoidable emotional connection to our humanity.

We should not, however, mistake the dearness of our humanness for an objectively superior value. Instead, in my view, we must strike a balance between valuing humanness as that which confers inherent worth on *all* human beings and understanding that it is *not the only source* of such worth. To put this claim in more philosophical language, being human is a sufficient but not necessary condition for deserving justice. Sentient nonhuman animals too (and sentient alien species we may someday meet) are subjects of their lives and must be treated with respect for those subjectivities.

In a discussion of how Englishwomen might move past parochialism in their views of Englishness, Virginia Woolf offers grist for thinking about how we can respect our emotional connection to our humanity without endorsing the arrogance of human exceptionalism. In *Three Guineas* Woolf notes that a woman of her time cannot logically be committed to national identity, since "by law she becomes a foreigner if she marries a foreigner" (128). The result of this, for Woolf, is a sense of international solidarity: "As a woman my country is the whole world" (129). But Woolf realizes that in spite of this principled rejection of nationalism, there might remain "some obstinate emotion, some love of England dropped into a child's ears by the cawing of rooks in an elm tree, by the splash of waves on a beach, or by English voices murmuring nursery rhymes" (129). So she recommends that the Englishwoman use "this drop of pure, if irrational, emotion" to work to "give England first what she desires of peace and freedom for the whole world" (129).

Woolf's discussion resonates for me because of its parallel with the situation for those of us who think critically about humanism. We may understand the destructive force of human exceptionalism without quite being able to discard our "pure, if irrational" partiality to humanness. If we were to follow Woolf's advice, we would seek to give human beings first what we seek of peace and freedom for all sentient beings. But there Woolf's counsel falls short. To work for justice for humans only, even if ostensibly temporarily, is to fall prey to the misconceptions I delineate in the introduction when discussing McBryde Johnson's assertion that getting "past species" is a "luxury way beyond [her] reach." Justice for sentient beings need not be divided into "human rights" and "animal rights." On the contrary, the "animal rights movement is a part of, not opposed to, the human rights movement" (Regan, *Case for Animal Rights*, xiii).

All sentient beings deserve to be treated as ends in themselves—as subjects rather than objects. As Martha Nussbaum argues, "Animals other than human beings possess dignity for the very same reason that human beings possess dignity: they are complex living and sentient beings endowed with capacities for activity and striving" ("Human Dignity and Political Entitlements," 367). To bring about "peace and freedom for the whole world," we must work against exploitation, abuse, and murder for all beings who are conscious, who are capable of experiencing the world, who are capable of suffering.

ACKNOWLEDGMENTS

In some ways this book returns me to ethical questions I began grappling with as an undergraduate at the University of Chicago—questions about the ethics of fiction, to use Wayne Booth's phrase, or about the status of "artworks as moral objects," as I titled my BA thesis. I therefore want to thank my professors from those early years of my intellectual development, especially Joel Snyder and the late Wayne Booth, Herman Sinaiko, and Ted Cohen. Since nearly that long ago, two of my graduate school advisors, Suzanne Raitt and John Whittier-Ferguson, have remained steadfast mentors and supports.

Thanks to my writing buddies, Cara Kinnally and Molly Scudder, and my writing group, Elena Coda, Jennifer Kaufman-Buhler, Rebekah Klein-Pejšová, Erin Moodie, and Toni Rogat. And thanks to my accountability partners, Jennifer William and Elaine Francis, and, from University of Georgia, Elizabeth McCarty. I am grateful to my fellow deaf academics, Stephanie Kerschbaum, Rebecca Sanchez, Teresa Blankmeyer Burke, and Mel Chua for their advice and camaraderie. My family—including my father and stepmother, mother, brother and sister-in-law, nieces, spouse, in-laws, and children—has been warmly encouraging. My mother, Deena Linett, is especially supportive of me and my work. My spouse, Dominic Naughton, offers insightful feedback and consistent support. And the ethical force of our children Ruth's and Lev's views about human beings and other animals inspires me every day.

I am indebted to Michael Davidson, Janet Lyon, and Rosemarie Garland-Thomson for their excellent advice and for writing whose brilliant inquiries into modernism, disability, and bioethics inspire my work. Many thanks to the series editors of Crip, Robert McRuer, Ellen Samuels, and Michael Bérubé, for bringing this project to New York University Press; to Eric Zinner and Dolma Ombadykow for seeing the manuscript through the review process; to production editor Alexia Traganas and the cover design team, and to the anonymous readers for the press for their enthusiasm and excellent suggestions.

For support in writing this book I am grateful for a Center for Humanistic Studies fellowship and a Provost's Enhancing Research in the Humanities and Arts grant, both from Purdue University. A version of chapter 2, entitled "'No Country for Old Men': Huxley's *Brave New World* and the Value of Old Age," was published the *Journal of Medical Humanities* 40.3 (2019): 395–415 (preceded by August 2017 online publication), and is adapted by permission from Springer Nature.

NOTES

INTRODUCTION

1 For example, Shreve writes, "Clearly it is unethical to study the unknown actions of stem cells in human subjects. One obvious solution is to insert the cells
into animals and watch how they develop" (n.p.) and describes experiments on
monkeys' brains without a hint of discomfort (without the squirming that Leon
Kass labels the "wisdom of repugnance") on the monkeys' behalf. The only beings
whose "rights and protections" he considers are human-ape chimeras, and then
only because of their partial humanity: "If such chimeras were to be created,
what legal rights and protections should they have, *distinct from other animals*?"
(emphasis added).

2 Cora Diamond similarly discusses the power of the vivid descriptions of slaves'
anguish in the abolitionist writings of Quaker John Woolman. "The power of the
arguments . . . comes from imaginative descriptions making evident the injustice
of the capture and transportation of slaves. Woolman attempts, in several very
moving passages, to make his readers understand the 'inexpressible Anguish of
soul' of those who survive, uncaptured, an attack by slavers, and also of the cap-
tives themselves. . . . These arguments bear the weight of the work; they open the
reader's eyes to the cruelty and injustice of the slave trade" (126). Diamond's point
here is that it was not by an appeal to rights that Woolman convinced his readers
of the injustice of slavery, but by vivid descriptions that appeal to their compassion.

3 Charles Altieri objects that Nussbaum's ethical criticism praises literature for its
concreteness and yet "has to interpret the value of that engagement in terms of
the very philosophical methods and generalisations from which the concrete
reading deviates" (35). While I do see this as a tension within Nussbaum's brand of
ethical criticism, I don't see it as a flaw. Literary criticism of any stripe can both attend to the concreteness of literature and generalize about it, even in philosophical terms, and while these two efforts sometimes engage in a sort of tug-of-war,
neither precludes the other.

4 Nussbaum argues that "for any character with whom the form invites our participatory identification, the motives for mercy are engendered in the structure of
literary perception itself" ("Equity and Mercy," 109).

5 Some critics, as will become clear in chapter 3, do excuse the murder. They have
swallowed the novel's excessive sympathy with Tarwater and its dismissal of

Bishop Rayber's value. They are set up to accede to these attitudes by the ableism that devalues intellectually disabled people within and outside of the text.

6 The implied author is a concept developed by Wayne Booth in *The Rhetoric of Fiction*, and used to discuss ethics in *The Company We Keep* (especially in the chapter entitled "Implied Authors as Friends and Pretenders"), where he considers readers' ethical and friendly relations with the implied authors of texts. Altieri discusses the powers and limitations of Booth's account of the ethics of fiction (28, 41).

7 It is true, as Altieri points out, that Nussbaum turns from Proust and James to the more straightforward Dickens to make her most persuasive cases for literature's ethical stance (29), suggesting that only certain kinds of literature work well for her argument. Altieri focuses mostly on Nussbaum's earlier *Poetic Justice* (1995), though she makes her argument for literature's ethical import in slightly different forms in the other articles and books I cite here. In *Not for Profit* (2010), for example, as I mention below, she gives a complicated account of how literature contains an antidote to its own refusal to grant readers imaginative access to stigmatized characters.

8 I want to note that Nussbaum is not contrasting literature to thought experiments; that is my addition. I also do not mean to suggest that readers are not free to disagree with thought experiments and to construct, as a result, counter thought experiments. They do that all the time. But the thought experiments are *designed* to be as convincing as possible in leading readers along a certain route, whereas literary representations are obviously far more open-ended.

9 In a much discussed move, bioethicist Leon Kass referred to Nathanial Hawthorne's story "The Birthmark"—in which a scientist trying to perfect his wife's beauty by removing her birthmark ends up killing her—as a way to warn against stem-cell research and therapeutic cloning (he assigned the story as preliminary reading to the rest of the President's Council on Bioethics in 2001 [Gillespie]). In its use of the story's basic plot as a scare tactic, such a strategy is opposed to the approach I take in this study. Squier discusses Kass's strategy in her Coda.

10 Keen does discuss readers who respond against the grain on 74ff.

11 In *Adulthood Rites* (1988), Octavia Butler explores different ways language could potentially manifest when she has an Oankali man explain to his mixed human-Oankali child about a large caterpillar-like being back on the "ship." When the child asks, "Can it talk?" his father explains, "In images, in tactile, bioelectric, and bioluminescent signals, in pheromones, and in gestures" (262).

12 And this world-making subject was necessarily heterosexual, with the possibility of sexual deviance a threat to the world-making project (which included heterosexual reproduction), and especially in the eugenics period, to the body politic. As Michael Davidson writes, "Historically, the merging of disability and sexuality has occurred through the pathologizing of the 'invert' as mentally defective, and by sexualizing the cognitively disabled person as a sexual threat to the gene pool. The castrating of mental patients during the eugenic 1920s . . . is only one version

of a more pervasive form of negative eugenics based around the control and monitoring of disability" (*Invalid*, 121).

13 This mindset was of course not confined to science. Davidson notes that many futurists and other avant-garde artists "endorse[d] an embodied future against a disabled past" (*Invalid* 68).

14 Now that the "we" ostensibly includes racial minorities, the "school-to-prison pipeline" works to segregate those whom slavery and Jim Crow laws can no longer remove from the midst of the white/nonracialized majority. For a disability studies analysis of this "New Jim Crow" (as Michelle Alexander labels it in her book of the same name), see Nirmala Erevelles, "Crippin' Jim Crow." Erevelles points out that disability is "implicated in the uneasy alliance between race, class, and criminalization" (84).

15 Karen Barad discusses the ways nonliving entities co-create agency in a process she calls "intra-action" (128). Focusing on "matter's dynamism," she offers a "posthumanist performative approach" to understanding the role of the human in the material world (135). In a similar vein, Mel Chen argues that "animacy is political, shaped by what or who counts as human, and what or who does not" (*Animacies*, 30).

16 In *Choreographies of the Living*, Carrie Rohman analyzes and counters the belief that the aesthetic impulse is restricted to human beings. In spite of art's ancient origins, we suppress any connection between art and our nonhuman relatives in the same way Wolfe describes anthropological dogma here. Building on work by Gilles Deleuze and Elizabeth Grosz, Rohman asserts that "human creativity is only the most recent iteration of an artistic impulse that belongs to the living in general" (7).

17 This phrasing is an inversion of a phrase Meilaender uses in his discussion of lives with "shape and not just duration," which I quote in chapter 2 (*Should We Live*, 15).

18 Francis Fukuyama uses Huxley's society as a grounding for his argument that "the most significant threat posed by contemporary biotechnology is the possibility that it will alter human nature and thereby move us into a 'posthuman' stage of history" (7).

19 Puar notes elsewhere that a "brutal humanism exists as a form of speciesism that cleaves . . . raced and sexed humans from other humans" ("Precarity Talk," 171).

20 The phrase "lower on the scale" of course partakes of human exceptionalism.

21 In calling Singer an animal rights pioneer, I am using the word "rights" loosely, in accordance with common parlance. But when speaking more narrowly, Singer is not actually an advocate for animal *rights*; he is an advocate for equal consideration of animals' interests. Tom Regan, on the other hand, argues that animals have rights, where rights are defined as entitlements that cannot be overridden for the benefit of others, even if overriding them would do a great deal of good. For example, if I have a right to life and/or bodily integrity, you cannot kill me and distribute my organs even though they could keep several other people alive. As

David DeGrazia names them in *Animal Rights: A Very Short Introduction*, these are "utility-trumping rights" (15)—but as he notes, in the strict sense of the term *rights*, the idea that they trump utility is built in.

22 Taylor suggests that "It is arguably because of Singer that animal rights and disability rights are nearly always seen as at odds" (*Beasts*, 124). Mark Bernstein's argument for the moral equality of human beings and animals, on the other hand, avoids ableism, in large part because he is not ascribing relative values to different subgroups of human and nonhuman beings. When he does mention disability, it is to argue that our obligations to those who are more vulnerable are, if anything, stronger than our obligations to those who are less vulnerable (64). Although Bernstein does seem to assume the vulnerability of disabled people stems from our bodies, an understanding of the social model allows us to read this as vulnerability due to injustice and oppression.

23 Alison Kafer and Eunjung Kim rightly point out that such an argument could slip into the suggestion that disability is the "only or primary discourse of disqualification. On the contrary, however, race, gender, class, and species have also been used to justify the inferior status of other groups. Ascriptions of femininity, for example, have been used to justify the marginalization of, among others, indigenous peoples, colonial subjects, and disabled people" (127). It is possible, though, I think, to examine the ways disability *has* been used to justify exploitation without implying that it is the *only* category that has been used to justify exploitation or that it is the most basic or primary ground for denials of justice.

24 Regan does join Singer and McMahan, however, in irresponsibly using mentally disabled human beings as objects of comparison with nonhuman animals to make the case for animal rights. He writes, for example, that "the magnitude of the harm that death is, is a function of the number and variety of opportunities for satisfaction it forecloses, and there is no credible basis on which to claim that the death of a normal, adult animal is not a greater loss, and thus a greater harm, than the death of a retarded human, one who possesses fewer desires, less competence to act intentionally, and is less responsive to others and the environment generally" (*Case for Animal Rights*, 314). Here Regan not only assumes that the question of the harm of death is settled—although philosophers continually debate in what the harm of death consists—but also demonstrates his lack of knowledge of mentally disabled adults and his overvaluation of certain kinds of intelligence as prerequisites for being responsive to others and the environment.

CHAPTER 1. BEAST LIVES

I thank Sarah Nolan for research assistance relating to this chapter.

1 In this discussion Chambers is relying on John Fowles's metaphor of the boxing match, suggesting that we see authors as fixing fights. I return to this idea in chapter 3.

2 Victor Shklovsky articulates the Russian formalist view of defamiliarization in his essay "Art as Technique," where he writes that "art exists that one may recover the

sensation of life; it exists to make one feel things, to make the stone *stony*" (Newton, 4). In *The Secret Life of Stories*, Michael Bérubé productively applies Shklovsky's ideas to the ways intellectual disability makes narrative processes strange (45–46). In *Bodyminds Reimagined*, Sami Schalk analyzes the ways black women's speculative novels defamiliarize "(dis)ability, race, gender, and sexuality [and] encourage . . . us to question our assumptions about the definitions, meanings, and boundaries of these categories" (134). And in *Invalid Modernism*, Michael Davidson explores the defamiliarization caused by disability in the context of modernist aesthetics (9).

3 Cole agrees, writing that "the learning of these years colored all of Wells's thought and profoundly shaped his role as a public intellectual" (13).

4 Donna Haraway describes Freud's take on the Darwinian "wound" to human narcissism: "The second wound is the Darwinian, which put *Homo sapiens* firmly in the world of other critters, all trying to make an earthly living and so evolving in relation to one another without the sureties of directional signposts that culminate in Man" (11).

5 Wells's "Human Evolution: An Artificial Process" appears as Appendix 5 in the 1993 Variorum edition of *The Island of Doctor Moreau* edited by Robert Philmus; hereafter, "Philmus" is used in citations. In *Animal Theory* Derek Ryan describes a typical view of humanness that fits Wells even though Wells was consciously questioning human superiority: "The relationship between human being and animal being is most commonly characterised by both a hierarchical and a supplementary arrangement. That is, the human is seen as the *highest* kind of animal and it is viewed in this way because of what the human *adds* to its base animal being" (50).

6 Cary Wolfe warns that this view is no longer tenable: "In the light of developments in cognitive science, ethology, and other fields over the past twenty years . . . it seems clear that there is no longer any good reason to take it for granted that the theoretical, ethical, and political question of the subject is automatically coterminous with the species distinction between *Homo sapiens* and everything else" (*Animal Rites*, 1).

7 Citations to the novel itself refer to the Broadview critical edition unless otherwise noted. References to related materials by Wells, Darwin, and Huxley included in the Broadview edition are cited as "Harris," the editor of that edition. References to the Variorum edition, edited by Robert Philmus, are cited as "Philmus;" additional Wells materials found in that edition are also cited as "Philmus."

8 Wells believed that the other part of human beings was artificial, created by our cultures, which grew from our ability to speak and to write ("Human Evolution: An Artificial Process," Philmus, Appendix 5).

9 A moment of differentiating knowledge of suffering from sensory experience of that suffering also arises in Conrad's *Heart of Darkness* when Marlow knows an African is being beaten for allegedly starting a fire and doesn't seem affected by the situation. But later when he passes near the man, he cannot tolerate the sound

of the man's sigh: "The hurt nigger moaned feebly somewhere near by and then fetched a deep sigh that made me mend my pace away from there" (26).

10   Brian Luke describes a strategy vivisectors use to this day to stave off interference from bystanders: in a process known as "debarking," some vivisectors sever the vocal chords of dogs so that they cannot howl or bark and attract attention. "If we cannot see them or hear them, we cannot sympathize with them, a point well appreciated by the founder of professional vivisection, Claude Bernard" (142).

11   Mason Harris, the editor of the Broadview edition, writes about one contemporaneous review: "Mitchell expresses surprise at Wells's gruesome presentation of vivisection, as though Wells were writing on the anti-scientific side of the debate over vivisection" (186). Harris also includes a review by R. H. Hutton, an opponent of Huxley, in the *Spectator* (188–190). Hutton is delighted by what he takes to be the novel's antivivisectionism. He writes that Wells "may, we hope, have done more to render vivisection unpopular, and that contempt for animal pain, which enthusiastic physiologists seem to feel, hideous, than all the efforts of the societies which have been organized for that wholesome and beneficent end" (189). More contemporary reviewers also see the novel as more thoroughly antivivisectionist than Wells seems to have intended. Frank McConnell, for example, writes that Wells shows animals' "inalienable right to survive, regardless of human beliefs about their usefulness or efficiency" (93).

12   In an essay called "Comparative Theology" Wells baldly asserts that "to a certain type of men and perhaps to all women a purely scientific method has ever been unsatisfactory" (*Early Writings*, 45).

13   Bernstein's thesis is that there is a moral equality between human and nonhuman animals that leaves us no right to subordinate nonhumans to our needs (viii).

14   As Mark Rowlands argues, Moreau's wantonness *should* be a problem, since if there is no vital interest of human beings that is ensured by vivisection, then one is allowing nonvital interests (of human beings) to outweigh vital interests (of animals). "In the impartial position, not knowing whether you are human or animal, it would be irrational to choose a world where non-vital interests are allowed to override vital interests" (125). The "impartial position" is a variation, used in animal ethics, of John Rawls's conception of the "original position."

15   Michael Parrish Lee points out that Prendick's error "underscores his readiness to believe that the human might readily transform into the bestial. Indeed, his encounter with the Beast Folk throws his own humanity into question, as evident in his suicidal certainty that Moreau can turn him into a 'beast'" (261).

16   In *The War of the Worlds* (1898), Wells similarly suggests that humans can be (treated as) animals. For example, the narrator realizes that "men, the creatures who inhabit this earth, must be to [the Martians] at least as alien and lowly as are the monkeys and lemurs to us" (5). The Martians obtain blood "from a still living animal, in most cases from a human being" (141) much as human beings use those we view as "animals" for our own sustenance.

17 John Huntington remarks that the beast people "prove [their] humanity by degenerating beneath it" (66) in accord with Wells's view of human beings as beastly.

18 Wolfe describes the dramatic overvaluation of language in the Western philosophical tradition, noting that "the basic formula . . . has been: no language, no subjectivity" (*Zoontologies*, xv–xvi). I briefly discuss a further conflation of speech and language (language can be visual rather than oral, as signed languages make clear) in *Bodies of Modernism* (89–91). In "Eating Well," Derrida discusses the strange fact that "thou shalt not kill" has always been understood to refer only to other human beings; it has never been taken to mean "Thou shalt not put to death the living in general" (279).

19 Glendinning agrees, writing that "the binary logic behind the process of eliminating 'the animal' implies that his goal is the god-like one of creating the human or super-human, not just some form chosen at random" (589).

20 Indeed, animal research generally relies on a sort of double-thinking about their status. As Sherryl Vint puts it, "They must be sufficiently different from humans for it to be morally defensible to torment them for research and kill them when that research is complete. At the same time, however, they must be sufficiently similar to humans for the research results to be deemed pertinent to human health" (91).

21 Margaret Atwood points out the novel's allusion to Comus, the son of Circe, who could turn men to animals (e.g., swine) and who "leads a band of creatures, once men, who have drunk from his enchanted cup and have turned into hybrid monsters. They retain their human bodies, but their heads are those of beasts of all kinds" (159).

22 Prendick accounts for his sense of familiarity by saying perhaps he had seen the face before, when he was semiconscious, but still wonders how it would be possible to forget so striking a face (79). Once readers are aware of Moreau's project, however, we are more likely to explain his sense of familiarity by noting that he has seen M'Ling's individual features on the animals of whom he is composed. It is their totality that is so surprising, and it is the contrast between the familiar features and the shocking whole that gives rise to the uncanny.

23 It is likely that this same combination of familiarity and difference sparked Wells's childhood "profound fear of the gorilla," who looked enough like a human being to startle a child (*Experiment in Autobiography*, 54).

24 Considering J. L. Austin's use of "a marriage with a monkey" to exemplify failed performatives, Chen addresses the negative side, the fear of such fascination, linking it to a process of shoring up normative identities. Chen writes that "Austin is responding to a sensed threat. Someone's heteronormative and righteous marriage must be protected against the mockery of performative improprieties. . . . Arguably, then, it is not just marrying monkeys, but those who occupy proximal category membership, that is, those who *approximate* marrying monkeys, who are consigned to queer life" (96).

25 This persistent humanism is visible especially in contrast with the work of the painter and writer Leonora Carrington, where, as Janet Lyon argues, "species-hybridity . . . is so robustly ordinary a condition that the term 'hybrid' has no purchase; it can only register as an aberration from the standpoint of humanism" ("Carrington's Sensorium" 163).

26 For a discussion of the relation of Wells's Beast People to genetic hybrids, see Chris Danta, "The Future Will Have Been Animal." Susan Squier also discusses hybridity with regard to Moreau and other texts, noting that the concept of hybridity always contains an "implicit racial . . . ideology" (95). Edwards gives the most thorough exploration of the science in and the scientific context of the novel.

27 In an article in *BioEdge*, Hyun says that he is not concerned about "moral human-ization" because scientists will "target where the human cells will go" (Symons). But in the same article an opposing view is offered by David King, who finds "these experiments disturbing. . . . The concern about mixing species touches something deep in the human psyche and our culture that is hard to put into words. It is not about some 'wisdom of nature,' but about the unwisdom of scien-tists" (Symons).

28 I view objections to Singer's elevation of nonhuman beings' interests quite dif-ferently than I do objections to his comparisons between intellectually disabled human beings and nonhuman animals. The former objections seem grounded in an investment in a metaphysical, ultimately religious faith in the unique value of human beings that causes immense suffering to nonhuman beings; and so I support Singer's work in elevating their interests. But the latter objections rightly condemn the separation of intellectually disabled human beings from the rest of "us," a separation that elevates nondisabled human beings above both nonhuman animals and intellectually disabled human beings. I do not find it either ethical or logically necessary to judge the value of lives based on their intellectual (or other) capacities (see Kittay, "The Personal," 408). Bernstein argues that capacities are not a sound basis for giving preference to a being's interests (27ff) and includes a section entitled "The Problem with Valuing Capacities" (111–128).

29 Melinda Hall writes that "transhumanists, the strongest proponents of enhance-ment, do not endorse the concept of the species-typical body as normative, as they find all current human bodies wanting and in need of improvement" (xii).

30 Related ideologies of cure are identified by Lennard Davis's phrase "enforcing nor-malcy" and Robert McRuer's term "compulsory able-bodiedness" (2).

31 An earlier version of this line read: "You could hardly feel a particle of my disgust if you were surrounded by all the most horrible cripples and maniacs it is possible to conceive" (Philmus 168).

32 Wells did see some generative possibilities in disability. In his *Experiment in Autobiography*, he noted a benefit that resulted from his own convalescence from tuberculosis: "Yet, though I did not realize it, I was getting through something of very great importance in my education during these months of outward inaction. I was reading . . . poetry and imaginative work with an attention to language and

style that I had never given these aspects of literature before" (250). This benefit had to be realized later, however, when he was no longer ill, and he does not generalize this potential.

33 Influential criminologist Cesare Lombroso defined criminality as atavism as well, and lumped it with disability (and other undesirable traits such as Jewishness; see Harrowitz). As explained by his daughter, Gina Lombroso-Ferrero, he believed that the "aetiology of crime, therefore, mingles with that of all kinds of degeneration: rickets, deafness, monstrosity, hairiness, and cretinism, of which crime is only a variation" (Harris 243). Wells cites Lombroso in "The Province of Pain" and explores atavism in *Moreau* in the eventual reversion of the Beast People; in a later novella, *The Croquet Player*, he uses the skull of a Neanderthal to focus the narrator's fear of human beastliness (Harris, 250).

34 Francis Galton famously wrote, "What nature does blindly, slowly and ruthlessly, man may do providently, quickly and kindly" (n.p.).

35 I am indebted to Sarah Cole for alerting me to the character of Karenin.

36 Danta writes, "*The Island of Doctor Moreau* helps us to see that, rather than dispelling the old superstitions of the mythological domain of monstrosity, the chimeras of modern molecular biology have instead brought us closer than ever to perceiving our own monstrosity" ("The Future" 697).

37 Meat-eating is associated in the novel with savagery and animality and is therefore prohibited for the Beast People. But as E. E. Snyder points out, while the Beast People are required to refrain from eating flesh to become more human, the human beings are allowed to eat rabbit, as well as mutton, and Prendick is revived after being shipwrecked by drinking a bloody concoction (216). Moreau seems to abstain from meat, however. Lee demonstrates the similarity of the role of meat-eating in *Moreau* to the role of meat-eating in late-Victorian vegetarian arguments: it was seen as animalistic while vegetarianism was believed to promote human evolution (262).

38 As Rohman describes this moment, "Being embodied, experiencing pain, having instincts and fears, these qualities mark one's humanity as profoundly as any other qualities" (*Stalking*, 75–6).

39 In "Equity and Mercy" Nussbaum points out that juries should not disregard emotion, because "sentiment, passion, and sympathy would be a prominent part of the appropriate (and rational) deliberative process, where those sentiments are based in the juror's 'reading' of the defendant's history" (120). Vint also notes this aspect of *Moreau*, arguing that by displaying Moreau's "disembodied perception of self," Wells "anticipates the critique of objectivity offered by feminist critics of science like Haraway and Sandra Harding, who point out that such a construction of objectivity is connected to a series of intellectual moves that separate man from body and nature and posit the scientist as the neutral, unmarked, and unconnected observer—a distorted and limited perspective" (89).

40 One of the questions motivating Taylor's study of animal and disability oppression raises the related issue: "How does an animal become an object?" (*Beasts*, xv).

41 Sherborne suggests that this aspect of the novel was inspired by Swift and shows that "we are not, as Christianity claims, heavenly spirits trapped in material bodies but animals whose evolution has left us tormented by regressive desires and impossible ideals" (113).

42 In *Evolution and Ethics*, T. H. Huxley calls "pain or suffering" the "baleful product of evolution." He adds that "the consummation [of "pain or suffering"] is not reached in man, the mere animal; nor in man, the whole or half savage; but only in man, the member of an organized polity. And it is a necessary consequence of his attempt to live in this way; that is, under those conditions which are essential to the full development of his noblest powers" (Harris 220–21).

43 McConnell agrees, writing that the novel's "final effect is not to dignify the animal in us as much as it is to degrade the human" (104).

44 The developing science of evolution also implied the possibility of degeneration, a possibility that caught Wells's imagination and that can be seen in the novel's interest in reversion. For a discussion of degeneration and Moreau, see McLean, chapter 3, "'An Infernally Rum Place: *The Island of Doctor Moreau* and Degeneration.'"

45 This exemplifies a point Ryan makes about Freud in *Animal Theory*: "Freudian psychoanalysis may seek to de-centre the human subject, but it is in danger of re-centring it elsewhere by using animals as vehicles in the process of arriving at a particular notion of what a healthy or unhealthy human subject is" (31).

46 Danta's observation about "Moreau's dream" applies also to Wells himself: "Moreau's dream of the anaesthetic body of the coming man—the body that has somehow evolved to do without the warning system of physical pain—is merely one more baseless attempt by humans to separate their species from the rest of the animal kingdom" ("The Future," 701). Snyder agrees, writing that "Moreau's claim is more ideological than factual. He argues for utility as a measure of progress, and requires some measure of what is good and what is not; he demands a purpose to evolution beyond pure survival" (224).

47 This is one way that, as Parrinder argues, Wells's optimism and pessimism about humanity are "inextricably . . . allied" in *Moreau* (*H. G. Wells* 27).

CHAPTER 2. OLD LIVES

I would like to thank Patrick Kain and Teresa Blankmeyer Burke for their advice about philosophical sources relevant to this chapter. I would also like to thank the anonymous reviewers for the *Journal of Medical Humanities* for their helpful suggestions.

1 Indeed, Chris Mooney claims that the field really took off in the early 1970s, when two pioneers of bioethics used ideas from *Brave New World* to challenge in vitro fertilization in leading American medical journals: Leon Kass in the *New England Journal of Medicine* and Paul Ramsey in the *Journal of the American Medical Association* (Mooney, 7). And the book's influence continues: according to Jennifer Doudna and Samuel Sternberg, "Rarely does the topic of germline gene editing

come up in the media nowadays without the book being directly or indirectly referenced" (240).

2 The term "compulsory youthfulness" descends from Adrienne Rich's "compulsory heterosexuality" through Robert McRuer's "compulsory able-bodiedness."

3 It is important to keep in mind that some abilities often improve in old age, that the narrative of decline is not the single narrative of aging. As Margaret Gullette persuasively argues, "Decline is a metaphor as hard to contain as dye. Once it has tinged our expectations of the future (sensations, rewards, status, power, voice) with peril, it tends to stain our experiences, our views of others, our explanatory systems, and then our retrospective judgments" (11). Gullette's assertion that decline is a culturally constructed narrative is bolstered by the research of S. van der Geest among the Aku people of southern Ghana. His findings on this point are summarized by Ehni et al.: "Interestingly, van der Geest observes that the local language of the people he studied does not have a term for 'old' as an adjective for people. Instead, the verb 'to grow' is used. The way to express 'I am old' in the language of the Aku people would be to say 'I have grown.' Ageing is thus seen as growth rather than as decline" (265).

4 A 2015 forum in the online journal *AgeCultureHumanities*, edited by Erin Lamb and entitled *Age and/as Disability*, brings age studies and disability studies together in exciting ways.

5 However, the important character of Crasweller, a hearty and strong man approaching the "fixed period" of sixty-seven years, demonstrates that Trollope was well aware that this is not true of all older people.

6 A response to the article by a Brown University philosophy professor similarly zeroes in on Emanuel's attitude toward people who are not productive: "Dr. Emanuel's suggestion that it would be good for 'each of us to ask whether our consumption is worth our contribution' will hardly attract those who think that even the unproductive have an unalienable right to life, liberty, and the pursuit of happiness" (Ackerman).

7 Dennett claims "that this is not a proposal designed primarily to save the taxpayers money or preserve the inheritances of the living, but a proposal designed to reduce the large and inevitably growing amount of pointless suffering that our other technologies have in store for us if we don't change something." But very soon afterward he makes the point quoted here about using up more than our fair share of the world's resources (n.p.). One redeeming feature of Dennett's proposal is that it would remove individual judgments about quality of life: he is aware that "wherever there are such decisions to be made, about quality of life, or degree of impairment or suffering, there are inevitable opportunities for undesirable motives to creep into the mix: greed or impatience or on the side of the soon-to-die guilt about staying alive beyond one's allotted span" (n.p.). Nevertheless, his project involves making sweeping claims about quality of life at the level of populations, as he seeks a method of universal, sudden, programmed death to avoid the physical and mental disabilities that can accompany old age.

8 In the conclusion to her wonderful article "Unspeakable Conversations," Harriet McBryde Johnson insists upon the "undeniable reality of disabled lives well lived" (519).

9 As Rebecca West describes it in a contemporaneous review, "Promiscuity is a social duty [in the Brave New World], since it discourages far more than puritanism the growth of that disintegrating factor, love" (199).

10 The 1946 Foreword can be found in the 2006 Harper Perennial edition of *Brave New World* and *Brave New World Revisited*.

11 Discussing *Brave New World* in the context of other dystopias, George Woodcock describes "falsification or destruction of history and the sense of the past" as common to "anti-Utopias" (90).

12 Thomas Cole reads *Oedipus at Colonus* differently, as a story that affirms the motif of life as a journey, and in Oedipus's case, a triumphant one. Quoting Christine Downing, he describes the ending of Oedipus's life this way: "His blessed death, Sophocles seems to be saying, is appropriate to one 'who has lived long enough to understand the meaning of his own story'" (xxxiv).

13 As Laura Frost points out, "As much as it is a nightmare of a totalitarian, genetically engineered future . . . *Brave New World* is also a cautionary tale about a world in which artifacts of high culture are held under lock and key while the populace is supplied with 'imbecile' entertainment" (447).

14 And as Lenore Manderson notes, the absence of change can sometimes be a pathology: "Pathology is not an absolute. . . . Rather it exists only in relation to a given, defined situation. . . . Aging and frailty instantiate this, for regardless of bodily and mental function and capability, a person is 'normal' (and not living in a pathological state) to the extent that there is consistency in relation to other older people and to how they were before. Biological variety and change are inevitable; thus pathology can include the absence of change at organic and phenomenological levels" (35).

15 Huxley borrowed this phrasing from his earlier novel *Crome Yellow* (1921), where Mr. Wimbush comments on farming techniques: "'Personally,' he said, 'I rather like seeing fourteen pigs grow where only one grew before. The spectacle of so much crude life is refreshing'" (19).

16 In Julian Huxley's story "The Tissue-Culture King" (1927), the Moreau-like scientist takes tissue cultures from the king of an African tribe, telling the people that this increases and spreads the protective power of the king's body. Like Aldous Huxley's Director, the scientist calls this process *"mass production"* (157).

17 Evelyn Cobley describes the society as "an efficient system from which all wasteful residues have been eliminated" (285).

18 This death conditioning contrasts with the withholding of information from the clones in Ishiguro's *Never Let Me Go*, discussed in chapter 4; the clones are taught that they will eventually donate organs and "complete," without quite understanding what those processes mean.

19 Nancee Reeves points out that a wide variety of late nineteenth-century speculative fiction included euthanasia schemes, although she notes that "in the majority
of late-Victorian future fiction, euthanasia is merely implied" (103).

20 In a brief article about the influence of James Fries, one of the foremost proponents of "healthy aging," Aimee Swartz writes, "Today, with data strongly con
firming the hypothesis, compression of morbidity has become widely recognized
as the dominant paradigm for healthy aging, at both individual and policy levels,
and is thought to have laid the foundation for successful health promotion and
programs" (1163).

21 For Huxley, such managed deaths at prescribed times are a crucial means of
population control. In the novel he has the Director refer to population control
in the first chapter, saying that "our business is to stabilize the population at this
moment" (4). In Brave New World Revisited (1958), he places great importance on
the issue, writing that "the problem of rapidly increasing numbers in relation to
natural resources, to social stability and to the well-being of individuals—this is
now the central problem of mankind" (242).

22 In his late utopia Island (1962), Huxley shows the importance of meaningful deaths
by having Susila explain the "art of dying" to Will and then depicting her mother-
in-law Lakshmi's death as solemn and profound (280ff). As Lakshmi is dying, Susila
reminds her to be present: "You've got to know you're here. All the time" (298). This
mindful dying is diametrically opposed to the deaths in Brave New World.

23 One philosopher who objects to the idea that it is useful to view life as a narrative is Galen Strawson, who does not dismiss the importance of viewing life in
this way for many, but objects to it as a universal necessity for a good life, because
"many of us are not Narrative in this sense" ("Unstoried," 285). In an earlier article
entitled "Against Narrativity," Strawson argues that both the descriptive claim, that
everyone views his or her life as a story, and the normative claim, that everyone
ought to view his or her life as a story, are false.

24 Meilaender writes that "our lives have a narrative shape, making our experience
something other than a succession of bare, momentary presents" (Should We Live,
31). David Carr notes that "we may not find it possible to separate 'living one's
life' from 'reflecting on one's life'" (180). Small, however, questions the value of life
narratives as they pertain to old age, especially in her chapter 3; but what she really seems to be objecting to is not narrative in general, but narratives of relentless
questing or progress. Small points out that we cannot fit old age into a continual
progress narrative, but she thereby overlooks the winding-down stage of narrative: the denouement.

25 Within the study of narrative it is also common to parallel the dynamics of plot
with those of human lives. As Peter Brooks writes in Reading for the Plot, "We
live immersed in narrative, recounting and reassessing the meaning of our past
actions, anticipating the outcome of our future projects, situating ourselves at the
intersection of several stories not yet completed" (3).

26 As Jackie Leach Scully points out, this does not mean we identify ourselves or our life narratives in narrow, wholly consistent terms. She writes: "Narrative identity indeed may be more tolerant of indeterminacy, disjunction, and ongoing reinterpretation . . . than we generally assume" (*Disability Bioethics*, 130).

27 This situation is obviously dramatically different from ours, since for us "aging is . . . not just an accumulation of years but an advancing and changing point of view" (Carr, 183).

28 In *Island*, the problems described here are solved differently: families are broadened by including twenty other sets of biological families in each child's life. The resulting family-networks are described as "inclusive, unpredestined and voluntary" (103).

29 In Trollope's *The Fixed Period* (1882), the plan to euthanize everyone at age sixty-seven fails largely because a daughter intercedes to extend the life of her father, and even the son of the zealous narrator says he would not like to "deposit" his own father (150). Huxley sees that the absence of family bonds is a necessary precondition of the Brave New World's excision of old age.

30 Carr writes similarly that aging can be seen not as a series of events but "as a changing perspective on the whole life . . . and as a creative process of self-formation and self-interpretation" (184).

31 Deery writes aptly: "Instead of being scientists and leaders, the women we encounter perform auxiliary, service roles in nursing, teaching, secretarial and factory work—the sort of jobs their contemporaries were in fact given in Huxley's society. These women therefore don't do science; they have science done to them" (264).

32 The Yeats phrase I quote in the introduction to this chapter seems appropriate because the novel focuses almost exclusively on the struggles of its male characters, and when it refers to older people becoming reflective, it is always to old *men*. But certainly the Brave New World, like our own, is even more intolerant of old women. As Thomas Cole writes about his grandmothers' shame and revulsion about aging, "These feelings reflect our culture's intractable hostility to physical decline and mental decay, imposed with particular vengeance on older women" (xxiv).

33 In an article advocating human genetic enhancement, Nick Bostrom argues that enhancement could just as likely have a positive effect on people with disabilities as a negative one. He writes that "the practice of germ-line enhancement might lead to better treatment of people with disabilities, because a general demystification of the genetic contributions to human traits could make it clearer that people with disabilities are not to blame for their disabilities and a decreased incidence of some disabilities could lead to more assistance being available for the remaining affected people to enable them to live full, unrestricted lives through various technological and social supports" (109). This seems contrary to what we see in both fiction and real life: without a critical mass of people with a given need (for example, elevators or captions or ramps), there is less incentive, not more, to meet that need. In theory there might be more money available for interventions, but

who with the power to enact them will *care* about the few people who need them? Certainly in the Brave New World, no accommodations are made for Linda.

34 In *Crome Yellow* (1921), killing nonhuman animals when they are no longer productive is labeled as sensible by the eugenicist Mr. Scogan but as cruel by Anne Wimbush: "'But how practical, how eminently realistic!' said Mr. Scogan. 'In this farm we have a model of sound paternal government. Make them breed, make them work, and when they're past working or breeding or begetting, slaughter them.' 'Farming seems to be mostly indecency and cruelty,' said Anne" (18).

35 Similar ideas animate the euthanasia plan in Trollope's *The Fixed Period*: "A judge shall be deaf on the bench when younger men below him can hear with accuracy. His voice shall have descended to a poor treble, or his eyesight shall be dim and failing. At any rate, his limbs will have lost all that robust agility which is needed for the adequate performance of the work of the world. It is self-evident that at sixty-five a man has done all that he is fit to do" (8–9).

36 For a discussion of the difficulties of "putting oneself in another's shoes" see Scully, *Disability Bioethics*, 52–75.

37 Holstein, Waymack, and Parks argue similarly that "human beings should be viewed as beings-in-relationship—as being *necessarily* and not only contingently ensconced in relationships of care" (xiv).

38 Firchow describes this state of affairs by saying that "in the Fordian society, the individual is no longer free to endanger himself or his group by refusing to indulge his impulses" (314).

39 Deery points out that the society places on women the obligation to consent to sex, especially with higher-caste men: "For women, it seems, 'free love' means always having to say yes" (261).

40 Adorno disagrees with Huxley, however, about the possibilities of collectivist societies and critiques the novel for its unwitting nostalgia and reactionary politics (106, 112). He contends that "unreflective individualism asserts itself as though the horror which transfixes the novel were not itself the monstrous offspring of individualist society" (115).

41 In his review Bertrand Russell stresses that open futures are illusory because we are all indoctrinated (badly in our culture, well in the Brave New World), but that we rely on our belief in them: "We have a notion that we can choose what we will be, and that we should not wish to be robbed of this choice by scientific manipulators. . . . What we cling to so desperately is the illusion of freedom, an illusion which is tacitly negated by all moral instruction and all propaganda. To us human life would be intolerable without this illusion" (211–12).

42 James Fries has said, "We cannot compress morbidity indefinitely, but the paradigm of a long, healthy life with a relatively rapid terminal decline is most certainly an attainable ideal at both a population level and individual level" (Swartz, 1166).

43 Rosemarie Garland-Thomson's article "Misfits: A Feminist Materialist Disability Concept" explores the idea of fits and misfits between varying bodies and minds and varying environments.

44 Meckier points out that Newman's and Biran's views are diametrically opposed to those expressed by D. H. Lawrence in *Apocalypse*, arguing that in *Brave New World* Huxley is grappling with many of Lawrence's views ("On D. H. Lawrence and Death").

45 John's objections likely owe something to H. G. Wells's Mr. Catskill in the utopian novel *Men Like Gods* (1923) and/or to Charlotte Haldane's Christopher in *Man's World* (1926). Mr. Catskill protests to the Utopians, "You have been getting away from conflicts and distresses. Have you not also been getting away from the living and quivering realities of life?" (Wells, *Men Like Gods,* 99). Haldane's Christopher similarly worries that "the individual has been gradually pushed out" and proclaims, "Perverse, reactionary, I am. But my emotions are myself. I refuse to purge myself of them as of waste matter. I will keep them!" (181, 101). Huxley set out to satirize Wells's utopia in *Brave New World*, though the novel subsequently grew into a much more complex project (Bradshaw, 161).

46 Huxley apparently agreed to a great extent with this belief, writing that "abolishing obstacles, ["man"] abolishes half his pleasures. And at the same time he abolishes most of his dignity as a human being" (qtd. in Firchow, 315). In *Island*, he has a character say that "it wouldn't be right if you could take away the pain of a bereavement; you'd be less than human" (112).

47 Rentsch suggests that we see old age as "a time of life in which the crossing of finitude and meaning, fulfillment and limitedness can be recognized and understood" (359). H. G. Wells's character Barnstaple similarly values the chance (when he thinks he is about to be killed) "to look death in the face for a time, to have leisure to write *finis* in one's mind, to think over life and such living as one had done and to think it over with a detachment, an independence, that only an entire inability to alter one jot of it now could give" (*Men Like Gods*, 226).

48 Harris does also discuss circumstances in which older people's lives might be considered worth less than younger people's lives, especially in his section on "the fair innings" argument (90–94). Silvers offers a brief critique of the "fair innings" argument (217). And Donovan argues that most of the time, "either/or dilemmas in real life can be turned into both/ands" (76).

49 Trollope's character Crasweller names the knowability of the "fixed period" as one of its worst aspects: "The fixed day, coming at a certain known hour, the feeling that it must come" (157).

50 Melinda C. Hall establishes that for transhumanists, embodiment generally and disability in particular are understood as risk (23 and passim).

CHAPTER 3. DISABLED LIVES

I am grateful to John Duvall, Rosemarie Garland-Thomson, and Rachel Adams for reading and commenting on earlier versions of this chapter.

1 Tod Chambers notes that "bioethicists in analyzing moral problems have often drawn upon literary texts as sources for 'rich cases,' for they have long recognized

that the traditional genre of the ethics case was limited in its portrayal of the complexity of the moral landscape of actual medical practice" (79).

2 Eva Kittay writes that "only by considering [her intellectually disabled daughter, Sesha] in the fullness of her joys and capacities can we view her impairments in light of her life, her interests, her happiness—and not as projections of her 'able' parents or of an able-biased society" ("When Caring," 560).

3 In a recent address to the American Philosophical Association, Kittay asserted that "the idea that one can compare intrinsic properties across species without regard to the species compared is flawed and unsupported" ("Moral Significance," 30). Kari Weil discusses the way dogs "read" scents, highlighting the complex interpretation of smells in which dogs engage (10).

4 Certainly some literary representations similarly strip minor disabled characters of context. In *Extraordinary Bodies*, Rosemarie Garland-Thomson writes that "textual descriptions are overdetermined: they invest the traits, qualities, and behaviors of their characters with much rhetorical influence simply by omitting—and therefore erasing—other factors or traits that might mitigate or complicate the delineations. . . . Consequently, literary texts necessarily make disabled characters into freaks, stripped of normalizing contexts and engulfed by a single stigmatic trait" (10–11). I disagree that this is a *necessary* feature of literary representation, however, and would argue that in many cases, even in spite of itself, literature provides background that fleshes out even its stigmatized characters.

5 For early explorations of resistant or oppositional reading, see Judith Fetterley and Patrocinio Schweickart.

6 As I discuss in the introduction, Singer's view of which capacities to value most highly is both ableist and speciesist (see Taylor, 146).

7 Singer outlines these views in several places, including *Practical Ethics* and *Should the Baby Live? The Problem of Handicapped Infants*, which he wrote with Helga Kuhse. I discuss this argument further below.

8 Far from being a thing of the past by the end of World War II, eugenics flourished in the deep south through the 1940s and 1950s (Larson, 138, 157), with the highest number of eugenic sterilizations in Georgia occurring in 1963 (Kaelber, "Georgia"). Indeed, Wendy Kline argues that the baby boom of the 1950s was the "triumph eugenicists had been looking for" (156).

9 Kathleen Patterson writes that O'Connor "knew first hand that the way others viewed her could be as disabling as her physical condition" and that her "assumptions guarantee that her readers see disability as one of many components in the social construction of identity" (95, 96). Jeffrey Folks ascribes to O'Connor "a genuine compassion toward all adversity and a genuine openness to all otherness" resulting from her religious beliefs combined with her experiences with lupus (82).

10 Davidson makes a related point when he notes that "whereas Romantic poets could celebrate the simple fool . . . modernist writers tended to treat mental dis-

ability as a pathological counterpart to cultural decay" ("Paralyzed Modernities" 77). In a similar vein, Lyon describes Woolf's reaction to "idiocy": it "represents the limits of her imagination, and thus the undoing of her last, best defense against her own dissolution" ("Asylum Road" 569).

11 Garland-Thomson makes a vital case for conserving disability and disabled lives across several essays and lectures (e.g., "Eugenic World Building and Disability," "A Habitable World," "Human Biodiversity Conservation"). Kafer's *Feminist, Queer, Crip* describes possibilities for desiring disabled futures. In *Frontiers of Justice*, "The Capabilities of People with Cognitive Disabilities," and other work, Martha Nussbaum argues that theories of justice have not "adequately addressed" the needs of cognitively disabled people ("Capabilities," 77). Kittay's and Carlson's edited collection, *Cognitive Disability and Its Challenge to Moral Philosophy*, takes up the question of how moral theories might be adjusted to incorporate the rights of intellectually disabled people. In *Love's Labor*, Kittay delves into the ethics and politics of caring for dependent people. In *The Faces of Intellectual Disability*, Carlson continues her exploration of the role and meaning of intellectual disability in philosophy and culture. And in *The Capacity Contract*, Stacy Simplican analyzes issues of citizenship for intellectually disabled people. Simplican, it must be noted, objects to interventions into Rawlsian contract theory such as Nussbaum's, which in her view do not go far enough to reject the idea of capacity as the ground for justice (86).

12 For an informative discussion of weed metaphors and other comparisons of "unfit" human beings to objects, see Gerald O'Brien; for discussions of selective abortion, see Marsha Saxton and Ruth Hubbard.

13 O'Connor refers to both old and young Tarwater as "Tarwater," which can be confusing. Hereafter I will refer to old Tarwater as Mason, and to young Tarwater as Tarwater.

14 In this case, Sheppard is fatally wrong. Norton is so swayed by Rufus's talk of heaven that he kills himself in an effort to be reunited with his dead mother, whom he thinks he sees waving to him when he looks through a telescope his father has bought for Rufus.

15 In spite of her efforts to distance herself from the devaluation of Bishop, Susan Srigley does not always take a compassionate or just view of Bishop: she refers to him as being mentally dead (119–120) and calls him an "idiot" not only when quoting the text but also when speaking in her own voice. Srigley understands the text's use of Bishop as a symbol of the pull of faith, but does not remark the dehumanization involved in this symbolic use.

16 The same phrase is used in "The Lame Shall Enter First," where Sheppard thinks his own son is mediocre, even though he has "had every advantage" (*Complete*, 449). Sheppard wants to provide these advantages to the Tarwater-like character Rufus, who disdains them.

17 In a letter to Grace Terry, O'Connor explained "that Tarwater's call is real, that his true vocation is to answer it. Tarwater is not sick or crazy but really called to be

a prophet—a vocation which I take seriously, though the modern reader is not liable to" (Cash 69).

18 In one manuscript version, Rayber's son is named George Fall (Driggers and Dunn 94).

19 Tarwater later similarly protests that he'd "as soon baptize a dog as him. It would be as much use" (144).

20 The injustice of the claim that disabled people have no future is brought home by comparison to Emily Rapp's heartbreaking memoir about her son Ronan, who died of Tay-Sachs shy of his third birthday. Rapp writes that Ronan "had, literally, no future" (53).

21 Nicholas Agar defends genetic engineering by saying that it is reasonable for parents to try to "give their children the best possible starts in life" (*Liberal Eugenics* 14). In *Choosing Children* Jonathan Glover tends to talk more about "human flourishing" but agrees that it is reasonable for parents to want to give their children "a better start in life" (34). The idea of a "start" participates in rhetoric of a race or path to achievement that seems influenced by a capitalist model of success.

22 Singer's assumptions that someone with Down syndrome cannot be expected to participate in good conversations, help aging parents, and so on, are being belied by people with Down syndrome doing those things now that they are being educated instead of institutionalized. For a discussion of Singer's assumptions about people with Down syndrome, see Bérubé, "Equality, Freedom, and/or Justice For All," from which I quote in the introduction.

23 The insistence on the child's *potential* as the source and object of parental love helps to explain the position Singer takes about a family who takes care of an unresponsive teenager, a position detailed in Harriet McBryde Johnson's "Unspeakable Conversations." Stipulating that such a teenager is absolutely unconscious and has absolutely no chance of improvement, Singer says that continuing to care for such a person is "weird," whereas Johnson says that it could be "profoundly beautiful" (514). Eunjung Kim comments about Singer's view that it implies that "it is purposeless, worthless, or pointless to care for an unresponsive human being under the condition of the 'absolute impossibility' of improvement, as if the potential to improve were the only justification for care" (95).

24 Singer writes, "The principle of equal consideration of interests prohibits making our readiness to consider the interests of others depend on their abilities or other characteristics, apart from the characteristic of having interests" (*Practical Ethics*, 21). But as we see in his qualification of his statement that "the moral worth of individuals is not dependent on their abilities" with the clause, "except where they have very limited intellectual capacities" ("Shopping" 315), he believes there are intellectual disabilities severe enough to warrant viewing a human being as *not having interests.*

25 Harriet McBryde Johnson refers to this as Singer's "replacement-baby theory" (510).

26 As Tara Powell writes, "Several critics have called Rayber 'the mechanical man,' as his relationship with reality is mediated both literally and figuratively by 'mechanism'" (44).

27 I discuss the representation of deaf characters in McCullers, Eudora Welty, and Elizabeth Bowen in *Bodies of Modernism*, chapter 3.

28 As a religious Christian, O'Connor values the afterlife more than the mortal life for all her characters, as can be seen in stories such as "The River." She can thus, admittedly, seem callous about the deaths of many of her characters. But my claim here is not that she values Bishop's mortal life too little in an absolute sense; it is rather that she values it too little relative to the lives of characters without intellectual disabilities.

29 Carlson gives many examples of earlier and contemporary philosophers proclaiming the subordinate status of "idiots" and "imbeciles," often vis-à-vis animals (see e.g., 107–113).

30 McMahan does acknowledge what Kittay argues in her article, that every child is "some mother's child" (Kittay, "Personal" 412) when he writes that "each severely retarded human being is someone's child. . . . And the rest of us are morally bound to respect these people's feelings and commitments" (*Ethics*, 232). In his view we need to care about the interests of nondisabled people; if they care about mentally disabled people, then we should care about them too, but only by extension. Carlson writes that in such an indirect-duty view, "the intellectually disabled are not persons. They are owed respect and justice only by virtue of their relationship to non-disabled family members who *are* persons" (2).

31 The textual descriptions of Bishop do not seem to indicate that he has Down syndrome (if a fictional character can be said to "have" a condition), though it doesn't seem important to me whether he does or not. Yaeger's assumption may be an example of what Ellen Samuels describes as a "fantasy of identification" that seeks to include "a verifiable, biological mark of identity" (2).

32 Lyon's main focus is intellectual disability, and she gives an insightful reading of what it means for Woolf to gradually come to see intellectual disability in what at first appeared "normal." She notes, too, that Woolf can use Septimus, who is mad, as "an aesthetic conduit," whereas the "maimed file of lunatics" she encounters in the street represent "impasses of the face beyond which her aesthetics cannot and will not go" ("Asylum Road" 569).

33 I am grateful to Stephanie Larson for pointing out the dog imagery. In a very early manuscript version of *Violent*, Rayber and his wife adopt a baby gorilla; when she is stolen and killed they have a son to fill the gap (Driggers and Dunn, 92). In a later version, Rayber tells Tarwater that his son Bishop is "a kind of superior vegetable" (Driggers and Dunn, 100). This textual history demonstrates O'Connor's investment in humanism, confirming that her comparisons of Bishop to a dog are not meant to be transgressive or posthumanist.

34 This translation is from the Douay-Rheims Bible, the version O'Connor used for the title of the novel.

35 That Grimes's assertion was maintained through peer-review and copyediting, at the journal of *Religion and Literature*, no less, is an alarming sign of a continuity between Nazi views of disabled people and those of our own society.

36 Simplican demonstrates that such exclusion on the basis of capacity is of long and distinguished standing and that disability has been "part of the conversation about political subjectivity *all along*, even before political theory took up the question of identity politics" (26).

37 In Kittay's article "On the Margins of Moral Personhood," she lays out her argument "against the view that such intrinsic psychological capacities as rationality and autonomy are requisites for claims of justice, a good quality of life, and the moral consideration of personhood" (100). After engaging in detail with McMahan's denial of full personhood to what he calls the "congenitally severely mentally retarded," she argues that we have overvalued the role rationality can play in being a part of a moral community and undervalued other qualities such as "giving care and responding appropriately to care, empathy and fellow feeling; a sense of what is harmonious and loving; and a capacity for kindness and an appreciation for those who are kind" (122). As Kelly Oliver points out, Kittay does not challenge the idea that only humans are persons ("Service Dogs," 248). Oliver writes: "Many proponents of rights for disabled persons and for their inclusion in the moral community insist on their inherent dignity or worth as human beings, apart from any specific abilities. Yet, too often, these arguments are based on redrawing a human-animal divide that places all animals on one side and all humans on the other" ("Service Dogs," 249).

38 As Eli Clare writes, "At the center of cure lies eradication, and the many kinds of violence that accompany it" (26). But he also cautions us to pay attention to cure's complexity: "As an ideology seeped into every corner of white Western thought and culture, cure rides on the back of *normal* and *natural*. Insidious and pervasive, it impacts most of us. In response, we need neither a wholehearted acceptance nor an outright rejection of cure, but rather a broad-based grappling" (14).

39 In addition to Getz and Grimes, many other critics respond to Bishop in the same contemptuous way the characters in the novel do. P. Travis Kroeker calls him a "hideous mistake of nature" (145). Jordan Cofer makes no evaluative comment on Tarwater's murder of Bishop but describes the rape of Tarwater as "heinous" (93). And John Desmond describes Rayber's relationship with Bishop as "emotionally powerful, psychologically credible, and moving" (144). Given that Rayber would have drowned Bishop except for a "failure of nerve" (O'Connor, *Violent*, 169), calling this relationship "moving" demonstrates a disquieting degree of ableism.

40 Undoubtedly because of its clear symbolic importance, O'Connor includes the fountain scene twice. The first instance, from the point of view of the narrator but focalized mildly by Rayber, reads: "They had come out into the center of the park, a concrete circle with a fountain in the middle of it. Water rushed from the mouth of a stone lion's head into a shallow pool and the little boy was flying toward it, his arms flailing like a windmill. In a second he was over the side and

in. 'Too late, goddammit,' Rayber muttered, 'he's in'" (145). The second instance, focalized by Tarwater, reads: "They had walked deeper into the park. . . . The path widened and they were faced with an open space in the middle of the park, a concrete circle with a fountain in the center of it. Water rushed out of the mouth of a stone lion's head into a shallow pool below and as soon as the dim-witted boy saw the water, he gave a whoop and galloped off toward it, flapping his arms like something released from a cage. . . . 'Too late, goddamit' [sic], the schoolteacher muttered, 'he's in'" (164). In the version from Tarwarter's point of view O'Connor expands the scene in ways that highlight the symbolism of baptism. For example, "A blinding brightness fell on the lion's tangled marble head and gilded the stream of water rushing from his mouth" (164).

CHAPTER 4. CLONED LIVES

1   A paper published in *Science* in August 2017 discusses progress in using the gene-editing technique CRISPR-Cas9 to edit virus genes out of pigs so that organs grown in them will be more safely implantable into humans (Niu et al). This scientific "progress" stands to open another arena in which nonhuman animals can be exploited.

2   Gabriel Rosenberg writes that "technologies of death making are being optimized within the spaces of the slaughterhouses, and the speciative difference that excludes humans from violence is only a contingent, biopolitical effect and hardly timeless and universal" (494).

3   A few critics do question the clones' human status, but as Rachel Carroll rightly claims, "It is not the human status of the clone which is in question in this novel so much as the normative discourses which conspire to contest it" (60). Nathan Snaza similarly writes that "the ethical problem of the novel is less the question of the humanity of the clones than it is the question of how humanely the clones should be treated" (215). Although his focus is on the idea of humanizing education, Snaza sees Hailsham, as I do, as "an attempt at free range production of organs in an industry where factory farming is the standard" (215).

4   Tommy tells Kathy, "You have to think about how they'd protect themselves, how they'd reach things" (178). Kathy too thinks that "for all their busy, metallic features, there was something sweet, even vulnerable about each of them" (188).

5   Even Jeremy Bentham, widely cited father of the animal rights movement, just before asking why "the law [should] refuse its protection to any sensitive being," still asserts that it "ought to be lawful to kill animals, but not to torment them" (562).

6   In this discussion Agamben draws on Hannah Arendt's explication of the two Greek terms for what we call "life."

7   The Agamben connection is not Black's main topic, however. She explores the role of art, replication, originality, and humanness in the Hailsham universe. While she focuses on the inhuman—the mechanical or manufactured—our arguments dovetail in our shared resistance to valuing only "purely" human lives. She writes that "Ishiguro's inhuman style suggests that only by recognizing what in ourselves

is mechanical, manufactured, and replicated—in a traditional sense, not fully human—will we escape the barbarities committed in the name of preserving purely human life" (786).

8   The denial of souls was of course instrumental in enslaving nonwhite peoples, and their supposed lack of artistic production was used as evidence. As Josie Gill writes, "The Guardians' reduction of the students' art and creativity to functioning as evidence of their humanity echoes the artificial relationship between art and humanity that historically characterized Europeans' judgment of the nonwhite subject" (851).

9   As Jacques Derrida points out "The 'Thou shalt not kill'—with all its consequences, which are limitless—has never been understood within the Judeo Christian tradition, nor apparently by Levinas, as a 'Thou shalt not put to death the living in general'" ("Eating Well," 279).

10 This revulsion is still Madame's dominant feeling about the clones years after Hailsham has closed. When she sees Kathy and Tommy outside her house, "without doubt, she saw and decided in a second *what we were*, because you could see her stiffen—as if a pair of large spiders was set to crawl towards her" (248).

11 Eluned Summers-Bremner argues that animals in *Never Let Me Go* "indicate the donors' compromised humanity, and, as such, ordinary humanity's fears about dying" (154). She argues that humans animalize the clones to try, unsuccessfully, to stave off fears of mortality. I don't share her sense of an impasse in relating to Kathy as a fellow human being, however, and I see no evidence for her suggestion that the animals Tommy draws are mechanical because he is not completely human (157).

12 Anne Whitehead similarly suggests that in "holding open the status of the clones, Ishiguro seems to (re)direct us to the ethical question of whether we can, or should, rely on such absolute categories of difference as 'human' and 'nonhuman'" (65). Neither Whitehead nor Walkowitz expands on her claims about nonhuman animals.

13 In *Frontiers of Justice*, Martha Nussbaum lists "bodily integrity" as one of the capabilities necessary for flourishing for animals as well as for humans (395).

14 For a reading of bestiality laws that define and prohibit sexual contact with animals while exempting animal husbandry practices, see Rosenberg, "How Meat Changed Sex."

15 James McWilliams opens his book *The Modern Savage* with a story of watching a cow "explode into rage" when her calf was taken from her at birth, and how much it reminded him of the feelings he had when his son was taken for medical treatment immediately after his birth—the baby was given to him soon thereafter, but when the medical staff took the baby, he felt "the floor rock beneath [him]" (1–2).

16 Carroll makes interesting use of this aspect of the novel in her exploration of the clones' nonnormative heterosexuality; she argues that they embody "a heterosexual identity which is disempowered and marginalised by heteronormativity" (60). She points out the ways in which the clones are ousted not only from what Michael Warner calls "reprosexuality" (a sexuality based on the logic and temporality of

reproduction and "generational transmission") but also from kinship relations that structure obligation and responsibility. Their exclusion from the sphere of kinship contributes to their being viewed as expendable (65).

17 David DeGrazia discusses the harm to animals of confinement as well as the harms of suffering and death (57–59).

18 In *The Buried Giant*, Ishiguro explores a related phenomenon, "a society that was suffering from a kind of collective amnesia." In that case, however, the amnesia acts to help the people "avoid another cycle of violence" ("Interview: Kazuo Ishiguro").

19 Amy Fitzgerald explains the history of slaughterhouses, which began to be moved out of the public gaze in the late 18th century; in the second half of the 20th century, they were moved to small rural communities where workers are often poorly paid immigrants.

20 Writing from an animal rights perspective, Deborah Slicer uses the same metaphor of schizophrenia to describe our relationship to animals: "As a final consideration, we might consider the affective schizophrenia of a country that spends more money than any other in the world on its 'pets,' while spending more than any other on animal research, much of it involving the use of cats and dogs, hamsters and bunnies. How and why do we circumscribe our collective and individual imaginations in this manner?" (119). While the metaphor of schizophrenia is inaccurate and rather ableist, both Slicer and Pollan are describing a powerful contradiction in our thinking about and treatment of animals.

21 For Ishiguro, the absence of rebellion is part of the theme of "the human capacity to accept what must seem like a limited and cruel fate" ("I Remain Fascinated").

22 The novel doesn't mention the idea that the clones would not exist at all if it weren't for the donation program, but this is another argument often used about farm animals. Taylor discusses this argument in *Beasts* (168–169).

23 James McWilliams also notes the assumption of consent in narratives of "backyard butchery" (104–105, 106).

24 The intensification of industrial animal agriculture is traced in detail in Ellen Silbergeld's *Chickenizing Farms and Food*, especially chapters 2 and 3.

25 In fact, regulations in animal agriculture and worker safety are both narrow and weak. Silbergeld discusses the history of regulations in worker health and food safety in her chapter 1.

26 Ishiguro noted in an interview with the *Paris Review* that he always chooses settings "with great care, because with a setting come all kinds of emotional and historical reverberations" (Hunnewell). Certainly in this case the setting reverberates emotionally, historically, and ethically.

27 The rumors that students who are in love (in a heterosexual relationship) can apply for deferrals represent the clones' attempt to employ heterosexuality as proof of humanness—an attempt that is realistic, given the society's and the novel's heteronormativity, but fruitless.

28 Myra Seaman describes the clones' process of grappling with "the great divide between their understanding of themselves as humans and their society's consid-

eration of them as non-humans—as mere bodies lacking deep interior selves or souls, artificial products of a human science whose sole purpose is to extend the lives of 'genuine' humans" (265).

29 Luke describes the work of James Serpell, who "infers [from his observation that only in cultures that domesticate animals are animals viewed as subhuman] that we denigrate animals *because* we domesticate them—without this denigration, our sympathies would more seriously interfere with the work of slaughtering an animal who has come to trust us through a previously established relationship of feeding and protection. If he is correct here, then the notion of nonhuman inferiority is a thoroughly political doctrine propagated to facilitate animal exploitation" (137).

30 Cora Diamond describes welfarism as the view "that we should avoid causing animals unnecessary suffering, avoid causing them suffering except so far as is necessary to the practices within which we use them. As is pointed out by proponents and opponents of welfarist views, what counts as unnecessary infliction of suffering will be determined by those engaging in the practices in which animals are used" (141).

31 According to humanefacts.org, "even at small slaughter facilities that comply with the strictest humane labeling requirements, animals experience confusion, stress, and terror. Many endure the same horrific agonies that animals in industrial slaughterhouses suffer. These include regular incidents of unsuccessful bolt stunning, in which the animal is not rendered unconscious by the firing of a bolt into his brain, but remains awake and crying out as a second or even third bolt is shot into his skull." Although the rhetoric here is inflammatory, the facts seem to be backed up by multiple sources describing how difficult it is to effectively stun cattle on the first try every time, even when *not* being rushed to stun "four hundred head of cattle every hour."

32 About language use, Derrida writes: "Of course, if one defines language in such a way that it is reserved for what we call man, what is there to say? But if one reinscribes language in a network of possibilities that do not merely encompass it but mark it irreducibly from the inside, everything changes. I am thinking in particular of the mark in general, of the trace, of iterability, of *différance*. These possibilities or necessities, without which there would be no language, *are themselves not only human*" ("Eating Well," 284–285).

33 Bernstein similarly writes that he has conceded for the sake of argument that "no nonhuman animals have even the capacity to entertain future-directed states, that they are incapable of having reflexive thoughts, and that they lack the ability to form plans and projects. In truth, I believe that we have strong empirical evidence that many nonhuman animals have all of these powers. . . . I ask skeptics about this point to peruse the last three to four years of the *New York Times*. You will find quite a few articles and reviews on the latest research on animals, and almost all of it suggests that we humans have been denigrating their abilities, skills, talents, and intelligence for millennia" (146).

34 Douglas Coupland explains that "small, cramped office workstations built of fabric-covered disassemblable wall partitions and inhabited by junior staff members" were referred to as "veal-fattening pens," named after "the small preslaughter cubicles used by the cattle industry" (20). I am grateful to Jennifer Kaufmann-Buhler for pointing this out to me.

35 To be precise, Bradley restricts his argument to the claim that death is bad for a cow; he does not commit himself to arguing that killing a cow is morally wrong. But I fail to see how, in the absence of pressing need (e.g., in self-defense or if there was no other possible food source), we should be permitted to cause harm to a cow by killing it.

36 Bradley seems to be building here on Regan, who writes that "an untimely death is not in the interests of its victims, whether human or animal, independently of whether they understand their own mortality, and thus independently of whether they themselves have a desire to continue to live" (*Case for Animal Rights*, 117–118).

37 In explaining her view that animals need not be conscious of a deprivation in order to be harmed by it, nor have a conscious interest in a good in order to benefit from it, Nussbaum gives this example: "The ability to have loving and supportive relationships with other animals and humans can be a good, even if the animal, raised in isolation, is not aware of the deprivation or pained by it" (*Frontiers*, 386).

38 To be an end in oneself entails having rights that cannot be violated for others' gain. As Regan puts it, "Like us, animals have certain basic moral rights, including in particular the fundamental right to be treated with the respect that, as possessors of inherent value, they are due as a matter of strict justice. Like us, therefore . . . any harm that is done to them must be consistent with the recognition of their equal inherent value and their equal prima facie right not to be harmed" (*Case for Animal Rights*, 329).

39 As I mention in the introduction, Diamond shows that for Weil, "rights can work for justice or injustice"; they have "a moral noncommitment to the good" (128). As an example she discusses the idea that farmers during the Irish famine had a "right" to make profits even though so many hundreds of thousands of Irish people were starving (123–124).

40 Kittay's argument focuses on the rights and moral value of intellectually disabled human beings. In both "The Personal Is Philosophical Is Political" and "At the Margins of Moral Personhood" she argues "against the view that such intrinsic psychological capacities as rationality and autonomy are requisite for claims of justice, a good quality of life, and the moral consideration of personhood" ("At the Margins" 100). Taylor, for her part, focuses on the links between disability oppression and animal oppression.

41 DeGrazia discusses the possibility that it is not *as* wrong to kill a nonhuman animal as it is to kill a human being because "under normal circumstances, death harms humans more" (65); but his discussion elides what he means by "normal circumstances" and how his view might affect views of disabled human beings. His claim is also vulnerable to Bernstein's critique about the "disvalue

of death argument" described above. Nevertheless, DeGrazia's discussion shows that even if killing an animal is *less* wrong than killing a human being, it is still wrong because it forecloses all opportunities for the animal's future pleasure and satisfaction.

42 The reference in the novel is to prison camps where *soldiers* were incarcerated. They were not states of exception, but places governed by rules and subject to the Geneva Convention. Concentration camps, on the other hand, were states of exception subject to no oversight and designed for rounding up, exploiting, abusing, starving, and in many camps gassing undesirable civilians.

43 The scene where Miss Lucy mentions the electrified fences around prison camps highlights the psychological fences around Hailsham. First and most powerfully, there is the rhetoric of the "special" students devoting their bodies to others by "donating" their organs and thereby "completing" their lives/missions. Second, there are the stories designed to make Hailsham students fear the world outside of the school grounds (stories about people who left Hailsham in the "old days" when the Guardians were strict, who ended up dead and dismembered). Third, there is the near-total isolation of the students and their resulting inability to imagine living in the outside world. Fourth, there is the vague but ever-present sense of being watched and tracked, such as when they have to tell the caretaker of the Cottages when they will be back from excursions (in the movie version this sense is made tangible through the tracking bracelets the students have to scan every time they come and go from the Hailsham buildings and then the Cottages). Fifth, there is the revulsion they encounter from anyone who finds out they are clones (the art gallery scene stresses that the owner of the art gallery speaks to them only because she has no idea). Sixth, as Mark Currie points out, there are the relative privileges granted to the clones by the institutions that govern their lives, privileges that provide the illusion of freedom (102–103). Seventh, there are the small vicarious outlets such as watching *The Great Escape*; prompting and watching Tommy's rages (instead of being simply mean, the other students' provocations of Tommy can be understood as something they need to vicariously let off their own fear and rage); protecting Miss Geraldine from an imaginary plot to kidnap and kill her—that is, from a plot very much like the real plot against their own lives. These outlets defuse the students' rebellious instincts by giving them temporary and harmless vent. Finally, studies of incarcerated people describe a process of institutionalization that infiltrates the beings of those who are subjected to it. Judi Chamberlin writes, for example, that "mental hospitals have been called 'total institutions,' in which even such ordinary decisions as when to eat, go to the toilet, and go to bed are made by others. A natural consequence of being subjected to such a regimen is a feeling of depersonalization." As Chamberlin describes, depersonalization robs its victims of autonomy and "promotes weakness and dependency" (6). The students at Hailsham have never known any other home than the institution that shapes their every activity. Ishiguro's layered depiction of their psychology is richly apt.

44 The other terms in Nussbaum's list are "inertness" and "ownership," both of which could also be said to apply to the cloned people in *Never Let Me Go*. Langton discusses Nussbaum's argument in her overview of feminism in philosophy and adds "reduction to body," "reduction to appearance," and "silencing" to the list, as well as contributing her different view of denials of autonomy that I mention above. Reduction to body, though, could be considered simply another way of saying objectification, the aspects of which Nussbaum is laying out.

45 Clearly the fact that the clones do not own their own bodies is at the heart of the crime being committed against them. As Judith Thomson writes in her famous article defending abortion, "My own view is that if a human being has any just, prior claim to anything at all, he has a just, prior claim to his own body" (54).

46 In a discussion of replicants and clones in popular film, Debbora Battaglia describes a "replication problematic" at the base of which is the "notion of supplement as something that supplies, or makes apparent, insufficiencies" (496).

47 I disagree here with Black who writes, "Like *homo sacer*, Ishiguro's students can be killed but not sacrificed; their deaths by organ removal create no source of transcendent meaning for them or for their community" (789).

48 Yugin Teo raises this question as well: "One of the ethical controversies surrounding Hailsham, indeed, is whether such institutions that provide a nurturing environment for the clones are ultimately doing more harm than good by sheltering them in a bubble when they are growing up and giving them a false impression of life before releasing them into the wider world to face their harsh realities as organ donors" (133). This question of whether they should have known more, sooner, about their own futures is highlighted by the plotline around Miss Lucy. Ishiguro's 2015 novel, *The Buried Giant*, conversely, raises the question of how much it is best to know about one's own and one's people's past.

49 As Black astutely points out, taking their art foreshadows taking their organs: "When Miss Emily says that 'your art will reveal your inner selves' (*Never*, 254), her choice of phrase suggests that making such art actually prefigures the process of organ donation" (794).

50 Kelly Rich argues that "Hailsham's emphasis on a kind, beautiful environment plays an even stronger role [than the euphemistic language] in their repression" (633).

51 Here again the clones' animalization is crucial: just as we are taught not to grieve for the animals killed in slaughterhouses, the noncloned people of *Never Let Me Go* are taught not to grieve for the clones. As Kari Weil points out, "not only with regard to matters of killing but also with regard to matters of grief, nonhuman animals belong to *the constitutive outside of the human*, designating the boundary between what or who is and is not grievable according to what or who is or is not humanized" (113).

EPILOGUE

1 In *The Biopolitics of Disability*, David Mitchell and Sharon Snyder discuss the ways some disabled people are excluded from civic recognition; for example, "The

U. S. census does not include institutionalized people in most states while each prisoner is counted meticulously in the prison-industrial complex" (17).

2   Nil Zacharias notes in a *Huffington Post* blog that "factory farms raise 99.9 percent of chickens for meat, 97 percent of laying hens, 99 percent of turkeys, 95 percent of pigs, and 78 percent of cattle currently sold in the United States" (n.p.).

3   For a discussion of this phenomenon, see Hailee Gibbons.

4   A 2016 *Atlantic* article is much more subdued, but its title, "The Invisible Revolution," is dramatic, and it warns that "as a workforce ages, it becomes less productive. . . . Slowing productivity growth will be particularly challenging because as the country gets older, a larger share of the native born population will be retired. Medicare, Social Security, and other programs for the elderly require lots of tax income from a large and vibrant working force" (Thompson).

5   Ashley's parents have created a website, pillowangel.org, to advocate the "treatment" their doctors performed on their severely mentally and physically disabled daughter. The "treatment" included high-dose estrogen treatment to stop Ashley's growth, bilateral mastectomy, and hysterectomy. They argue that such procedures make it easier to care for severely disabled children as they grow into adult bodies. The justifications for the procedures offered by the parents and doctors are analyzed by Alison Kafer in *Feminist, Queer, Crip* (47–68) and meditated on by Eli Clare in *Brilliant Imperfection* (152–157).

6   As late as 1972, 97 percent of U. S. obstetricians admitted to believing that unmarried mothers on welfare should be sterilized (Hubbard and Wald, 25).

7   Singer's deference to an individual's preference for remaining alive is what grounds his view that infants can be killed "and no one count it murder" as Harriet McBryde Johnson puts it (507). Infants cannot conceive of what it means to be alive or to die, so they cannot have a true preference for remaining alive. Many other philosophers use this criterion to justify killing nonhuman animals, assuming that animals also cannot conceive of being alive or dead. But Johnson points out that this particular criterion is just as arbitrary as other criteria for valuing some lives over others. In an imagined conversation with her sister, she has Beth ask: "That overarching respect for the individual's preference for life—might some say it's a fiction, a fetish, a quasi-religious belief?" (518). As I quote in chapter 4, Martha Nussbaum believes that sentient beings have the right to remain alive *"whether or not they have a conscious interest*, unless and until pain and decrepitude make death no longer a harm" (*Frontiers*, 393, emphasis added).

8   For more on this notion, see Colin Gavaghan, *Defending the Genetic Supermarket*. Merryn Ekberg identifies six arguments in defense of the new eugenics (or as she calls it, the new genetics), several of which can be seen in Agar's and Singer's defenses:

> These contested arguments are that the old eugenics was racial politics whereas the new genetics is preventive medicine. Second, the old eugen-

ics was discriminatory towards women whereas the new genetics offers new opportunities for women. Third, the old eugenics was discriminatory against the disabled whereas the new genetics offers new opportunities for the disabled. Fourth, the old eugenics was oriented around an ethos of collectivism and the promotion of social rights whereas the new genetics is focused on an ethos of individualism and the protection of individual rights. Fifth, the old eugenics was coercive whereas the new genetics is voluntary. Finally, the old eugenics was based on flawed science whereas the new genetics is grounded in accurate science. (581)

9 Legal scholar and *Washington Post* blogger Eugene Volokh describes (with approval) court rulings that allow involuntary sterilization of intellectually disabled people and a California Supreme Court decision that *"struck down as unconstitutional a state law that categorically barred such sterilizations,* and that had been passed in reaction to the sterilization movement exemplified in *Buck v. Bell."*

10 Iceland is just the most extreme example. In the United States, a 2012 review of research studies found a mean termination rate after diagnoses of Down syndrome to be 67 percent (Natoli et al.), which is significantly lower than the often-cited 90-percent rate, a number that came from a European study from 1999. However, given earlier screening methods, women are receiving diagnoses sooner. Because of the greater practical, ethical, and emotional complications of abortion at later points in their pregnancies, earlier testing may lead American women to choose selective abortions at higher rates.

11 Ekberg points out that while contemporary geneticists discredit eugenicists for targeting "complex medical and behavioural traits we now understand as being shaped by an interaction between many genes and an uncertain environment . . . they continue to receive research grants to search for genes responsible for" the same traits targeted by their predecessors, such as "intelligence, addiction, criminality, insanity, sexuality and illiteracy" (590).

12 Elizabeth Barnes builds her chapter "Bad-Difference and Mere-Difference" around these terms as she offers a philosophical argument for the neutrality of disability.

BIBLIOGRAPHY

Ackerman, Felicia Nimue. "Response to Emanuel." "The Conversation." *Atlantic Magazine*, December 2014. http://www.theatlantic.com/.

Adams, Carol J. *The Sexual Politics of Meat: A Feminist-Vegetarian Critical Theory.* 1990. New York: Bloomsbury, 2016.

Adams, Tim. "For Me, England Is a Mythical Place." *Guardian*, February 19, 2005. https://www.theguardian.com/.

Adorno, Theodor. "Huxley and Utopia." 1983. In *Prisms*, translated by Samuel and Shierry Weber, 95–117. Cambridge, MA: MIT Press, 1967.

Agamben, Giorgio. *The Open: Man and Animal.* Translated by Kevin Attell. Stanford, CA: Stanford University Press, 2004.

———. *Homo Sacer: Sovereign Power and Bare Life.* Stanford, CA: Stanford University Press, 1998.

Agar, Nicholas. *Truly Human Enhancement: A Philosophical Defense of Limits.* Cambridge, MA: MIT Press, 2013.

———. *Liberal Eugenics: In Defense of Human Enhancement.* Malden, MA: Blackwell, 2004.

Alexander, Michelle. *The New Jim Crow: Mass Incarceration in the Age of Colorblindness.* New York: The New Press, 2012.

Altieri, Charles. "The Literary and the Ethical: Difference as Definition." In *The Question of Literature: The Place of the Literary in Contemporary Theory*, edited by Elizabeth Beaumont Bissell, 19–47. New York: Manchester University Press, 2002.

Attridge, Derek. *J. M. Coetzee and the Ethics of Reading: Literature in the Event.* Chicago: University of Chicago Press, 2004.

———. *The Singularity of Literature.* New York: Routledge, 2004.

Atwood, Margaret. *In Other Worlds: SF and the Human Imagination.* New York: Doubleday, 2011.

Barad, Karen. *Meeting the Universe Halfway: Quantum Physics and the Entanglement of Matter and Meaning.* Durham, NC: Duke University Press, 2007.

Barnes, Djuna. *Nightwood.* 1937. Preface by Jeanette Winterson. New York: New Directions, 2006.

Barnes, Elizabeth. *The Minority Body: A Theory of Disability.* New York: Oxford University Press, 2016.

Battaglia, Debbora. "Multiplicities: An Anthropologist's Thoughts on Replicants and Clones in Popular Film." *Critical Inquiry* 27.3 (2001): 493–514.

Baynton, Douglas C. *Defectives in the Land: Disability and Immigration in the Age of Eugenics*. Chicago: University of Chicago Press, 2016.

———. "Disability and the Justification of Inequality in American History." In *The Disability Studies Reader*, 4th edition, edited by Lennard J. Davis, 17–33. New York: Routledge, 2013.

Belshaw, Christopher. "Death, Pain, and Animal Life." In *The Ethics of Killing Animals*, edited by Tatjana Visak and Robert Garner, 32–50. New York: Oxford University Press, 2016.

Ben-Moshe, Liat, Chris Chapman, and Allison C. Carey, eds. *Disability Incarcerated: Imprisonment and Disability in the United States and Canada*. New York: Palgrave Macmillan, 2014.

Bentham, Jeremy. *The Works of Jeremy Bentham, Published under the Superintendence of His Executor, John Bowring*, vol. 1. Edinburgh: William Tait, 1843.

Bernstein, Mark. *The Moral Equality of Humans and Animals*. New York: Palgrave, 2015.

Bérubé, Michael. *The Secret Life of Stories: From Don Quixote to Harry Potter, How Understanding Intellectual Disability Transforms the Way We Read*. New York: New York University Press, 2016.

———. "Equality, Freedom, and/or Justice for All: A Response to Martha Nussbaum." In *Cognitive Disability and Its Challenge to Moral Philosophy*, edited by Eva Feder Kittay and Licia Carlson, 98–109. Malden, MA: Wiley Blackwell, 2010.

Black, Shameem. "Ishiguro's Inhuman Aesthetics." *Modern Fiction Studies* 55.4 (2009): 785–807.

Booth, Wayne C. *The Company We Keep: An Ethics of Fiction*. Berkeley: University of California Press, 1988.

Bostrom, Nick. "Human Genetic Enhancement: A Transhumanist Perspective." In *Arguing about Bioethics*, edited by Stephen Holland, 105–114. New York: Routledge, 2012.

Bozarro, Claudia, Joachim Boldt, and Mark Schweda. "Are Older People a Vulnerable Group? Philosophical and Bioethical Perspectives on Aging and Vulnerability." *Bioethics* 32.4 (2018): 233–239.

Bradley, Ben. "Is Death Bad for a Cow?" In *The Ethics of Killing Animals*, edited by Tatjana Visak and Robert Garner, 51–64. New York: Oxford University Press, 2016.

Bradshaw, David. "Huxley's Slump: Planning, Eugenics, and the 'Ultimate Need' of Stability." In *The Art of Literary Biography*, edited by John Batchelor, 151–171. Oxford, UK: Clarendon Press, 1995.

Brannigan, Michael. "Wisdom Does Come with Age." Bioethics Today: A Program of the Alden March Bioethics Institute at Albany Medical Center, November 13, 2014. http://www.amc.edu/.

Brantlinger, Patrick. *Dark Vanishings: Discourse on the Extinction of Primitive Races, 1800–1930*. Ithaca, NY: Cornell University Press, 2003.

Brome, Vincent. *H. G. Wells: A Biography*. 1951. Kelly Bray, Cornwall: Stratus Books, 2001.

Brooks, Peter. *Reading for the Plot: Design and Intention in Narrative*. New York: Vintage, 1985.

Butler, Judith. *Frames of War: When Is Life Grievable?* New York: Verso, 2016.

———. *Precarious Life: The Powers of Mourning and Violence.* New York: Verso, 2004.

Butler, Octavia. *Lilith's Brood: Contains the Complete Series: Dawn, Adulthood Rites, and Imago.* New York: Grand Central Publishing, 2009.

Carlson, Licia. *The Faces of Intellectual Disability: Philosophical Reflections.* Bloomington: Indiana University Press, 2010.

Carr, David. "The Stories of Our Lives: Aging and Narrative." In *The Palgrave Handbook of the Philosophy of Aging,* edited by Geoffrey Scarre, 171–185. New York: Palgrave Macmillan, 2016.

Carroll, Rachel. "Imitations of Life: Cloning, Heterosexuality and the Human in Kazuo Ishiguro's *Never Let Me Go.*" *Journal of Gender Studies* 19:1 (2010): 59–71.

Cash, Jean W. "O'Connor on *The Violent Bear It Away*: An Unpublished Letter." *English Language Notes* 26.4 (1989): 67–71.

Chamberlin, Judi. *On Our Own: Patient Controlled Alternatives to the Mental Health System.* Philadelphia: Haworth Press, 1978.

Chambers, Tod. "Eating One's Friends: Fiction as Argument in Bioethics." *Literature and Medicine* 34.1 (2016): 79–105.

Charise, Andrea. "'Let the Reader Think of the Burden': Old Age and the Crisis of Capacity." *Occasion: Interdisciplinary Studies in the Humanities* 4 (May 31, 2012): 1–16.

Charon, Rita. *Narrative Medicine: Honoring the Stories of Illness.* New York: Oxford University Press, 2008.

Chen, Mel Y. *Animacies: Biopolitics, Racial Mattering, and Queer Affect.* Durham, NC: Duke University Press, 2012.

Chesterton, G. K. *Eugenics and Other Evils.* New York: Cassell and Company, 1922.

"The Chimera Quandary: Is It Ethical to Create Hybrid Embryos?" *All Things Considered.* August 7, 2016. http://www.npr.org/.

Chivers, Sally. *The Silvering Screen: Old Age and Disability in Cinema.* Toronto: University of Toronto Press, 2011.

Clare, Eli. *Brilliant Imperfection: Grappling with Cure.* Durham, NC: Duke University Press, 2017.

Clayton, Jay. "Victorian Chimeras, or, What Literature Can Contribute to Genetics Policy Today." *New Literary History* 38.3 (2007): 569–591.

Cobley, Evelyn. *Modernism and the Culture of Efficiency: Ideology and Fiction.* Toronto: University of Toronto Press, 2009.

Coetzee, J. M. *The Lives of Animals,* edited and introduced by Amy Gutmann. Princeton, NJ: Princeton University Press, 1999.

Cofer, Jordan. *The Gospel According to Flannery O'Connor: Examining the Role of the Bible in Flannery O'Connor's Fiction.* New York: Bloomsbury Academic, 2014.

Cole, Sarah. *Inventing Tomorrow: H. G. Wells and the Twentieth Century.* New York: Columbia University Press, 2019.

Cole, Thomas. *The Journey of Life: A Cultural History of Aging in America.* New York: Cambridge University Press, 1992.

Combs, Robert. "The Eternal Now of *Brave New World*: Huxley, Joseph Campbell, and *The Perennial Philosophy*." In *Huxley's* Brave New World: *Essays*, edited by David Garrett Izzo and Kim Kirkpatrick, 161–171. Jefferson, NC: McFarland, 2008.

Conrad, Joseph. *Heart of Darkness*, 4th Norton Critical Edition, edited by Paul B. Armstrong. New York: W. W. Norton, 2006.

Costa, Richard Hauer. *H. G. Wells*, revised edition. Boston: Twayne Publishers, 1985.

Coupland, Douglas. *Generation X: Tales for an Accelerated Culture*. New York: St. Martin's Press, 1991.

Currie, Mark. "Controlling Time: *Never Let Me Go*." In *Kazuo Ishiguro: Contemporary Critical Perspectives*, edited by Sean Matthews and Sebastian Groes, 91–103. New York: Continuum, 2009.

Danta, Chris. *Animal Fables after Darwin: Literature, Speciesism, and Metaphor*. New York: Cambridge University Press, 2018.

———. "The Future Will Have Been Animal: Dr. Moreau and the Aesthetics of Monstrosity." *Textual Practice* 26.4 (2012): 687–705.

Darwin, Charles. *The Expression of the Emotions in Man and Animals*. 1872. New York: D. Appleton & Company, 1913.

———. *The Descent of Man and Selection in Relation to Sex*, vol. 1, 2nd edition. New York: D. Appleton, 1898.

Davidson, Michael. *Invalid Modernism: Disability and the Missing Body of the Aesthetic*. New York: Oxford University Press, 2019.

———. "Paralyzed Modernities and Biofutures: Bodies and Minds in Modern Literature." In *The Cambridge Companion to Literature and Disability*, edited by Clare Barker and Stuart Murray, 74–89. New York: Cambridge University Press, 2017.

———. "Pregnant Men: Modernism, Disability, and Biofuturity in Djuna Barnes." *Novel: A Forum on Fiction* 43:2 (2010): 207–226.

Davies, Caroline. "Martin Amis in New Row over 'Euthanasia Booths.'" *Guardian*, January 24, 2010.

Davis, Angela. Foreword. In *Disability Incarcerated: Imprisonment and Disability in the United States and Canada*, edited by Liat Ben-Moshe, Chris Chapman, and Allison C. Carey. New York: Palgrave Macmillan, 2014.

Davis, Lennard. *Enforcing Normalcy: Disability, Deafness, and the Body*. New York: Verso, 1995.

De Boever, Arne. *Narrative Care: Biopolitics and the Novel*. New York: Bloomsbury Academic, 2013.

Deery, June. "Technology and Gender in Aldous Huxley's Alternative (?) Worlds." *Extrapolation* 33.3 (1992): 258–273.

DeGrazia, David. *Animal Rights: A Very Short Introduction*. New York: Oxford University Press, 2002.

Dennett, Daniel C. "Whole-Body Apoptosis and the Meanings of Lives." *On the Human: A Project of the National Humanities Center*, December 12, 2011. https://nationalhumanitiescenter.org/.

Derrida, Jacques. *The Animal That Therefore I Am*. Edited by Marie-Louise Mallet. Translated by David Wills. New York: Fordham University Press, 2008.

———. "'Eating Well,' or The Calculation of the Subject." In *Points: Interviews, 1974–1994*, edited by Elisabeth Weber. Translated by Peggy Kamuf and Others, 255–287. Stanford, CA: Stanford University Press, 1995.

Desmond, John. "By Force of Will: Flannery O'Connor, the Broken Synthesis, and the Problem with Rayber." *Flannery O'Connor Review* 6 (2008): 135–146.

Diamond, Cora. "Injustice and Animals." In *Slow Cures and Bad Philosophers: Essays on Wittgenstein, Medicine, and Bioethics*, edited by by Carl Elliott, 118–148. Durham, NC: Duke University Press, 2001.

Diken, Bülent. "Huxley's *Brave New World*—and Ours." *Journal for Cultural Research* 15.2 (2011): 153–172.

Donovan, Josephine. "Animal Rights and Feminist Theory." In *The Feminist Care Tradition in Animal Ethics*, edited by Josephine Donovan and Carol J. Adams, 58–86. New York: Columbia University Press, 2007.

Doudna, Jennifer, and Samuel H. Sternberg. *A Crack in Creation: Gene Editing and the Unthinkable Power to Control Evolution*. Boston: Houghton Mifflin Harcourt, 2017.

Drake, Stephen. "Connecting Disability Rights and Animal Rights—A Really Bad Idea." Not Dead Yet, October 11, 2010. http://notdeadyet.org/.

Driggers, Stephen G., and Robert J. Dunn, with Sarah Gordon. *The Manuscripts of Flannery O'Connor at Georgia College*. Athens: University of Georgia Press, 1987.

Dunaway, David King. "Huxley and Human Cloning: *Brave New World* in the Twenty-First Century." *Aldous Huxley Annual* 2 (2002): 165–179.

Eagleton, Terry. *Literary Theory: An Introduction*, anniversary edition. Malden, MA: Blackwell Publishing, 2008.

Edwards, Ronald. *The Edge of Evolution: Animality, Inhumanity, & Doctor Moreau*. New York: Oxford University Press, 2016.

Ehni, Hans-Joerg, Selma Kadi, Maartje Schermer, and Sridhar Venkatapuram. "Toward a Global Geroethics—Gerontology and the Theory of the Good Human Life." *Bioethics* 32.4 (2018): 261–268.

Ekberg, Merryn. "The Old Eugenics and the New Genetics Compared." *Social History of Medicine* 20.3 (2007): 581–593.

"Elder Abuse Facts." National Council on Aging. https://www.ncoa.org.

Emanuel, Ezekiel J. "Why I Hope to Die at 75." *Atlantic Magazine*, October 2014. http://www.theatlantic.com/.

Erevelles, Nirmala. "Crippin' Jim Crow: Disability, Dis-Location, and the School-to-Prison Pipeline." In *Disability Incarcerated: Imprisonment and Disability in the United States and Canada*, edited by Liat Ben-Moshe, Chris Chapman, and Allison C. Carey, 81–99. New York: Palgrave Macmillan, 2014.

Evans, Oliver. *The Ballad of Carson McCullers: A Biography*. New York: Coward McCann, 1966.

Faulkner, William. "Appendix: Compson, 1699–1945," *The Sound and the Fury*, Norton Critical Edition, edited by David Minter. New York: W. W. Norton, 1994.

Fetterley, Judith. *The Resisting Reader: A Feminist Approach to American Fiction.* Bloomington: Indiana University Press, 1978.

Firchow, Peter. "Science and Conscience in *Brave New World.*" *Contemporary Literature* 16.3 (1975): 301–316.

Fitzgerald, Amy J. "A Social History of the Slaughterhouse: From Inception to Contemporary Implications." *Human Ecology Review* 17.1 (2010): 58–69.

Foer, Jonathan Safran. *Eating Animals.* New York: Little, Brown, 2009.

Folks, Jeffrey J. "The Enduring Chill: Physical Disability in Flannery O'Connor's *Everything That Rises Must Converge.*" *University of Dayton Review* 22.2 (1993–1994): 81–88.

Freedman, Estelle B. *Redefining Rape: Sexual Violence in the Era of Suffrage and Segregation.* Cambridge, MA: Harvard University Press, 2013.

Freud, Sigmund. *A General Introduction to Psychoanalysis.* Translated by G. Stanley Hall. New York: Horace Liveright, 1920.

Frost, Laura. "Huxley's Feelies: The Cinema of Sensation in *Brave New World.*" *Twentieth-Century Literature* 52.4 (2006): 443–473.

Fukuyama, Francis. *Our Posthuman Future: Consequences of the Biotechnology Revolution.* New York: Farrar, Straus, and Giroux, 2003.

Fuller, Steve. "It's Time to Expand Our Definition of 'Human Being.'" *Discover Magazine* Blogs, February 2, 2015. http://blogs.discovermagazine.com/.

Gallop, Jane. "The View from Queer Theory." *AgeCultureHumanities: An Interdisciplinary Journal* 2 (2015).

Galton, Francis. "Eugenics: Its Definition, Scope, and Aims." *American Journal of Sociology* 9.1 (1904). http://galton.org/.

Garland-Thomson, Rosemarie. "Eugenic World Building and Disability: The Strange World of Kazuo Ishiguro's *Never Let Me Go.*" *Journal of Medical Humanities* 38 (2017): 133–145.

———. "A Habitable World: Harriet McBryde Johnson's 'Case for My Life.'" *Hypatia* 30.1 (2015): 300–306.

———. "Human Biodiversity Conservation: A Consensual Ethical Principle." *American Journal of Bioethics* 15.6 (2015): 13–15.

———. "Misfits: A Feminist Materialist Disability Concept." *Hypatia* 26.3 (2011): 591–609.

———. *Staring: How We Look.* New York: Oxford University Press, 2009.

———. *Extraordinary Bodies.* New York: Columbia University Press, 1997.

Gavaghan, Colin. *Defending the Genetic Supermarket: Law and Ethics of Selecting the Next Generation.* New York: Routledge-Cavendish, 2007.

General Accounting Office, Report to Congressional Requesters. "Humane Methods of Slaughter Act: USDA Has Addressed Some Problems but Still Faces Enforcement Challenges." Collingdale, PA: Diane Publishing, 2004.

Getz, Lorine M. *Nature and Grace in Flannery O'Connor's Fiction.* New York: Edwin Mellen Press, 1982.

Giannone, Richard. "Making It in Darkness." *Flannery O'Connor Review* 6 (July 2008): 103–118.

Gibbons, Hailee M. "Compulsory Youthfulness: Intersections of Ableism and Ageism in 'Successful Aging' Discourses." *Review of Disability Studies* 12.2–3 (2016): 70–88.

Gill, Josie. "Written on the Face: Race and Expression in Kazuo Ishiguro's *Never Let Me Go*." *Modern Fiction Studies* 60.4 (2014): 844–862.

Gillespie, Nick. "Anti-Science-Fiction." *Slate*, January 18, 2002. http://www.slate.com/.

Glendinning, John. "'Green Confusion': Evolution and Entanglement in H. G. Wells's *The Island of Doctor Moreau*." *Victorian Literature and Culture* 30.2 (2002): 571–597.

Glover, Jonathan. *Choosing Children: Genes, Disability, and Design*. Oxford: Clarendon Press, 2006.

Gooch, Brad. *Flannery: A Life of Flannery O'Connor*. New York: Little, Brown, 2009.

Green, Ronald M. *Babies by Design: The Ethics of Genetic Choice*. New Haven, CT: Yale University Press, 2007.

Griffin, Gabriele. "Science and the Cultural Imaginary: The Case of Kazuo Ishiguro's *Never Let Me Go*." *Textual Practice* 23.4 (2009): 645–663.

Grimes, Ronald L. "Anagogy and Ritualization: Baptism in Flannery O'Connor's *The Violent Bear It Away*." *Religion & Literature* 21.1 (1989): 9–26.

Gross, Aaron, and Anne Vallely, eds. *Animals and the Human Imagination: A Companion to Animal Studies*. New York: Columbia University Press, 2012.

Gullette, Margaret Morganroth. *Aged by Culture*. Chicago: University of Chicago Press, 2004.

Haldane, Charlotte. *Man's World*. New York: George H. Doran Company, 1927.

Hall, Melinda C. *The Bioethics of Enhancement: Transhumanism, Disability, and Biopolitics*. Lanham, MD: Lexington Books, 2017.

Hamilton, Christopher. "'This Damnable, Disgusting Old Age': Ageing and (Being) One's Body." In *The Palgrave Handbook of the Philosophy of Aging*, edited by Geoffrey Scarre, 305–324. New York: Palgrave Macmillan, 2016.

Haranjo-Huebl, Linda. "Toward a Consistent Ethic of Life in 'A Stroke of Good Fortune.'" In *Flannery O'Connor in the Age of Terrorism: Essays on Violence and Grace*, edited by Avis Hewitt and Robert Donahoo, 70–86. Knoxville: University of Tennessee Press, 2010.

Harari, Yuval Noah. "Industrial Farming Is One of the Worst Crimes in History." *Guardian*, September 25, 2015. https://www.theguardian.com/.

Haraway, Donna. *When Species Meet*. Minneapolis: University of Minnesota Press, 2008.

Harris, John. *The Value of Life: An Introduction to Medical Ethics*. New York: Routledge, 1985.

Harris, Mason. "Vivisection, the Culture of Science, and Intellectual Uncertainty in *The Island of Doctor Moreau*." *Gothic Studies* 4.2 (2002): 99–115.

Harrowitz, Nancy A. "Weininger and Lombroso: A Question of Influence." In *Jews and Gender: Responses to Otto Weininger*, edited by Nancy A. Harrowitz and Barbara Hyams, 73–90. Philadelphia: Temple University Press, 1995.

Haynes, Roslynn D. "The Unholy Alliance of Science in *The Island of Doctor Moreau*." *The Wellsian, Journal of the H. G. Wells Society* 11 (1988): 13–24.

———. *H. G. Wells: Discoverer of the Future: The Influence of Science on his Thought.* New York: New York University Press, 1980.

Hendershot, Cyndy. "The Animal Without: Masculinity and Imperialism in *The Island of Doctor Moreau* and 'The Adventures of the Speckled Band.'" *Nineteenth Century Studies* 10 (1996): 1–32.

Hiltzik, Michael. "Why Ezekiel Emanuel Is Wrong to 'Hope' for Death at 75." The Economy Hub. *Los Angeles Times*, October 16, 2014. http://www.latimes.com/.

Holloway, Kali. "Modern-Day Eugenics? Prisoners Sterilized for Shorter Sentences." *Salon*, July 28, 2017.

Holstein, Martha B., Mark H. Waymack, and Jennifer A. Parks. *Ethics, Aging, and Society: The Critical Turn.* New York: Springer Publishing, 2010.

Hope, Tony. *Medical Ethics: A Very Short Introduction.* New York: Oxford University Press, 2004.

Horsburgh, Beverly. "Schrödinger's Cat, Eugenics, and the Compulsory Sterilization of Welfare Mothers: Deconstructing an Old/New Rhetoric and Constructing the Reproductive Right to Natality for Low-Income Women of Color." *Cardozo Law Review* 17.1 (1995): 531–582.

Hubbard, Ruth. "Abortion and Disability: Who Should and Should Not Inhabit the World?" In *Disability Studies Reader*, 4th edition, edited by Lennard Davis, 74–86. New York: Routledge, 2013.

Hubbard, Ruth, and Elijah Wald. *Exploding the Gene Myth: How Genetic Information Is Produced and Manipulated by Scientists, Physicians, Employers, Insurance Companies, Educators, and Law Enforcers.* Boston: Beacon Press, 1999.

Hunnewell, Susannah. "Kazuo Ishiguro, The Art of Fiction." *Paris Review* 184 (Spring 2008): 23–54.

Huntington, John. *The Logic of Fantasy: H. G. Wells and Science Fiction.* New York: Columbia University Press, 1982.

Huxley, Aldous. *Brave New World.* 1932. New York: HarperPerennial Modern Classics, 2006.

———. *Brave New World* Corrected Typescript. Harry Ransom Center, University of Texas at Austin, n.d.

———. *Brave New World* and *Brave New World Revisited.* New York: Harper Perennial, 2004.

———. *Island.* New York: Harper and Brothers Publishers, 1962.

Huxley, Julian. "The Tissue-Culture King." 1927. In *Great Science Fiction by Scientists*, edited by Groff Conklin, 147–170. New York: Collier Books, 1962.

"In Search for Cures, Scientists Create Embryos That Are Both Animal and Human." *All Things Considered*, May 18, 2016. http://www.npr.org/.

"'I Remain Fascinated by Memory': Spiegel Interview with Kazuo Ishiguro." *Spiegel Online*, October 5, 2005. www.spiegel.de.

Ingersoll, Earl G. "Taking Off into the Realm of Metaphor: Kazuo Ishiguro's *Never Let Me Go.*" *Studies in the Humanities* 34.1 (2007): 40–59.

"Interview: Kazuo Ishiguro." *Lightspeed Magazine* 63 (August 2015). http://www.lightspeedmagazine.com/.

Ishiguro, Kazuo. *The Buried Giant*. New York: Random House, 2015.

———. "Future Imperfect: Kazuo Ishiguro on How a Radio Discussion Helped Fill in the Missing Pieces of Never Let Me Go." *Guardian*, March 24, 2006. https://www.theguardian.com/.

———. *Never Let Me Go*. 2005. New York: Vintage International, 2006.

Johnson, Corey. "California Was Sterilizing Its Female Prisoners as Late as 2010." *Guardian*, November 8, 2013.

Johnson, Harriet McBryde. "Unspeakable Conversations." In *Disability Studies Reader*, 4th edition, edited by Lennard Davis, 507–519. New York: Routledge, 2013.

Kaelber, Lutz. "Georgia." Eugenics: Compulsory Sterilization in 50 American States. 2012. http://www.uvm.edu/.

Kafer, Alison. *Feminist, Queer, Crip*. Bloomington: Indiana University Press, 2013.

Kafer, Alison, and Eunjung Kim. "Disability and the Edges of Intersectionality." In *The Cambridge Companion to Literature and Disability*, edited by Clare Barker and Stuart Murray, 123–138. New York: Cambridge University Press, 2018.

Kalanithi, Paul. *When Breath Becomes Air*. New York: Random House, 2016.

Kamenev, Marina. "Sterilizing a Child, for a Better Life." *Atlantic*, September 19, 2013.

Kass, Leon. "Defending Human Dignity." In *Human Dignity and Bioethics: Essays Commissioned by the President's Council on Bioethics*, 297–329. Washington, DC, March 2008.

Keen, Suzanne. *Empathy and the Novel*. New York: Oxford University Press, 2007.

Kim, Eunjung. "Why Do Dolls Die? The Power of Passivity and the Embodied Interplay between Disability and Sex Dolls." *Review of Education, Pedagogy, and Cultural Studies* 34.3–4 (2012): 94–106.

Kittay, Eva Feder. "The Moral Significance of Being Human." *Proceedings and Addresses of the APA* 91 (November 2017): 22–42.

———. "The Personal Is Philosophical Is Political: A Philosopher and Mother of a Cognitively Disabled Person Sends Notes from the Battlefield." In *Cognitive Disability and Its Challenge to Moral Philosophy*, edited by Eva Feder Kittay and Licia Carlson, 393–413. Malden, MA: Wiley Blackwell, 2010.

———. "At the Margins of Moral Personhood." *Ethics* 116 (October 2005): 100–131.

———. "When Caring Is Just and Justice Is Caring: Justice and Mental Retardation." *Public Culture* 13.3 (2001): 557–579.

———. *Love's Labor: Essays on Women, Equality, and Dependency*. New York: Routledge, 1998.

Kittay, Eva Feder, and Licia Carlson, eds. *Cognitive Disability and Its Challenge to Moral Philosophy*. Malden, MA: Wiley Blackwell, 2010.

Kline, Wendy. *Building a Better Race: Gender, Sexuality, and Eugenics from the Turn of the Century to the Baby Boom*. Berkeley: University of California Press, 2001.

Kluchin, Rebecca M. *Fit to Be Tied: Sterilization and Reproductive Rights in America, 1950–1980*. New Brunswick, NJ: Rutgers University Press, 2009.

Korsgaard, Christine M. "A Kantian Case for Animal Rights." In *The Ethics of Killing Animals*, edited by Tatjana Visak and Robert Garner, 154–177. New York: Oxford University Press, 2016.

Kraynack, Robert P. "Human Dignity and the Mystery of the Human Soul." In *Human Dignity and Bioethics: Essays Commissioned by the President's Council on Bioethics*, 61–82. Washington, DC, March 2008.

Kroeker, P. Travis. "'Jesus Is the Bread of Life': Johannine Sign and Deed in *The Violent Bear It Away.*" In *Dark Faith: New Essays on Flannery O'Connor's* The Violent Bear It Away, edited by Susan Srigley, 136–156. Notre Dame, IN: University of Notre Dame Press, 2012.

Kuhse, Helga, and Peter Singer. *Should the Baby Live? The Problem of Handicapped Infants*. New York: Oxford University Press, 1988.

Lake, Christina Bieber. "The Violence of Technique and the Technique of Violence." In *Flannery O'Connor in the Age of Terrorism: Essays on Violence and Grace*, edited by Avis Hewitt and Robert Donahoo, 25–40. Knoxville: University of Tennessee Press, 2010.

Lamb, Erin, ed. "Age and/as Disability." Forum in *AgeCultureHumanities: An Interdisciplinary Journal* 2 (2015).

Langton, Rae. "Feminism in Philosophy." In *The Oxford Handbook of Contemporary Philosophy*, edited by Frank Jackson and Michael Smith, 231–257. New York: Oxford University Press, 2007.

Larson, Edward J. *Sex, Race, and Science: Eugenics in the Deep South*. Baltimore, MD: Johns Hopkins University Press, 1995.

Lee, Michael Parrish. "Reading Meat in H. G. Wells." *Studies in the Novel* 42.3 (2010): 249–268.

"Life Expectancy in the USA, 1900–98." Berkeley Department of Demography. University of California, Berkeley, n.d. demog.berkeley.edu.

Linett, Maren. *Bodies of Modernism: Physical Disability in Transatlantic Modernist Literature*. Ann Arbor: University of Michigan Press, 2017.

Livingston, Julie, and Jasbir Puar. "Interspecies." *Social Text* 29.1 (2011): 3–14.

Loftis, Sonya Freeman. "The Autistic Victim: *Of Mice and Men*." In *Disability Studies Reader*, 5th edition, edited by Lennard Davis, 470–480. New York: Routledge, 2016.

Luke, Brian. "Justice, Caring, and Animal Liberation." In *The Feminist Care Tradition in Animal Ethics*, edited by Josephine Donovan and Carol J. Adams, 125–152. New York: Columbia University Press, 2007.

Lyon, Janet. "Modernism, Debility, and Intellectual Disability." Paper presented at the Modern Language Association, Chicago, January 2019.

———. "Carrington's Sensorium." In *Leonora Carrington and the International Avant-Garde*, edited by Jonathan Paul Eburne and Catriona McAra, 163–176. Manchester, UK: Manchester University Press, 2017.

———. "On the Asylum Road with Woolf and Mew." *Modernism / modernity* 18.3 (2012): 551–574.

MacIntyre, Alasdair. *Dependent Rational Animals: Why Human Beings Need the Virtues*. Chicago: Open Court Publishing, 1999.

———. *After Virtue: A Study in Moral Theory*, 2nd edition. Notre Dame, IN: University of Notre Dame Press, 1984.

Manderson, Lenore. *Surface Tensions: Surgery, Bodily Boundaries, and the Social Self*. Walnut Creek, CA: Left Coast Press, 2011.

McConnell, Frank. *The Science Fiction of H. G. Wells*. New York: Oxford University Press, 1981.

McLean, Steven. *The Early Fiction of H. G. Wells: Fantasies of Science*. New York: Palgrave, 2009.

McMahan, Jeff. "The Comparative Badness for Animals of Suffering and Death." In *The Ethics of Killing Animals*, edited by Tatjana Visak and Robert Garner, 65–85. New York: Oxford University Press, 2016.

———. *The Ethics of Killing: Problems at the Margins of Life*. New York: Oxford University Press, 2002.

McRuer, Robert. *Crip Theory: Cultural Signs of Queerness and Disability*. New York: New York University Press, 2006.

McWilliams, James. *The Modern Savage: Our Unthinking Decision to Eat Animals*. New York: St. Martin's Griffin, 2015.

Meckier, Jerome. "On D. H. Lawrence and Death, Especially Matricide: *Sons and Lovers*, *Brave New World*, and Aldous Huxley's Later Novels." *Aldous Huxley Annual 7* (2007): 185–221.

———. "Aldous Huxley's Americanization of the *Brave New World* Typescript." *Twentieth Century Literature* 48.4 (2002): 427–460.

Meilaender, Gilbert. *Should We Live Forever? The Ethical Ambiguities of Aging*. Grand Rapids, MI: William B. Eerdmans Publishing, 2013.

———. *Neither Beast nor God: The Dignity of the Human Person*. New York: Encounter Books, 2009.

Mickelbart, Stacey. "From the Pen to the Plate." *Envision Magazine*, Purdue University College of Agriculture, Fall 2018.

Mitchell, David T., and Sharon L. Snyder. *Narrative Prosthesis: Disability and the Dependencies of Discourse*. Ann Arbor: University of Michigan Press, 2000.

Mitchell, David T., with Sharon L. Snyder. *The Biopolitics of Disability: Neoliberalism, Ablenationalism, and Peripheral Embodiment*. Ann Arbor: University of Michigan Press, 2015.

Mooney, Chris. "Irrationalist in Chief." *American Prospect* 12.17 (2001).

Mundy, Liza. "A World of Their Own." *Washington Post Magazine*. March 31, 2002. 22–43.

Murphy, Stephen T. *Voices of Pineland: Eugenics, Social Reform, and the Legacy of 'Feeblemindedness' in Maine*. Charlotte, NC: Information Age Publishing, 2011.

Murray, Thomas H. "What Do We Mean by 'Narrative Ethics'?" In *Stories and Their Limits: Narrative Approaches to Bioethics*, edited by Hilde Lindemann Nelson, 3–17. New York: Routledge, 1997.

Natoli, Jaime L., D. L. Ackerman, S. McDermott, and J. G. Edwards. "Prenatal Diagnosis of Down Syndrome: A Systematic Review of Termination Rates (1995–2011)." *Prenatal Diagnosis* 32.2 (2012): 142–153.

Newton, K. M., ed. *Twentieth-Century Literary Theory: A Reader*. New York: Macmillan, 1997.

"The Nobel Prize in Literature 2017." NobelPrize.org. Nobel Media AB 2019, February 11, 2019. https://www.nobelprize.org/.

Niu, Dong, H. J. Wei, L. Lin, H. George, T. Wang, I. H. Lee, H. Y. Zhou, et al. "Inactivation of Porcine Endogenous Retrovirus in Pigs Using CRISPR-Cas9." *Science*, August 10, 2017. DOI: 10.1126/science.aan4187.

Nozick, Robert. *Anarchy, State, and Utopia*. New York: Basic Books, 1986.

Nussbaum, Martha C. *Political Emotions: Why Love Matters for Justice*. Cambridge, MA: Belknap Press of Harvard University Press, 2013.

———. "The Capabilities of People with Cognitive Disabilities." In *Cognitive Disability and Its Challenge to Moral Philosophy*, edited by Eva Feder Kittay and Licia Carlson, 77–95. Malden, MA: Wiley Blackwell, 2010.

———. *Not for Profit: Why Democracy Needs the Humanities*. Princeton, NJ: Princeton University Press, 2010.

———. "Human Dignity and Political Entitlements." In *Human Dignity and Bioethics: Essays Commissioned by the President's Council on Bioethics*, 351–380. Washington, DC, March 2008.

———. *Frontiers of Justice: Disability, Nationality, Species Membership*. Cambridge, MA: Belknap Press of Harvard University Press, 2006.

———. *Hiding from Humanity: Disgust, Shame, and the Law*. Princeton, NJ: Princeton University Press, 2004.

———. "Objectification." *Philosophy & Public Affairs* 24.4 (1995): 249–291.

———. *Poetic Justice: The Literary Imagination and Public Life*. Boston: Beacon Press, 1995.

———. "Equity and Mercy." *Philosophy & Public Affairs* 22.2 (1993): 83–125.

———. "The Literary Imagination in Public Life." *New Literary History* 22.4 (1991): 877–910.

O'Brien, Gerald. "Anchors on the Ship of Progress and Weeds in the Human Garden: Objectivist Rhetoric in American Eugenic Writings." *Disability Studies Quarterly* 31.3 (2011).

O'Connor, Flannery. *The Habit of Being: Letters of Flannery O'Connor*. Edited by Sally Fitzgerald. New York: Farrar, Straus and Giroux, 1979.

———. *The Complete Stories*. New York: Farrar, Straus and Giroux, 1971.

———. *Mystery and Manners: Occasional Prose*. New York: Farrar, Straus, and Giroux, 1969.

———. *The Violent Bear It Away*. New York: Noonday Press, Farrar, Straus & Giroux, 1960.

Oliver, Kelly. "Service Dogs: Between Animal Studies and Disability Studies." *philoSOPHIA* 6.2 (2016): 241–258.

———. "Subjectivity as Responsivity: The Ethical Implications of Dependency." In *The Subject of Care: Feminist Perspectives on Dependency*, edited by Eva Feder Kittay and Ellen K. Feder, 322–333. Lanham, MD: Rowman and Littlefield, 2002.

Owen, Wilfred. *The War Poems of Wilfred Owen*. Edited by John Stallworthy. London: Chatto and Windus, 1994.

Parrinder, Patrick. *Shadows of the Future: H. G. Wells, Science Fiction, and Prophecy*. Syracuse, NY: Syracuse University Press, 1995.

———. *H. G. Wells*. Edinburgh: Oliver and Boyd, 1970.

Partington, John S. *Building Cosmopolis: The Political Thought of H. G. Wells*. Aldershot, UK: Ashgate, 2003.

Patterson, Kathleen. "Negotiating Elevators and Hay Lofts: Disability and Identity in Flannery O'Connor's Short Fiction." In *Literature and Sickness*, edited by David Bevan, 95–104. Atlanta, GA: Rodopi, 1993.

Pollan, Michael. *The Omnivore's Dilemma: A Natural History of Four Meals*. New York: Penguin Books, 2007.

Powell, Tara. *The Intellectual in Twentieth-Century Southern Literature*. Baton Rouge: Louisiana State University Press, 2012.

Puar, Jasbir K. "Precarity Talk: A Roundtable with Lauren Berlant, Judith Butler, Bojana Cvejić, Isabell Lorey, Jasbir Puar, and Ana Vujanović." *TDR: The Drama Review* 56:4 (2012): 163–177.

———. "Prognosis Time: Towards a Geopolitics of Affect, Debility and Capacity." *Women & Performance: A Journal of Feminist Theory* 19.2 (2009): 161–172.

Quinn, Mary Joy, and Susan K. Tomita. *Elder Abuse and Neglect: Causes, Diagnoses, and Intervention Strategies*, 2nd edition. New York: Singer Publishing, 1997.

Quinones, Julian, and Arijeta Lajka. "'What Kind of Society Do You Want to Live In?' Inside the Country Where Down Syndrome Is Disappearing." *CBS News: On Assignment*, August 14, 2017. Web.

Rapp, Emily. *The Still Point of the Turning World: A Memoir*. New York: Penguin, 2013.

Rawls, John. *A Theory of Justice.*, revised edition. Cambridge, MA: The Belknap Press of Harvard University Press, 1999.

Reeves, Nancee. "Euthanasia and (d)Evolution in Speculative Fiction." *Victorian Literature and Culture* 45.1 (2017): 95–117.

Regan, Tom. *The Case for Animal Rights*. Updated with a new preface. Berkeley: University of California Press, 2004.

———. *Defending Animal Rights*. Urbana: University of Illinois Press, 2001.

———. "The Case for Animal Rights." In *In Defense of Animals*, edited by Peter Singer, 13–26. New York: Basil Blackwell, 1985.

Rentsch, Thomas. "Aging as Becoming Oneself: A Philosophical Ethics of Late Life." In *The Palgrave Handbook of the Philosophy of Aging*, edited by Geoffrey Scarre, 347–364. New York: Palgrave Macmillan, 2016.

Rich, Kelly. "'Look in the Gutter': Infrastructural Interiority in *Never Let Me Go*." *Modern Fiction Studies* 61.4 (2015): 631–651.

Rohman, Carrie. *Choreographies of the Living: Bioaesthetics in Literature, Art, and Performance*. New York: Oxford University Press, 2018.

———. *Stalking the Subject: Modernism and the Animal*. New York: Columbia University Press, 2009.

Rolston, Holmes, III. "Human Uniqueness and Human Dignity: Persons in Nature and the Nature of Persons." In *Human Dignity and Bioethics: Essays Commissioned by the President's Council on Bioethics*, 129–153. Washington, DC, March 2008.

Rosen, Christine. *Preaching Eugenics: Religious Leaders and the American Eugenics Movement*. New York: Oxford University Press, 2004.

Rosenberg, Gabriel. "How Meat Changed Sex: The Law of Interspecies Intimacy after Industrial Reproduction." *GLQ* 23.4 (2017): 473–507.

Rowlands, Mark. *Animals Like Us*. New York: Verso, 2002.

Russell, Bertrand. "We Don't Want to Be Happy." 1932. In *Aldous Huxley: The Critical Heritage*, edited by Donald Watt, 210–212. Boston: Routledge and Kegan Paul, 2013.

Ryan, Derek. *Animal Theory*. Edinburgh: Edinburgh University Press, 2015.

Samuels, Ellen. *Fantasies of Identification: Disability, Gender, Race*. New York: New York University Press, 2014.

Sandel, Michael. *The Case against Perfection: Ethics in the Age of Genetic Engineering*. Cambridge, MA: The Belknap Press of Harvard University Press, 2011.

Sanger, Margaret. *The Pivot of Civilization*. New York: Brentano's, 1922.

Savulescu, Julian. "Procreative Beneficence: Why We Should Select the Best Children." *Bioethics* 15.5/6 (2001): 413–426.

Saxton, Marsha. "Disability Rights and Selective Abortion." In *Disability Studies Reader*, 4th edition, edited by Lennard Davis, 87–99. New York: Routledge, 2013.

Schalk, Sami. *Bodyminds Reimagined: (Dis)ability, Race, and Gender in Black Women's Speculative Fiction*. Durham, NC: Duke University Press, 2018.

Schechtman, Marya. *Staying Alive: Personal Identity, Practical Concerns, and the Unity of a Life*. New York: Oxford University Press, 2014.

Schweik, Susan M. *The Ugly Laws: Disability in Public*. New York: New York University Press, 2009.

Schweickart, Patrocinio P. "Reading Ourselves: Toward a Feminist Theory of Reading." In *Gender and Reading*, edited by Elizabeth A. Flynn and Patrocinio P. Schweickart, 31–62. Baltimore, MD: Johns Hopkins University Press, 1986.

Scully, Jackie Leach. *Disability Bioethics: Moral Bodies, Moral Difference*. Lanham, MD: Rowman and Littlefield, 2008.

———. "Moral Bodies: Epistemologies of Embodiment." In *Naturalized Bioethics: Toward Responsible Knowing and Practice*, edited by Margaret Urban Walker, 23–41. New York: Cambridge University Press, 2008.

Seaman, Myra. "Becoming More (than) Human: Affective Posthumanisms, Past and Future." *Journal of Narrative Theory* 37.2 (2007): 246–275.

Sherborne, Michael. *H.G. Wells: Another Kind of Life*. London: Peter Owen, 2010.

Shloss, Carol. *Flannery O'Connor's Dark Comedies: The Limits of Inference*. Baton Rouge: Louisiana State University Press, 2012.

Shreeve, Jamie. "The Other Stem-Cell Debate." *New York Times Magazine*, April 10, 2005.

Silbergeld, Ellen K. *Chickenizing Farms and Food: How Industrial Meat Production Endangers Workers, Animals, and Consumers*. Baltimore, MD: Johns Hopkins University Press, 2016.

Silvers, Anita. "Aging Fairly: Feminist and Disability Perspectives on Intergenerational Justice." In *Mother Time: Women, Aging, and Ethics*, edited by Margaret Urban Walker, 203–226. Lanham, MD: Rowman and Littlefield Publishers, 2000.

"The Silver Tsunami: Business Will Have to Learn How to Manage an Ageing Workforce." *Economist* February 4, 2010.

Simplican, Stacy Clifford. *The Capacity Contract: Intellectual Disability and the Question of Citizenship*. Minneapolis: University of Minnesota Press, 2015.

Singer, Peter. *Practical Ethics*, 3rd edition. New York: Cambridge University Press, 2011.

———. *Animal Liberation,* updated edition. New York: Harper Perennial, 2009.

———. "Preface to the 2009 Edition." *Animal Liberation*. New York: HarperCollins, 2009.

———. "Shopping at the Genetic Supermarket." In *Disability: The Social, Political, and Ethical Debate*, edited by Robert M. Baird, Stuart E. Rosenbaum, and S. Kay Toombs, 309–331. Amherst, NY: Prometheus Books, 2009.

Slicer, Deborah. "Your Daughter or Your Dog? A Feminist Assessment of the Animal Research Issue." In *The Feminist Care Tradition in Animal Ethics*, edited by Josephine Donovan and Carol J. Adams, 105–124. New York: Columbia University Press, 2007.

Small, Helen. *The Long Life*. New York: Oxford University Press, 2007.

Snaza, Nathan. "The Failure of Humanizing Education in Kazuo Ishiguro's *Never Let Me Go*." *Lit: Literature Interpretation Theory* 26:3 (2015): 215–234.

Snyder, E. E. "Moreau and the Monstrous: Evolution, Religion, and the Beast on the Island." *Preternature: Critical and Historical Studies on the Preternatural* 2.2 (2013): 213–239.

Sorabji, Richard. *Animal Minds and Human Morals: The Origins of the Western Debate*. Ithaca, NY: Cornell University Press, 1993.

Squier, Susan Merrill. *Liminal Lives: Imagining the Human at the Frontiers of Biomedicine*. Durham, NC: Duke University Press, 2004.

Srigley, Susan. *Flannery O'Connor's Sacramental Art*. Notre Dame, IN: University of Notre Dame Press, 2004.

Stramondo, Joseph. "Disabled by Design: Justifying and Limiting Parental Authority to Choose Future Children with Pre-Implantation Genetic Diagnosis." *Kennedy Institute of Ethics Journal* 27.4 (2017): 475–500.

Strawson, Galen. "The Unstoried Life." In *On Life Writing*, edited by Zachary Leader, 284–301. New York: Oxford University Press, 2015.

———. "Against Narrativity." *Ratio* 17.4 (2004): 428–452.

Summers-Bremner, Eluned. "'Poor Creatures': Ishiguro's and Coetzee's Imaginary Animals." *Mosaic* 39.4 (2006): 145–160.

Swartz, Aimee. "James Fries." *American Journal of Public Health* 98.7 (2008.): 1163–1166.

Swirski, Peter. *Of Literature and Knowledge: Explorations in Narrative Thought Experiments, Evolution, and Game Theory*. New York: Routledge, 2007.

Symons, Xavier. "Scientists Closer to Growing Human Organs in Pigs." *BioEdge: Bioethics News from Around the World*, January 28, 2017.

Taylor, Sunaura. *Beasts of Burden: Animal and Disability Liberation*. New York: The New Press, 2017.

———. "Beasts of Burden: Disability Studies and Animal Rights." *Qui Parle: Critical Humanities and Social Sciences* 19.2 (2011): 191–222.

Teo, Yugin. "Testimony and the Affirmation of Memory in Kazuo Ishiguro's *Never Let Me Go*." *Critique: Studies in Contemporary Fiction* 55:2 (2014): 127–137.

Terry, James S., and Peter C. Williams, "Literature and Bioethics: The Tension in Goals and Styles." *Literature and Medicine* 7 (1988): 1–21.

Thompson, Derek. "The Invisible Revolution: How Aging Is Quietly Changing America." *Atlantic*, October 6, 2016.

Thomson, Judith Jarvis. "A Defense of Abortion." *Philosophy & Public Affairs* 1.1 (1971): 47–66.

Trollope, Anthony. *The Fixed Period*. 1882. Edited by R. H. Super. Ann Arbor: University of Michigan Press, 1990.

Tsao, Tiffany. "The Tyranny of Purpose: Religion and Biotechnology in Ishiguro's *Never Let Me Go*." *Literature & Theology* 26.2 (2012): 214–232.

Valente, Joseph. "Modernism and Cognitive Disability: A Genealogy." In *A Handbook of Modernism Studies*, edited by Jean-Michel Rabaté, 379–398. Hoboken, NJ: John Wiley & Sons, 2013.

Vande Kieft, Ruth M. "Judgment in the Fiction of Flannery O'Connor." *Sewanee Review* 76.2 (1968): 337–356.

Vint, Sherryl. "Animals and Animality from the Island of Moreau to the Uplift Universe." *Yearbook of English Studies* 37.2 (2007): 85–102.

Volokh, Eugene. "Sterilization of the 'Intellectually Disabled.'" *Washington Post*, April 18, 2014.

Walkowitz, Rebecca L. "Unimaginable Largeness: Kazuo Ishiguro, Translation, and the New World Literature." *NOVEL: A Forum on Fiction* 40.3 (2007): 216–239.

Weil, Kari. *Thinking Animals: Why Animal Studies Now?* New York: Columbia University Press, 2012.

Wells, H. G. *The Island of Doctor Moreau*. Broadview edition, edited by Mason Harris. Buffalo, NY: Broadview Press, 2009.

———. *The Island of Doctor Moreau: A Variorum Text*. Edited by Robert M. Philmus. Athens, GA: University of Georgia Press, 1993.

———. *The War of the Worlds*. 1898. New York: Signet Classic, 1986.

———. *Early Writings in Science and Science Fiction*. Edited, with critical commentary and notes, by Robert M. Philmus and David Y. Hughes. Berkeley: University of California Press, 1975.

———. *Experiment in Autobiography: Discoveries and Conclusions of a Very Ordinary Brain*. 1934. Philadelphia: J. B. Lippincott, 1967.

————. *A Modern Utopia.* 1905. Lincoln: University of Nebraska Press, 1967.

————. *Men like Gods: A Novel.* New York: Macmillan, 1923.

————. *The World Set Free. A Story of Mankind.* New York: E. P. Dutton, 1914.

————. *Anticipations of the Reaction of Mechanical and Scientific Progress upon Human Life and Thought.* New York: Harper and Brothers, 1901.

Wendell, Susan. *The Rejected Body: Feminist Philosophical Reflections on Disability.* New York: Routledge, 1996.

West, Rebecca. "Aldous Huxley on Man's Appalling Future." 1932. In *Aldous Huxley: The Critical Heritage,* edited by Donald Watt, 197–202. Boston: Routledge and Kegan Paul, 2013.

Whitehead, Anne. "Writing with Care: Kazuo Ishiguro's *Never Let Me Go.*" *Contemporary Literature* 52.1 (2011): 54–83.

Whitman, James Q. *Hitler's American Model: The United States and the Making of Nazi Race Law.* Princeton, NJ: Princeton University Press, 2017.

Woiak, Joanne. "Designing a Brave New World: Eugenics, Politics, and Fiction." *Public Historian* 29.3 (2007): 105–29.

Wolfe, Cary. *What Is Posthumanism?* Minneapolis: University of Minnesota Press, 2010.

————. *Animal Rites: American Culture, the Discourse of Species, and Posthumanist Theory.* Chicago: University of Chicago Press, 2003.

Wolfe, Cary, ed. *Zoontologies: The Question of the Animal.* Minneapolis: University of Minnesota Press, 2003.

Woodcock, George. "Utopias in Negative." *Sewanee Review* 64.1 (1956): 81–97.

Woolf, Virginia. *Between the Acts.* 1941. Annotated and with an introduction by Melba Cuddy Keane. New York: Harcourt, 2008.

————. *Three Guineas.* 1938. Annotated and with an introduction by Jane Marcus. New York: Harcourt, 2006.

————. "Mr. Bennett and Mrs. Brown." In *The Virginia Woolf Reader,* edited by Mitchell A. Leaska, 192–212. New York: Harvest Books, 1984.

Yaeger, Patricia. "Flannery O'Connor and the Aesthetics of Torture." In *Flannery O'Connor: New Perspectives,* edited by Sura P. Rath and Mary Neff Shaw, 183–206. Athens, GA: University of Georgia Press, 1996.

Zacharias, Nil. "It's Time to End Factory Farming." *Huffington Post* blog, October 19, 2011. https://www.huffingtonpost.com/.

INDEX

Adams, Carol, 122–23, 132

Adorno, Theodor, 67, 69, 82, 175n40

Agamben, Giorgio: *The Open: Man and Animal*, 10–11, 15, 47; *Homo Sacer: Sovereign Power and Bare Life*, 28, 119–20, 139–45

Aging, 13, 26–27, 29, 148–49; in *Brave New World*, 61–88; "compulsory youthfulness," 26, 61, 72, 77, 79, 171n2; and disability, 63–66; elder abuse, 29, 148; "healthy aging," 26, 71, 74, 148, 173n20; value of old age, 79–80, 87–88, 176n48

Altieri, Charles, 2, 161n3, 162n6, 162n7

Animals: animal studies and disability studies, 16–25; animality in Wells's *Moreau*, 31–60; ethics of humane farming in Ishiguro's *Never Let Me Go*, 117–46; factory farming, 8, 28, 29, 118, 126, 128–30, 137, 147–48, 189n2; disabled people viewed as, 25, 52–53, 63, 97–98, 110, 115; welfare of, 135–39. *See also* Humanness

Ashley X, 100, 151, 189n5

Attridge, Derek, 2, 4, 25

Atwood, Margaret, 167n21

Barnes, Djuna, 110

Barnes, Elizabeth, 155, 190n12

Baynton, Douglas, 19, 53, 97, 110

Bentham, Jeremy, 17, 23, 182n5

Bernstein, Mark, 38, 135, 164n22, 166n13, 168n28, 185n33, 187n41

Bérubé, Michael, 5, 21, 92, 164–65n2, 179n22

Bioethics 1–3, 8, 25, 27, 33–34, 61, 89–90, 101–2, 154–55, 162n9, 170n1. *See also* Animals; Disability

Butler, Judith, 102, 112, 114, 128, 146

Butler, Octavia, 156, 162n11

Capacities, as basis of moral worth, 12, 13–14, 16–18, 20–22, 33, 44–45, 89, 91, 103, 108, 113, 136, 138–39, 158, 168n28, 177n6, 178n11, 179n24, 181nn36–37, 186n40

Carlson, Licia, 93, 178n11, 180nn29–30

Chen, Mel, 34, 48, 136, 163n15, 167n24

Chesterton, G. K., 153–154

Chimeras. *See* Hybrids, biological

Clare, Eli, 26, 51, 113, 142, 181n38, 189n5

Cloning, 118, 182n3, 183n11. *See also* Ishiguro, Kazuo

Cobbe, Francis Power, 37

Coetzee, J. M., 19, 147

Cole, Sarah, 43, 60, 165n3, 169n35

Cole, Thomas, 64–65, 172n12, 174n32

Cure, ideology of. *See* Clare, Eli; Disability: "curative imaginary"; Kafer, Alison

Darwin, Charles, 10, 11, 12, 31–32, 34, 45, 52–53, 59, 110

Davidson, Michael, 51, 100, 162n12, 163n13, 165n2, 177n10

Davis, Lennard, 20, 105, 168n30

Deafness, 97, 105, 175n35, 180n27; choosing, 101; in Lombroso, 169n33; in *Violent*, 104–107

ABOUT THE AUTHOR

Maren Tova Linett is Professor of English and Director of the Critical Disability Studies program at Purdue University. She is the author of *Modernism, Feminism, and Jewishness* and *Bodies of Modernism: Physical Disability in Transatlantic Modernist Literature* and the editor of two collections about modernist women writers.

Lightning Source UK Ltd.
Milton Keynes UK
UKHW040906160620
364880UK00009B/122